Vitamin En*Rich*ed

Never, never, never, never give up.
Winston Churchill

*A man can succeed at almost anything for which he
has unlimited enthusiasm.*
Charles Schwab

*The greatest use of life is to spend it for something
that will outlast yours.*
William James

*The secret to success is for a man to be ready for his
opportunity wherever it comes.*
Benjamin Disraeli

*Shoot for the moon. Even if you miss you'll land
among the stars.*
Les Brown

VITAMIN ENRICHED

Carl DeSantis
with Donald Michael Platt

Publishing, Inc.

Boca Raton, Florida

Just as life itself, companies like mine are always evolving to meet the changing needs of their customers. Therefore, from the time I stopped writing in the summer of 1998, some aspects of our company may have changed or some of the people I have written about may have moved on. For the period covered, however, it is as accurate as possible.

—Carl DeSantis

Copyright © 1999 by Carl DeSantis

Published by Transmedia Publishing, Inc.
6001 Broken Sound Parkway, N.W.
Boca Raton, Florida 33487

Publisher's Cataloging-in-Publication Data
DeSantis, Carl.
　　Vitamin enriched: a mega-prescription for wealth & health by the
　　founder of rexall sundown, inc.: carl desantis / Carl DeSantis with
　　Donald Michael Platt – Boca Raton, FL: Transmedia, 1999.

　　　　p.　ill.　cm.
　　ISBN 1-890819-03-4
　　1. DeSantis, Carl.　2. Rexall Sundown Company – history.
　　3. Businesspeople – United States – biography.　4. Pharmaceutical
　　industry – United States – history – 20th century.　5. Drugstores
　　– United States – history – 20th century.　I. Platt, Donald, Michael.
　　II. Title.
HD9666.95.D47　D47　　　1999　　　　　98-90144
381'.456151'092　　　　　dc—21　　　　　CIP

03　02　01　00　◆　5　4　3　2　1

Printed in the United States of America

Contents

CONTENTS

Foreword

Iam Carl DeSantis.

Until Rexall Sundown went public in 1993, I was blissfully anonymous. Since then, my name has been mentioned more and more frequently in the media.

I want to set the record straight and tell you about the real Carl DeSantis. That is why I have written this book.

I will share my thoughts and experiences, and perhaps you may glean something useful from them. I truly hope you will.

We are so often misunderstood along the way. We never have a second chance to make a first impression. Writing gives us the ideal platform and enough time to express exactly what we wish to communicate and, therefore, make a meaningful and lasting impression.

I believe and act upon the principles that we should always help needy individuals and give something back to society as a whole, no matter how much or little we have materially. Since my early childhood, I have wanted to touch people in a positive way. **Hopefully, I can convince you that to change someone's life for the better does not always involve dollars. It's all about being a caring and altruistic person. That is the one important message I hope to get across, no matter what else you may attempt to cull from my story.**

The creation of a flourishing corporation or the acquisition of great wealth should not be the sole basis for considering a person to be a successful human being. There are so many other ways to evaluate true success: Kindness, generosity of spirit, honesty, and keeping one's word. Those are the higher standards by which I hope to be measured.

I also want to tell you how I acquired Rexall in a relatively short time after going into business for myself, and perhaps inspire the reader to venture into something similar, that niche waiting to be filled, and to keep the entrepreneurial spirit alive and well in America.

Just do it! Follow your dream or star, or whatever else you want to call it. Long before the U.S. Army came up with the slogan, I frequently advised myself and others: "Be all you can be."

The day I purchased Rexall I experienced several strong emotions. One was a feeling of pride. Like nearly everyone else, I had grown up in an era when the name Rexall meant quality and value from your friendly drugstore in cities and towns throughout America – and much of the world.

Many of us still fondly remember products like *Plenamins, Cara Nome, Jonteel,* and the flurry of promotional sales that livened the days in many a town. Who amongst us would not like to sit one more time at a Rexall lunch counter and leisurely sip a soft drink or milkshake?

The Rexall story began on a train en route to Seattle one afternoon in 1903 when Louis K. Liggett conceived a plan that ultimately impacted the lives of nearly every American throughout the twentieth-century. Liggett had already established a powerful druggist's trade organization before he had the inspiration which would become Rexall Drugs and the first concept of franchising in America. Eventually another of Liggett's dreams came true – a Rexall drugstore in every county seat in each state. Ultimately, nearly 25,000 drugstores carried his Rexall banner and products.

Like Mr. Liggett, I too had a dream. I wanted to give the consumer the purest, highest quality manufactured vitamins and nutritional aids at lower and fairer prices than any other supplier. I not only made my dream a reality, and continue to do so, but in the process I purchased and saved the grand old Rexall name from dinosauric extinction.

That same day I purchased Rexall, I experienced another emotion – something spiritual – as if the essence of Louis K. Liggett had become part of my psyche. In any case, I then believed and still do to this day that I had become the keeper of his keys.

Today, we proudly display the Rexall name on our corporate mast. In this book you will learn about Rexall Sundown, Inc., and how we created or acquired: Sundown Vitamins, the nation's number one selling brand; SDV Vitamins, our mail order division; **the** Rexall, of course; our multilevel marketing subsidiary, Rexall Showcase International; Thompson Nutritional Products, a favorite of the health food stores; and Rexall Managed Care, which provides quality drugs and nutritional products to hospitals, nursing homes, and the burgeoning HMOs.

Yes, my acorn has grown into a many-branched great oak which continues to thrive. Yet, cultural and political clouds are hovering over us. Today, it seems that *all* businessmen have become the established villains in the current folklore of America, as portrayed in many films and entertainment TV shows. Their pernicious propaganda would have the audience believe that if you are a financial success, you must be a swindler or, at the very least, less than honorable.

That is yet another reason why I have decided to tell my story. I am an entrepreneur. I want the public to refocus on the entrepreneur's contributions to the growth and health of the American economy and its free way of life.

Those of us who start up businesses are a positive force. We create jobs. We are the innovators. We are the people who do make the better mousetrap – or develop a superior mouse.

A friend has compared entrepreneurs to artists, composers, and writers – Picasso, Beethoven, and Poe – because they are unique and also create. From a wisp of an inspiration, they can give birth to lasting institutions and inspire visual cultural icons from the Coca Cola bottle and the original T-Bird, to the classic Rexall logo.

I would never be so arrogant as to compare my accomplishments with those of Picasso and other geniuses; so, before I describe who I am, I'll begin by telling you who I am **not** and what I am **not**.

I am not a trust baby. I did not inherit Rexall or wealth; nor was I given any seed money by daddy or anyone else as a gift.

I did not marry material wealth, although my wife, who helped initiate our company, was a treasure in all other ways.

I did not and do not embrace the repugnant business practice that to make your first million you have to be deceitful or misappropriate it; then afterwards you wear the ethical robes.

I did not build my business with lucrative Federal Government contracts or SBA loans.

I did not create my company with money earned by "playing" the stock, bond, or commodity markets.

I did not buy and sell apartments for profit and raise the rents on working people.

I did not buy out companies to destroy them and, therefore, create more unemployment and increase welfare rolls as my bank account fattened.

I did not rise up the corporate ladder in major chains -- their loss, I feel, as you shall read.

I did not come up with an invention that made me a millionaire before I was thirty.

I am a self-made millionaire, as is said in the vernacular, who, more often than not, has used adversity as a bridge to success.

Therefore, I cannot help but think back to Sundown's humble origins, and that of my family. Early in our marriage, my pregnant wife and I were so down and out that we had to rely on donations of food from a church in order to survive; incredible as it may seem, at 2:20 PM on December 24, 1997, the DeSantis family reached a worth of **one billion dollars**, based on solely the value of our Rexall Sundown Corporate stock holdings. That placed us amongst an extremely select few, of this I am sure.

Because my wonderful, talented sons and daughter are already in place as the core of Rexall Sundown's management and poised for tomorrow's bright future, the DeSantis family saga is ongoing. The end, it appears, is nowhere in sight.

I believe that you too can eventually achieve the same level of success no matter your current economic status. That is why I want to tell you how I started my own business, the company that is Rexall Sundown today, about twenty years ago as a part-time endeavor in my home with my family. I was thirty-seven years old, which is proof positive that at whatever age you may be, it is never too late to start up a business or change careers.

At that time, I felt certain that there was a tremendous opportunity for success by working hard, providing a quality product at a fair price, and remaining ever vigilant in the search for new ideas and opportunities wherever they may present themselves.

In those early days, I did not envision the degree of success that would ensue. In less than two decades, a family venture, run from our bedroom, has grown to become Rexall Sundown, a company that employs over a thousand people on several campuses totalling almost a million square feet of space for administrative, research and development, manufacturing, packaging, and distribution. And, we have already begun to outgrow a number of those facilities.

I never vowed to become president, CEO, or Board Chairman of a big company. I never planned to be King of the Vitamin Hill. I never aimed to make a million dollars.

Yet the same ingredients for success are applicable whether you're running a fruit stand or a giant corporation. It's all about people – those you sell to and those who work with and for you.

By far, our greatest strength is our people. I have been told that I have a knack for sizing up people in an instant. I hire to compensate for my shortcomings because you can't be everything or everywhere.

How much do I care about the fine men and women who have worked with me over the years? Since we went public, dozens of employees have become multi-millionaires, and another one hundred or so have made considerably more than a quarter of a million dollars. Very many more.

Those are the things I want to tell you. How I got to share my success.

I want to encourage people to hang in there and tough it out during times of adversity, which can include serious illness. I have been there. During the crucial ten year period from about the time I acquired Rexall until after we took the company public, I suffered from a severe debilitating malady, which no doctor could cure, and nearly died from a life-threatening disease. Despite all my travails, I continued to play an active role in my company to ensure that Rexall Sundown would grow and prosper.

Although I will be describing my past and the birth of Rexall Sundown as a public company, I want to give you a look ahead to the future and somewhat of an education in vitamins and nutritional supplements along the way.

Rexall Sundown is a cutting edge company. We seek new, beneficial science based products that have passed rigorous testing to improve the quality of life.

I am fully cognizant of my own achievement and the role I've played in the growth of my company. But I'm truly more proud of the people who have made it their life's work to assure that Sundown – later Rexall Sundown – became a success.

Beyond numbers and statistics, my story is one of long term loyalty from our employees, distributors, customers, and associates. People who come to work for us **stay** with us. We consider them part of the Rexall Sundown family and we hope and believe that they will always consider themselves part of our extended family as well.

Like the Roman god Janus, as the twentieth-century comes to an end and the twenty-first-century approaches, we simultaneously look back to Rexall's illustrious past and ahead to yet a more glorious future for Rexall Sundown, Inc., one in which we shall contribute significantly to the health and wellness of America.

To my colleagues and employees, to our customers and distributors, and to my family, I dedicate this book.

Acknowledgments

I'd like to thank some of those who have enriched my life so much more than the dollars I've amassed.

My Family: Sylvia, Debbie, Dean, Damon, and my sister, Dorothy

Nick Palin	Ron Barnhart
Buck Prestidge	Donna Walsh
Joe Greene	Rodger Rohde
Brent MacLeod	Sol Schwartz
Sister Mary Lourdes	Jim Steinhauser
Sister Thomas Rose	Geary Cotton
Sam Cohen	Richard Burton, P.A.
Jerry Whimmer	Paul Chappelear
Jerry Kay	Ted Rogalny
Rich Wisely	Sid Garrison
Dick Kaplan	Sammy Rakofsky
Jerry Rayman	Luigi Carusillo
Peter Perri II	Father Carr
Maury Treble	Pat Sauls and Family
Stan Leedy	

The Employees and Associates (past and present) of *Rexall* **Sundown Company** (and You for whatever good you derive from this book.)

To those who have gone before me:
Mr. Fischer (Goldfarb & Fischer)   Barbara Gillis

ACKNOWLEDGMENTS

Marty Greenberg	Stanley Rosen
Seymour Gordon	Gene Gotto
Terry Justice	Mr. Dan Foreman

And finally, to a special gentleman, Donald Platt, who, without his intelligence, wit and understanding of patience, this book would never have been realized nor would our mutual respect and friendship have evolved. Thank you, Donald.

ONE

A Family Of Entrepreneurs

Is the child truly the father of the man, or is it a mix of nurture and nature; environment or heredity; genetic predisposition or background? You can use whatever terms you like and then math the percentages. By the time I finish my story, you may very well have the answer.

Both sides of my family were entrepreneurs. Men and women. Therefore, I believe that my success was due in great part to the influence of my background on my basic nature – as well as my innate drive and unwavering, optimistic belief in people.

I want to tell you about my childhood and boyhood in Miami to emphasize that there was nothing remarkable about my origins and upbringing. I also want to reassure you that someone like myself, who was molded from what might be called ordinary clay, can still rise to the top of the heap. Of course, you may very well catch glimpses along the way of similar possibilities for yourself that may bc likewise actualized.

One coincidence regarding my birth should be mentioned. I let out my primal scream in the city where Rexall was founded.

I was born in Boston, July 19, 1939, the second child

and only living son of Florence and Amarico DeSantis. My father was known as Ricardo, and a decade after his death was referred to as "Ricky" Ricardo thanks to the popularity of the *I Love Lucy* TV show.

I really never knew my father. He died when I was three.

I have only one memory of my father that reoccurs. I remember riding in the front seat next to him in a 1940 or '41 Plymouth that he owned. We were downtown in a rough section of Boston, near a Bowery area. My father picked up a man who got into the back seat and must have been inebriated. He puffed away on a cigar and burned a hole in the upholstery. I remember that my father got very angry. He threw the man out of his car while admonishing him severely.

Other than that, I don't have any memories of Boston because we moved to Florida after he died. All I know is what my mother told me. My father owned several beauty salons during the depression and early years of World War II, so he must have been a pretty fair entrepreneur. One salon was in Filene's, but not in its notorious bargain basement where shopper hand-to-hand fighting over merchandise was born. Additionally, other beauty salons of his own were scattered throughout Boston.

I learned more about my father's family about seven years ago when my children arranged a trip to Italy for me. We met our Italian relations who were descended from my paternal grandfather's brother. One DeSantis was Mayor of Avellino, a city near Naples. He lived in a grand villa, and with his children and brothers owned many buildings and several large and successful business enterprises.

My mother had met my father through the beauty business because she was a hairdresser. Mothers are protective of their children and are reluctant to tell you the entire story when there might be something negative. She told me simply that my father was a binge drinker. It was my understanding that he'd sometimes go away for two or three days over a long weekend and drink the entire time. Supposedly beer. I was never told what had really happened. Whatever, that experience certainly toughened her. So did the events that followed.

I was told that my father had a large family in the Dedham, Massachusetts area, where there was an Italian neighborhood. They had assured my mother that if my father should ever die, they would take care of everything and look out for us.

After my father passed away, she didn't hear from his family for months and felt abandoned. She did, however, became close with Aunt Gracie, one of my father's sisters. My aunt, who was a lovely lady, passed away a couple of years ago. She and her immediate family always stayed in touch.

My mother was not left alone for long. Her maiden name was Florence Gillis. Her parents, Margaret and Angus, who lived in Boston, were from Nova Scotia. They spoke Scotch and Gaelic around the house. My maternal grandparents had six children. My mother was one of three daughters.

My middle name is Angus. Carl Angus DeSantis. Only in America. What a country!

My grandfather was a builder, but not a carpenter-builder, although he could use hammer and nails and carve wonderful wood furniture and toys. His business was *Gillis and Sons,* and he completed about six hundred homes in Norwood and throughout the nicer areas outside of Boston. The Gillis family was quite well-off until the Crash of 1929 and the subsequent Great Depression of the 1930s.

When Angus Gillis was in his late sixties, he and

Margaret sold their homes and property in Boston and moved to Florida with three of their children. They were familiar with the Sunshine State because they'd had a summer place in St. Petersburg. My grandparents eventually purchased a home in Miami.

* * *

About eight months after my father's death and while still in mourning, my mother, my older sister Dorothy, and I moved in with my grandparents, Ma and Pa Gillis. They lived in the Allapattah section of Miami, close to Miami-Jackson High School. It was a middle class neighborhood of mixed religions and ethnicity. Their house was about twelve years old and typical Americana – single story, all wood, with a shade porch on a double-size lot with oak trees in back and a *porte cochere.*

The house had been upgraded and was fairly decent, but only a three-bedroom, and my grandparents, my mother's two sisters, an uncle who was drafted, and the three of us all lived there. I slept in the same room with my grandfather because he had a room unit air conditioner to help with his asthma.

Angus Gillis was a grand gentleman, a wonderful grandfather, and I loved him dearly. He was the man I grew up with. My true father-image, my mentor. I called him Pa, and my grandmother Ma – with the Boston accent I heard and acquired at that time.

Pa was portly, rotund, and balding, and always wore a brimmed hat. A man of few words, he liked to sit in his own chair on the shaded porch and listen to the radio. Although he loved all sports, boxing was his favorite. Radio commentators like Walter Winchell and Gabriel Heatter were his passion, and mine as well. Later after we got our first Muntz TV set, I enjoyed shows like *Omnibus,* the political conventions, and Senate hearings like those run by Estes Kefauver against syndicated crime and the big one against Senator Joseph McCarthy.

I looked up to Pa. I'd run errands for him and make regular trips to Mobley's Gas Station to get him a plug of apple tobacco. Pa always gave me a nickel for that particular errand, and I'd buy a NEHI or an RC Cola. I never saw him spit. He was too classy to use a spittoon. He certainly didn't swallow. But I never did learn how he got rid of the plug. Maybe, as I think about it, he cut it up and smoked it in his ever present corncob pipe.

Even though my grandfather was semi-retired and about seventy when I really began to know him, he built rocking horses, chairs, small children's furniture and put them in variety stores all over Miami on consignment. Pa didn't need the money for those carvings. He simply liked doing it, working with his hands in wood. I began to work in wood with him when I was six or seven years old.

My grandparents had separate bedrooms. I never knew anything about two people living together when I was a youngster. She was at one end of the house, he on the other. They loved each other very much, but I think I saw them show physical affection for each other only once. That happened during the Second World War. There was a knock at the door and someone advised them that Angus Jr. had been killed. I'd met my uncle Angie only one time.

I saw my grandparents hold hands and go into the room together. The only other time I saw any closeness between them was when my grandmother fell and fractured her wrist, and Pa held her. They were in their seventies then.

In later years, Pa was ill with circulatory problems. My grandparents died when I was in my teens.

I believe that my mother's sisters subliminally influenced my entrepreneurial bent. Aunt Barbara was an entrepreneur in her own right. She had her own beauty salon and also worked with a major chain of salons in South Florida called J. Baldi of Miracle Mile in Coral Gables. From her salon, she created false eyelashes from human hair, made and sold sandwiches in her shop, and dabbled in a variety of other opportunities to earn money.

Aunt Irene, who went off to California and married at least a couple of times, was very enterprising as a manicurist.

My mother was the exception in the family. After my father died, she wanted a guaranteed salary in a steady job while she brought us up. Like her younger sister, she too was a manicurist, and worked for a while at Roffler's Barber Shop in Coral Gables. Roffler would become a nationally known name later in the seventies and eighties. The Roffler Cut was a specific technique of cutting hair with a razor.

So, I grew up among entrepreneurs. Fertile soil for what I was to do and become.

* * *

Although my mother was not an entrepreneur, she strongly influenced me in one important area. She was my moral compass and mostly responsible for my growing up with no ethnic or religious prejudices.

Of course, as part of the old Confederacy, Florida practiced segregation when I was a boy in the 1940s and '50s, although I was not terribly aware of that great injustice until later. My grandparents had come from Massachusetts, the most liberal state of them all, yet they had separate plates and utensils for David, the black gentleman who used to cut the grass. I thought they were his plates; later I learned that they were ours but kept for his use only.

There were no African Americans at any of my public schools, only about five in my elementary Catholic school, and very few in college. 1964 was still a ways off.

My own problems dealing with prejudice arose from my last name, although, generally, I played up my Gaelic Scot heritage, for that was the side of the family that raised me. I was called wop and guinea long before I knew what they meant – except I knew that those names were pejorative from the bigot's tone of voice. In communication we can learn more from the tone than the words.

Another experience regarding prejudice came when I heard about Miami Beach having restricted areas and hotels – no Jews allowed. Rent the award winning film, *Gentleman's Agreement*, and you'll know exactly what I am referring to.

My mother had changed jobs to work as a manicurist in a hotel barbershop for a gentleman she had known in Boston. She came home after her first day and was upset that the hotel was restricted. She hadn't known that until she went to work there.

Aunt Irene, who had moved to Los Angeles, California, encountered the same situation. People have forgotten that the City of Angels had many restricted neighborhoods in those days. Aunt Irene told my mother that she would make more money where Jews were accepted.

As it turned out, and somewhat ironically, my mother did not work for long at the restricted hotel. At that time, she was seeing the only man I was ever aware of she dated, Ross Sobel, who was Jewish.

Ross was a golf pro and a sweetheart of a man. Once he brought me an autographed baseball from an All-Star game. All the great ones had signed it – DiMaggio, Williams, Musial.

My mother went with Ross for quite a while, and he got her a position as manicurist in a hotel that accepted Jews. Aunt Irene had been right. The money was better with the Jewish clientele.

My mother almost married Ross. I never learned why she didn't. Then many years later, I met a fine gentleman, Ron Barnhart, when I was managing a Super-X drugstore in Miami Beach. Ron sold cigars through Faber, Coe & Gregg, a tobacco wholesaler, and he was married to Gloria Sobel, Ross' daughter whom my mother had known when she was just six years old. Small world. Ron would later help start my company and sell to retail stores in the early days before our multi-talented, staunch, and loyal Nick Palin came aboard. Ron never enjoyed the administrative side of our business and left for other, more creative enterprises.

Back to prejudice: I've been on the receiving end of ethnic slurs since childhood because of my last name – *if you are Italian, you must be mafioso.* I also experienced some unexpected serious discrimination in the early years of our marriage when my wife and I moved back to Miami. Because of my last name, the phone company thought I might be Cuban and gave me a rough time. In the 1960s, Cubans who had escaped the Castro revolution had to put down a several hundred dollar deposit for their phones in Miami. That could not be done today.

There was another type of prejudice I was aware of, which bothers me to this day. The Guerins, a family that had gone through World War II in Italy, moved next door. They were in the terrazzo business. George, who was one of their sons, had been affected by the bombing and appeared to be a bit slow. It always upset me when the other kids would pick on him. Yet, George had value and feelings, and could accomplish certain tasks, sometimes to the level of genius.

I learned a significant lesson from George: Each person, regardless of ethnicity, IQ, economic class, has something positive to offer. I also discovered more about myself from his brother, John, who was about a year and a half older than I. Because he had not yet mastered English, he was in my grade, but a straight-A student and a super athlete.

John was in our group of twelve to fourteen year old boys. We'd wrestle all day, and were so competitive that we often had to be pried apart from our lock holds by his parents. When their efforts failed, our mothers would hose us down. As we matured physically, we became more competitive and rougher. Although we boxed without gloves – and losened some teeth – John was always a good friend. When I last saw him, he owned his own air conditioning refrigeration company.

Those wrestling bouts with John taught me more about myself. I learned that I hated to lose and always wanted to win. I have not changed.

TWO

Young Entrepreneur And The Great Raccoon Escape

I went into my first business ventures when I was thirteen – all kinds of odd enterprises. I had a good friend, Pat Sauls, and we used to run around together on a regular basis. Like me, Pat had an entrepreneurial spirit.

Just about every boy cuts grass – his own and the neighbors' lawns – to earn extra money. Back in the early 1950s, most lawn mowers were hand or electric. They didn't have power mowers.

Because Pat and I were very successful hustling up business, we were able to purchase three or four lawn mowers, and ended up hiring a slew of other kids to work the lawns that Pat and I didn't have the time for. We did about fifty-plus lawns each month, and since I had a knack for numbers, I was in charge of the books. We got from three to seven dollars for each lawn. If we priced a job out at seven, we'd give a guy five to do it and pocket the other two.

Pat Sauls was my partner and cohort in other businesses. We used to go over to the Rickenbacker Causeway in Key Biscayne, which had, back in its wild days, a sizable population of raccoons. You weren't really allowed to take them off Key Biscayne, but Pat and I did anyway.

We'd go out at three in the morning with old bird traps – a box, a stick, and a string. When the raccoon entered and ate the bait, the box fell over it. We'd throw a net over the raccoon and bring it home. We were careful never to hurt any of the animals.

We trapped a lot of raccoons over there and at one time we had over thirty of those masked critters. We kept them in the back of Pat's folks garage, which was a torn up old house behind his home. We wired up the fence, separated some raccoons, and mated others. Our plan was to sell them for their pelts or for their meat.

Then one day we discovered that the raccoons were considerably smarter than we were. Although we had lined our fences with heavy barbed wire so that they couldn't possibly get through, somehow all forty-plus raccoons ended up outside, all over the neighborhood, on everyone's roofs. That was the great raccoon escape – everything but a raccoon Steve McQueen on a motorcycle.

The police came and wanted to know where those raccoons had come from. They were everywhere, and we weren't licensed. But our neighbors were great. No one turned us in.

Pat was a fine young man, and I knew his whole family. I saw him about fifteen years ago. As I recall, he has a horse ranch in the middle of Florida in Ocala. We chatted for a while. He's done quite well on his own.

* * *

Then there was my parakeet venture. I already had a pair, and Pat knew an older woman who bred them. Although he didn't want to get involved, I decided to become a parakeet breeder.

At the same time, I had a *Miami Herald* route, and I'd saved some money, about two cents for every nickel earned. I used part of my savings to buy a budgie business. Budgies – that's what they used to call parakeets.

Back then you could buy a budgie at a retail selling price from about $2.50 to $4.00. I fixed up my own garage, which wasn't quite as big as Pat's, with breeder boxes. Then I gave the woman, whom Pat knew, $20 down for my first group of breeders and put them in the garage.

I knew all the names then, but today my memory isn't that good to recall all of them. I remember that I had Latinas and Harlequins, and there were different ways to tell the males from females, one being the color of the area adjacent to their beaks.

Even as a thirteen year old I knew the value of advertising. Back then we had mimeograph machines at school, and I used them to print my ads for the budgies. Then I'd insert them in the *Miami Heralds* I delivered.

When I'd get phone calls from potential customers, I would bring the budgies over to their houses and sell them for three to five bucks. I ended up selling quite a few birds, and averaged about $30 a week extra.

After six months in the parakeet business, we were ready to sell out. There's a lot of work attached to caring for birds, and I'd gotten tired of it. Also, the budgies had gotten mites, and I had to spray them. Ugh!

Because I was so successful, someone offered to buy us out. We sold the parakeet business for a little over $400.00, and Pat and I split the profits.

* * *

By the time I sold the parakeet business, I had discovered something else about myself. Once I succeed at something, once I've proven myself, I tend to want to move on to something else – but not necessarily for the dollars. I liked the action, the challenge of it all.

For example, I really loved woodwork after learning it from grandfather Angus. Miami-Jackson High had good equipment – planers, joiners, the works – and you could buy all the wood from fine ash to Philippine mahogany at school. I took Wood Shop and got more involved with it after school.

Burdines Department Store in Greater Miami held an annual furniture competition open to all school children. One year, I entered three items: A coffee table, a lamp, and a four-drawer chest. I won second prize, which made me happy, because quite a large number of students from all the Dade County schools had participated. I've always loved working with my hands and doing those kinds of things. My efforts all ended up at my house as our finest furniture back then.

*   *   *

Everything was coming up roses for me financially my last year at Corpus Christi and while I was in high school. I had other jobs and a car, a '41 Plymouth I had bought for fifty-five dollars in the 9th grade and used to deliver newspapers.

Of course I was too young to be driving, but I went out early in the morning. When I first got my *Miami Herald* route, I used a bicycle for a while, but I couldn't make enough money. The big routes had over three hundred homes on the delivery route, and I had only one hundred and fifty. That wasn't enough to make a lot of money, and the big routes were available only for those who had cars.

So I bought the car and took out the rumble seat to make room for the papers. My mother didn't find out about it right away. I kept it at my buddy's house for a long time. I was fourteen or fifteen at the time, and had only two days to learn my new route, which included multi-hundreds of residences. The supervisor and his father took me around in the mornings and told me who was who.

To make matters more confusing, some customers took the paper daily only, others Sunday only, and the rest got it all week. To make my life easier, I bought a paintbrush and some paint. In the wee hours of the morning, I marked the curb in front of each house with yellow paint – X for Sunday only, a zero for daily only, and XO for the entire week. My own variation of Passover. If anyone was upset because I had painted their curb, I never heard about it.

They didn't rubber band the papers for the deliverer in those days. I had to learn how to fold them and put them all together. The papers would arrive at a gas station at about four in the morning. I'd be there even though I had stayed out until about eleven-thirty at night. Then I'd fold them all and start delivering.

I worked that route for about a year and probably made about sixty dollars a week, which was very good money at that time. I had a tendency to spend it as fast as I made it. I later sold my car for sixty-five dollars and made a small profit.

About fifteen years ago, I went back to the neighborhood of my old paper route, and there was still some paint left where I'd made my marks. I have not changed. I still like to leave my marks in all my endeavors.

* * *

One job was never enough for me. It helped that I had never required much sleep.

When I was fourteen, I hired on with Lawn Lite Manufacturing. They made aluminum lawn furniture on Biscayne Boulevard. They did not do the extruding. They put the pieces together with straps. That's the kind of work I did for one summer. I learned the entire business and for a while thought about getting into it, but never did.

I also worked as a lifeguard because I was a fair swimmer and good diver.

I even used to be in radio speech, along with being the school announcer on our own high school radio show. The teacher who put me in there was Fred Fischer. I worked for the school about a half hour every two weeks, when I'd be on the radio discussing everything that happened at Miami-Jackson.

Because Fred thought I was a fairly good speaker, he got me involved with a local disc jockey who was connected with a black station at the time – it was Negro then. This was in the 1950s, and Florida continued to be racially segregated – separate drinking fountains, schools, seats on public transportation, the works.

I became the white counterpart deejay and put on a lot of Bo Diddley, Earl Bostic, Jackie Wilson, the "Midnighters", and other hot, popular artists like them. Many of the listeners calling into the show were in their twenties, and I'd talk to them as an equal although I was only sixteen. That was great fun.

While in the 11th grade I worked at Margaret Anne Table Supply and Kwik-Chek, now known as Winn Dixie. I was produce manager and assistant manager of the store, working more than forty-five hours a week. My mother used to call me the Onion Boy. She repeatedly said that her son was going to be an onion boy, and that really stuck in my craw. I'd tell her not to worry, that I was going to make it, but she'd continue to say, "All you'll ever be is my Onion Boy." She said it with love, but it hit home, believe me.

THREE

Looking Beyond The Marker

Miami today is a radically different city than it was when I was growing up in the 1940s and '50s. Racial segregation was still an ugly blight. So were the WASP enclaves that excluded Catholics and Jews. Castro's revolution was years away, so we did not yet have the great influx of Cubans who enriched and further diversified the city.

Miami was not a "major league" city when I was growing up. Decades would pass before it acquired National League, NFL, NHL, NBL, and NBA franchises.

Air conditioning was not yet a birthright, and we were lucky if our fans worked. That's why I was happy to sleep in Pa's room.

Miami has not changed completely, however. Its beaches are still spectacular. We continue to wage our eternal war against palmetto bugs and german cockroaches, and intensely watch the hurricane reports and chart their movements with diagrams that resemble fancy football plays.

I have gone through many hurricanes in Florida. Big blows, we used to call them. Long before Andrew, one was clocked at 162 mph. I remember surviving three very strong hurricanes, and when we were living in Allapatah, we had to stay in a shelter for almost a week. Everyone was moving around the neighborhoods in canoes and row-boats. When we were finally allowed to return to our home, we faced the kind of damage and mess all too commonly shown on TV after all natural disasters.

The destruction and threat to life is worse now because we have five times the population and construction. I never suffered any business losses because we essentially battened down the hatches. Today at our firm, we have a major disaster recovery plan for the corporation in a worst case scenario, complete with back-up generators, which costs a fortune, but is absolutely essential in South Florida.

* * *

I had a wonderful childhood in old Miami. My nickname was Skippy. I guess that moniker came about because my pace was faster than walking, although not quite running. And I was a real goody two-shoes who could do no wrong as far as Pa and Ma were concerned. Within the family, I was placed on a pedestal, always the best in everyone's eyes. I guess it's because I was the only boy among so many women, which was unfortunate for my sister.

Dorothy was almost a year older and a very lovely girl. She and I were a lot closer than most brothers and sisters. We seldom argued. We truly respected each other; as a result, we were always in each other's corner. She is still a wonderful lady.

Unfortunately, Dorothy was often berated unnecessarily by Ma, our grandmother. My sister was always taking the brunt of the family's hang-ups. She wasn't in real trouble, but her body filled out quite early.

Although Dorothy developed a beautiful figure, she was not yet aware of the boys' newly found interest in her. All of them wanted to look her over, which drove our grandparents crazy. They consistently blamed her for teasing the boys, which she really didn't do consciously. She just couldn't avoid the attention. She was a real Dolly Parton. 38 or 40 D at thirteen when the hormones of her male schoolmates were really kicking in, and there was nothing she could do about it.

In the third grade I went to Corpus Christi, a Catholic elementary school in Greater Miami. I fared well there. My competitive nature manifested itself early – from first memory, to tell the truth.

I always sat at the front of the class, always raised my hand and gave all the answers first. Always a good boy. I wanted to be the best student. And I was.

My mother was very protective. I survived the childhood trauma of being the last boy in my class to wear long pants. I was about ten at the time, and most of the boys had been wearing long pants since they were eight. I was always a little embarrassed to be her Little Lord Fauntleroy with the short pants, little bow tie, starched shirt, shined shoes – everything so nice and proper.

I still remember that long overdue day when I put on my first pair of long pants. My mother cried in front of me and said, "You're getting to be a big boy." That really pleased me. I wanted to be a big boy.

I continued to do all the right things at Corpus Christi. I was a school crossing guard, one of the youngest altar boys, took Latin real early and learned to do the Mass.

I also won many awards for the school. In South Florida, they had a competition called the "Quizdown" that took place in Miami at the old Olympia Theater – the last I heard it was Gusman Hall. Catholic and public schools all competed. I represented Corpus Christi for four straight years.

Seven students from each school were on the team. A moderator asked us difficult questions, like the *$64,000 Question* quiz show we saw on TV. We competed in front of an audience of hundreds, plus it was broadcast over WQAM, a major Miami radio station.

I always answered correctly, never missed once, and we'd win a set of *Collier's Encyclopedia.* Talk about coincidences – many years later, I met the President of Sales for P. F. Collier's Encyclopedia, by then, owned by the Macmillan Publishing Company, and he would help play a meaningful role in the success of one of our newest divisions. Back to the quiz show – we'd also win about five hundred dollars, which would go into the school's endowment fund. I was in all the yearbooks at Corpus Christi until I entered Miami-Jackson High School in the Allapattah section of Miami.

About that time, my mother, sister, and I moved out of my grandparents' house. My mother wanted her own life, and her parents were getting more difficult to deal with. My wonderful and caring Aunt Barbara stayed there to watch over them.

We moved into a lower middle-class to working class neighborhood, and that's when I discovered that there was more to life than scholastics. I began to break away from a lot of ties to my mother – apron strings, they used to be called – and started running around with a less-than-reputable group of teenagers between school hours and my jobs. More about that later.

The Catholic schooling at Corpus Christi had been considerably more advanced than the public school system. When I entered the 9th grade at Miami-Jackson, I didn't have to take a book home. I already knew the subjects and had all the answers.

In fact, I ended up teaching Algebra to the class. I had approval to take over whenever the teacher was out, which I did once for a period of three straight weeks with the less-than-adequate substitute. I also taught Business Math during Student's Days. My skills with numbers would later serve me well in retail – and recreational gambling in casinos, which means, despite some spectacular wins, I usually broke even in the long haul. Be assured, breaking even in any casino is a major win!

I was on the debate team too. I had developed a naturally deep, commanding voice, and enjoyed speaking before any audience. We were part of the NFL, National Forensic League, and competed against other high schools. They'd give you a subject and time to work on it. Should we be in the Korean War? Should the death penalty be abolished? The usual.

We competed two to a team in a real debate held with judges, teachers, and college professors. It was like a tag team, with a process of elimination. If you won you'd go to the next round. Many schools were represented, and, as I recall, twenty-four teams. My partner was Delores Rosendo, a very bright girl and a fast talker. We didn't win the finals, but we were in the select top fcw.

My grades in high school varied. In Debate and Math I earned grades of A and B; and a D in the Humanities, or subjects where I cut classes. My buddies and I wouldn't go back to school after lunch. Consequently, I did poorly in courses everyone should have gotten an A in because of my lack of attendance.

While in high school, I went out for a variety of sports. Those experiences taught me lessons that became part of my lifelong approach to business, and just about everything else.

I was amongst the fortunate boys who matured earlier than most, which was certainly more advantageous for me than what my sister had experienced. I was built fairly well by the time I entered high school. I weighed about 160 with a V-shaped torso tapered like a manta ray, a rippling washboard stomach, and all the biceps and musculature that went along with it.

I was in a weightlifting group at school – not just power lifting but body building, which interested me a lot. I liked looking good. I still do.

I tried all the sports. I loved baseball and was a pretty good pitcher for Miami-Jackson's summer team. I also went out for Junior Varsity Football. If I was seventeen today and had my high school weight of 160 pounds, they probably wouldn't even let me try out for the team. But we're talking of another era, before steroids, more than forty years ago.

I had big plans for myself in football. I saw little glory in being a linebacker. I didn't think I'd be all that good as a running back, but I knew I could pass accurately.

The school had set up a criteria of five specific tasks for a boy to qualify for quarterback– sort of a mini pentathlon. Among them, we had to run the hundred yard dash in so many seconds, throw the ball so many yards, and zigzag through tires in so much time.

They gave us three turns at each skill. The minimum qualifying throw was around 30 yards. The boys who were bigger than I, with larger hands could throw the pigskin over 40 yards. Although they failed to qualify in some of the events I excelled at, my dexterity and speed zigzagging through tires didn't count as much as their passing did.

My first throw went for 22 yards, about normal for me. I improved on the next with a 24 yard toss. I saw my dreams of quarterback glory dissipating. Only later would I realize that those short distances had not been caused by lack of strength. My hands were too small to grip a football properly.

We had time to think between throws while we waited our turns. That was when I realized that I'd been shooting for the 30 yard marker.

I told myself, "You're aiming at the wrong thing, Carl. Aim for the fence."

The fence was about two hundred yards past the marker. I set my sights on it and again told myself to quit looking at the damn 30 yard marker.

I threw the ball as far as I could towards the fence and did get it beyond the 30 yard marker, although by only a few more feet. I did not become the quarterback. Instead, I played JV football as a linebacker.

But I had tossed the ball beyond the qualifying mark, which taught me a lesson I would later apply to everything I did in life: **Whatever you aim for, you've got to set your sights higher and farther than where you intend to go. Too many times people look only at the marker and not beyond it. They do not go very far.**

It became the same for me in baseball. **You should be looking for the home run all the time, not just to bring in a guy on base with a single. Go for the gold.**

And I applied that lesson to my diving. Although most of my competitions were at 3 meters, I used to practice on the 10 meter board. I believed that if I could dive well off the 10 meter board, I'd do better at 3 meters. Because I was a substitute, not on the first team, I spent more time at the swim meets as the announcer.

One summer, I worked at a place called The Castaways on Miami Beach on Sunny Isles Boulevard. It's closed now. I was a combination cabana boy and lifeguard.

The Castaways put on water shows once a week for the tourists. We would dive from the top of the hotel, which was only four stories, but still the pool looked terribly small from up there. Each story was 10 feet, so I was looking at 40 feet, maybe a little more.

You'd go right off the roof and you'd better aim yourself accurately at the kidney-shaped pool, which was about 17 by 30 feet, or you'd be part of the pavement. But those were things you knew you could do and didn't worry about because you were a teenager and, therefore, immortal.

I could really dive in my teens. I used to do back flips, swans, full-gainers, jack-knifes, the works. But be assured - - I was no Greg Louganis.

Although those dives worried my mother, I felt confident because I always had a great sense of balance in those days – ironic considering my extended malady, which I describe in a later chapter.

I was pretty good at track and field until I broke my tibia. At five-nine I jumped around 5'8", and put the shot, if I recall, over 16 feet. I could run fairly fast in the relay. We ran yards not meters in those days, and I did the hundred in 11.7; the school record was 10-point-something. Not too bad considering the things I did with my buddies – staying out late, smoking cigarettes, and drinking beer.

I was never good at basketball. I was too short and unorthodox, almost klutzy.

I also played sandlot football after school, without pads and other equipment, against kids who were playing real ball, all dressed in their uniforms. I held my own until, after one tackle, my leg was broken. The bone was protruding, and they carried me off the field.

I was taken to Jackson Memorial Hospital where my leg was set improperly. I had to change my gait to compensate for that bit of medical malpractice. My leg could probably be reset, but at fifty-eight why would I want to have it broken again?

Today, I swim regularly and do up to three sets of forty pushups most days. I'm still competing physically – mostly against myself – and against anyone who is willing to arm-wrestle.

In the meantime, I looked beyond the marker in another area when love came to this Andy Hardy.

* * *

All work and no play makes Jack a dull guy, and my name is Carl.

At the time I was at Miami-Jackson, the high school had, I think, around 2,000-plus students, of which about 50 percent were boys. So we had a nice selection of coeds, and they had a great choice among the boys – the kind we'd never have again, not even in college because of the way schedules were set up.

Think about it. Never again, would any of us be with 2,000 – or whatever number your own school had – boys and girls our own age in the confined space of a high school. It was literally a smorgasbord or Sunday buffet for all appetites of both sexes, in a finite space for nearly eight hours a day, five days a week. That's the way I look at it now.

While in the 10th grade, I saw a very beautiful, perfectly formed girl at Miami-Jackson High walking down the hall on her way to gym. I was also going to my PE class.

She had dark hair, almost raven black. She must have felt my eyes on her. She turned and flashed the most dazzling smile at me with the same perfect white teeth she has to this day.

If we'd been in a Disney animated film, birds would be chirping, cute little animals would have watched me and sighed with hearts floating above their heads – Thumper, Flower, the entire Bambi gang.

At that moment, I was totally captivated. She simply stole my heart. It was more than puppy love or a pimply crush. I just couldn't believe there was anyone that lovely on the face of this earth. I wanted to possess her, both body and soul. It suddenly hit me that somehow she would be my wife.

I went home that evening and spoke to my mother about the lovely brunette who had smiled at me. I told her that I'd seen the woman I was going to marry. Of course she laughed, and then advised me to finish high school, get myself together, go to college, and get a permanent job.

She emphasized that it was way too soon for me to talk of marriage. From her point of view, I was in the 10th grade, only fifteen, and completely inexperienced. That was true. I had not really dated anyone formally. I was in a group of common friends, both boys and girls.

The name of the beautiful brunette was Sylvia Chappelear. Her family on her father's side was of French heritage. I thought that Sylvia was more exquisite than the fine porcelain that came from one of the cities of her family's origins, Limoges. Sometime later, she learned that her mother, who was a Wadsworth, may very well have had direct blood ties with Henry Wadsworth Longfellow. After reading some of Mrs. Chappelear's prose, I could believe the likelihood of that relationship.

Sylvia had more than great looks. She was an outstanding athlete; had there been a Title IX in the 1950s, she definitely would have lettered in track and field. Sylvia's physical beauty was enhanced by her radiant soul and keen intelligence. We were in the same grade, and I tried to get into some of her courses. Sylvia was enrolled in honor classes, Spanish and other subjects that I had not qualified to take because, as I mentioned earlier, I was not being especially honorable academically. How's that for euphemistic expression?

I really can't call Sylvia my high school sweetheart. We did not go steady or even date regularly. For about a year it was basically a flirtatious situation.

I made plenty of futile overtures to Sylvia and tried to connect with her during the summer. I regretted that I had sold my Plymouth and no longer had a car to take her anywhere.

I bought a motorcycle, found out where she lived, and, with one of my buddies, rode over to her house at about one in the morning. I like to think that my late-night visit was due to youthful exuberance and inexperience rather than blatant stupidity. Her parents came out with a shotgun attitude and told me to leave Sylvia alone. Although I got their message in an eye-blink, I continued to pursue her.

Sylvia didn't really want to have anything to do with me. She was dating another fellow who attended the University of Florida at Gainsville. Back then, two or three years were ages of difference, and the girls in our high school who did date boys two or more years older wouldn't condescend to notice us. Sylvia's college beau was an old man in my book.

Nevertheless, during the summer between our 10th and 11th grades, I had the opportunity to see Sylvia on several occasions. Unfortunately, they were still only flirtatious and not magical moments.

That same summer, I purchased a 1951 Ford for $575.00, $100.00 down, and paid it off through the earnings from my various jobs. The Ford gave me the ability to date, and after school resumed and we were in the 11th grade, I timed it so that I would drive past Sylvia while she was waiting at a bus stop.

I offered her a ride, and my heart nearly burst when she got in the passenger side. Taking her home was the biggest thrill of my life.

At that time, she was still going out with her college man, which did not make any difference to me. I had made up my mind that she was **the one**. Whatever I had to do, I would win her over regardless of the fact that my rival was older and in college.

If I really want something, I accept no boundaries. I'll pursue it until I get it. That has always been my MO.

I was able to date Sylvia during our senior year even though she was still seeing Joe College, which is why we didn't go steady or anything like that. But I had improved my position. At that time, I learned that Sylvia was not all that sure how any of us were going to end up. Her indecision gave me hope. She was no longer all that committed to her college man.

Sylvia's plan was to let matters take their course during the summer. Her family was just getting by, not at food stamp level, but her father earned a meager living. He was hard working, honest and frugal but he could never seem to get ahead financially.

Although Sylvia had the ability and grades to earn a full Teacher's Scholarship and had scored very high on her SATs, she went to work for the phone company after graduation. I'd also done okay on the tests, which wasn't bad considering that I never studied in high school.

Sylvia's uncertainty continued into the Fall when I went away to Florida State University. Yes, in spite of my skirting the edge of academic suicide, I was a C+ student at Miami Jackson, and I did make it to college.

And I was still in love with Sylvia – aiming far beyond the mark of ordinary girls.

FOUR

The Gang's All Here

Along with my entrepreneurial endeavors, debate, athletics, and trying to date Sylvia, I still had enough free time to skirt the edges of trouble. Because my education had been so superior at Corpus Christi, I did not have to study for the classes I regularly attended. That gave me opportunities to change my circle of friends.

I discovered that I liked getting into situations which could be potentially dangerous. Dope wasn't prevalent then, but smoking cigarettes, drinking beer, cutting classes, and staying out late were popular forbidden activities.

Up to my arrival at Miami-Jackson, I had run with a goody two-shoes crowd at Corpus Christi. Stamp collector, academic types. We'd call them nerds, geeks, and dweebs today.

After school, I used to stop off at my friends' houses before I went home because my mother was working. I was espccially close with Khalil Hasham. We'd play with his chemistry sets and listen to long-hair music – Beethoven, Rachmaninoff, and Verdi. I loved all that stuff – operas, concertos, and symphonies – and while still in short pants I used to wave my arms conducting like a Toscanini. It was really in my blood.

After I found out that only a few people ever succeeded in the fine arts, I stopped considering a career in classical music. There was another reason. By the time I entered Miami-Jackson, I wanted to be a tough guy, a real man; and a real man wasn't supposed to like classical music.

I still loved the arts, but I rejected them because it was considered sissyish, and I didn't want to become a sissy, which was unfortunate, because to this day I still love that music.

But my group didn't. Because of peer pressure, I didn't listen to classical music or admit that I liked it. I wanted to play sports every day and get together with the guys at night.

While attending Miami-Jackson, I got in with a rather rough crowd. I liked to go out on the other side of the tracks, whether I was drinking beer or just hanging out with my buddies. I preferred to hang out with natural, basic guys. They didn't have jobs like I did, and if pushed to the wall, I'd have to say most of them were punks.

They were always running around the block, hiding behind houses or garages, and smoking at age twelve, which a good boy, as I had been at Corpus Christi, would never have done.

The guys weren't doing anything to hurt people in those days. They committed no crimes against persons. It was mostly hanging out. Stealing hubcaps, which I never did, was their biggest heist. They also enjoyed an occasional gang rumble.

We were a mini-version of the Little River Rats, although they were older and seemed to have gotten into more serious trouble, and numbered about eighty to a hundred in the total gang. My group had about fifteen to twenty boys. When there was talk of a rumble, usually with the Hialeah crowd, we'd meet over at the beach and have our big war on a Friday night.

I was always on the verge of getting into serious trouble but never did. Out of curiosity, I attempted to create a zip gun for myself and was about to test it with .22 shorts and longs. Then one day I came home and it was gone. My mother must have found the gun, but she said nothing. That was the end of my arms manufacturing enterprise.

I was present at only one fight that actually turned into a really tough one – when knives, bats, and maybe a few zip-guns came out. Some of the kids were beaten up, though, and a few were cut superficially, but no one was hurt badly, nothing too drastic – and that was as bad as it ever got. We have seen a radical change in gang behavior since then.

I've come to understand why I had run with my particular group. I'd been a mama's boy, and I wanted prove to myself that I was no longer a mama's boy. I was no longer Skippy. I was now Skip.

There was the teenage status thing too. I wanted to do it all, and prove to myself and my peers that I could be as tough as anyone.

Almost every night, I used to go to Lummus Park in Miami Beach. At that time, around 1954-55, I discovered girls other than the lovely Sylvia. She was still my unattainable ideal; the others were available. My hormones were kicking in big-time.

We wore jackets and pegged pants, and the girls who hung out with us – they were groupies, I guess – had the same jackets. We were more like the kids portrayed in *Grease.*

I was dating, yet not dating. You'd meet a girl at a park – not a bad girl, but the type who thought guys who smoked and drank were more mature and exciting than the good boys. And maybe she'd have six or seven girl friends. We'd all smoke cigarettes and drink beer or cokes, and that was our date. Then one of us would end up taking this one or the other home.

I usually stayed out of the brawls. I hung out with guys tough enough so that I wouldn't have to get into fights I could potentially lose. I'd had plenty of fights before high school at Corpus Christi. Always for a good cause, I like to think.

I remember one of them. Some guy said something to my older sister, pushed her, and caused her to cry. Although he was the toughest kid at school, I defended Dorothy and got into a fight with him.

I was terrified, absolutely terrified, and I hurt him badly. He couldn't believe it. Nor could I. I think my fear caused me to beat him.

To be honest, though, I felt good that I had clobbered a guy the whole school thought was a tough kid. That gave me more confidence that I could hold my own, yet I wasn't looking for trouble. I was never one to start a fight, although I thought I was pretty good at it.

I also got into some neighborhood fist fights, not just wrestling, and I always won – except – I don't think I'll discuss that one. It's interesting to me, and I've always said and still say it to my friends to this day: "How come we meet only the guys who beat up the other guy?"

Now somewhere, someone lost a fight. But how come we don't know him? The only guys who talked to me about the fights they'd been in always said, "Boy, I really beat this guy to a pulp." Even when they've got black eyes, broken noses, and missing teeth, they'll still say, "You should have seen the guy who lost." Well, who was the loser? How come we never meet the loser? Guys can be full of malarkey more often than people think.

Many of the kids I knew and some I ran with never amounted to much. A few spent some time in reformatories and even prison. But not all I knew were hooligans. There were success stories too.

One brilliant rogue, who didn't do much schoolwork, got a perfect 1600 on his SATs. He later became a tracker for NASA. Another is a major winner in yacht sales. A third became President of Caesar's World.

My running with the so-called tough guys taught me another lesson. No matter how negative the beginnings – and several made some very big mistakes – if a kid has the right stuff, he can eventually become a successful adult and contribute to his community.

FIVE

Almost A Criminalist

During my senior year at Miami-Jackson, many of my classmates whose minds I respected were making plans for college. I did not know them well; nor did I especially like them. They weren't the guys I hung out with. I was happier running with the lower middle class delinquents, the kids on the block who didn't have any money. Those were my friends.

The boys whose families had money – they were the guys I was watching, and they were moving on to college. I told myself I could do that too.

Because of my neighborhood gang-like experiences, I initially considered a career in Criminology. Florida State University offered a fine course in that field and was well respected for the criminalists it produced – and probably its criminals too these days.

I liked psychology too. I've always loved to watch human behavior. I am not ashamed to admit that I am an optimist about people and their potential.

I had seen the good side of the guys I ran with, and truly cared about them. Call it a spiritual side, whatever that may be. That's always been part and parcel of what I am about, which explains how and why I've run my company a certain way.

Therefore, along with Criminology, I considered majoring in Psychology, especially Child Psychology. An altruistic calling like being a priest, teacher, or psychologist may seem to be a far cry from the entrepreneur I became. I now believe we can have it both ways. I'm not being arrogant when I speak of my altruistic nature.

If I had to name those I admire most beyond the obvious like Malcolm Forbes, I definitely would include Albert Schweitzer, Mother Teresa, and Jimmy Carter as models for my humanitarian behavior. Before I ever heard of them, I gave away my lunch money when I couldn't afford it. That was in the third grade. When I didn't have lunch money, I gave away my sandwiches to a kid who was hungry and had no lunch. No one gave me awards or praise for what I did. I wasn't seeking them. I just did it spontaneously. I still do.

Anyway, I had seen the potential for becoming a better human being within each of my so-called tough gang buddies. That led to my strong interest in the rehabilitation aspect of Criminology.

Unfortunately, a number of the guys I ran with while in high school ended up in boys' reformatories for a while. I knew the good side of those boys. Many were fine fellows who came from wonderful families. I knew their parents. Their moms and dads were struggling the same as my mother was, and the kids were left unsupervised – and you know the saying, *an idle mind is the devil's workshop.*

They got involved in a lot of bad and outright stupid situations. I believed that there surely had to be a way to change them; I believed that there was still time to change them.

There is another factor too, which I think the Almighty has much to do with. Some people get caught or their lives can be ruined simply for being in the wrong place at the wrong time – which I can illustrate from personal experience.

*   *   *

When I was in high school and while Sylvia still had her college man, I was seeing a young lady named Joan who was a waitress at a Walgreens luncheonette on 200 East Flagler Street in downtown Miami. Those were the sweet old days when drugstores had soda fountains and served food. If you are too young to remember, several scenes in the classic film, *The Best Years of Our Lives,* will give you a good understanding of how elaborate the food and confectionery service could be in a major drugstore.

I can remember pharmacists taking turns making sundaes and scooping ice cream when the rush was for sweets for the sweeties rather than prescriptions.

One night around ten-thirty, I sat at Joan's counter while waiting for her to get off work. I was with another guy whose name is not important – although **he** was. We'll call him John. He had been in my group and had just been released on probation from Apalachicola, a boy's reform school.

There were a couple of sailors sitting on the stools along with us, and they started ribbing Joan, knowing full well that I was going with her. They talked loudly about her derrière and said crude things like, "Hey, honey, what a great ass you have."

The sailors were in their twenties, and to me, when you're a teenager, they were older people. **Old** old! And tougher.

One of them made several more comments that were

out of order, completely uncalled for, and I told him to back off. The sailor then verbally assaulted me with every known and some new, to me, profanities.

Remember, I was with a guy who had just been released from a boy's prison. He was sitting to my right, and was justifiably nervous. He said to me, "Skip, you probably shouldn't start anything because that'll bring the police, and I'll get in trouble. And probably get sent back to a juvenile detention center."

I suggested that he leave because I was not going to let these characters say anything more to my girlfriend. As John left, I pushed the most obnoxious of the sailors to shut him up. He had tattoos all over him – snakes and dragons on his arms. He pushed back. I hit him, but didn't hurt him bad enough. He whipped out a switchblade.

That was more terrifying to me than a gun, because you can see yourself ripped open and bleeding. I realized that I had gotten into a major fight.

People were screaming. This was Walgreens, not some sleazy bar.

I was yelling too because the sailor was coming at me with his knife. I threw down a big postcard rack between us. Postcards are very slick, and he slipped on them. As the sailor fell, I gave him a knee to the face and held on to his knife arm.

I heard somebody shout, "He's going to kill the kid!" Meaning the sailor was trying to kill me! I kept pummeling him in the face because I was terrified. By then he was bleeding all over the place.

It was a wild scene. Cops arrived, and they were prepared to call an ambulance. I think I had broken the sailor's nose.

The store manager was supposed to sign papers against us because the fight had occurred inside his store. That would have put me and the sailor in the hoosegow for sure. I saw myself suddenly burdened with a criminal record that would limit my future.

The Almighty intervened. The manager had been on his way out and wanted to go home, so he did not sign the papers. Instead, he said, "Get them out of here!"

Store employees cleaned up the mess, and the sailor left in an ambulance, if memory serves. My girl was crying, and my friend had wisely sneaked outside during the fight. I did not need to be told twice to leave. In a blur worthy of the Road Runner, I burst out of there with no arrest on my record.

It could have gone the other way and changed my life for the worst. And that was not the end of my fight with the sailor. Later, someone phoned to tell me that he'd gone AWOL and wouldn't return to his unit until he killed me. When I graduated high school I went on further alert, because he'd told some people he was going to be in the crowd and shoot me.

I was working at Margaret Anne Table Supply at that time. About two weeks after graduation, I was driving in the downtown section of Miami when the sailor pulled up along side my car. The obsessive troublemaker had really been looking for me, and he pulled out a revolver.

My heart dropped down to my stomach. I thought, "Oh, my God! I'm going to die because of the fight at Walgreens."

For whatever reason when we locked eyes, I yelled at him from the car, "Let's pull over, and we'll see how bad you are!" I was trying to sound tough, and instead, I put my foot down on the accelerator, gunned the engine, and barreled out of there at what seemed like 100 mph. Fortunately, I never saw him after that.

I did, however, encounter the manager again. Several

years later when I was an assistant manager at Walgreens in Miami, I attended a sales meeting and he was there in the capacity of advertising manager. He stared at me as if I looked familiar. Needless to say, I kept quiet. I saw no reason to remind him of our initial meeting.

SIX

Alone At Florida State

My mother had always struggled to make ends meet. Although her income was marginal, she hoped that her children would go on to college. Therefore, she was extremely pleased when I went to Florida State with a scholarship. Despite my long hours away from studying and missing classes, as I worked, dated, and ran with my gang, I had earned a scholarship from Winn Dixie, which covered only my tuition and books. I still had to come up with the money for my room and board from my many part-time jobs.

I have never forgotten how difficult it was to survive financially when I attended FSU. Today, at our company, we offer a number of scholarships to worthy students whose parents work for the firm. They are known as the DeSantis Family Scholarships.

My mother didn't have the time to counsel me properly about the distractions and pitfalls of college life even though she had been a graduate. If she had, I probably wouldn't have listened anyway.

Florida State University is 630 miles north of Miami at Tallahassee near the Alabama state line. For me that was the other end of the earth.

To be perfectly honest about it, from the day I arrived at FSU, I had the feeling that I wanted out. I did not fit in with the college crowd – frat life, sorority dates, the extended adolescence thing. Childish stuff.

College seemed to be so much of a sham back then. There were thousands of students – probably more today -- who seemed to be living off their parents in the Greek houses and drinking themselves into oblivion. Generally they were bright students, but it was their first time away from home with unlimited opportunities to raise hell and have kegs of beer in the houses and dorms without parental interference. I had already become worldly, having done all that at thirteen and fourteen, while they were just beginning to cut their umbilicals as college freshmen and coeds.

Another big difference was that I had earned the money for my beer, and they waited for mom and dad to send them their checks. I'm not absolutely certain, but I'm pretty sure those college kids didn't raise raccoons or have parakeet farms.

I knew that we had not run around with the same types of people. They came from, I wouldn't call it a better class, but certainly a different class. So, I didn't care to associate with them.

Although I never wanted any part of fraternities or sororities, I lived at first in the Pi Kappa Phi house, a fraternity for very bright students that also rented out rooms. I ended up dating a few girls who thought I was a legitimate PK person. They thought I was cute and all that, but my appeal was really only based on what they thought I was, a frat-rat who could invite them to parties. When they found out I only lived at the PK house and paid rent, they didn't want to have anything to do with me.

I had never liked phonies. I've already told you that I liked to befriend real people.

I later moved into what was then Magnolia Hall. I was still a roustabout and hung out with the ruffians in the dorms. I believe I haven't changed in that respect. Although I can relate and work well with corporate types, I enjoy going to places where I can mingle with the hard guys and challenge the body-builders who work out at Gold's Gym to bouts of arm wrestling. It keeps the boy in me alive. Never lose the child's sense of play.

Looking back, I believe that I went to college for several of the wrong reasons. I probably wanted to please my mother, and I thought a degree would open doors for me. While in grade school I'd heard many adults say things like: "Well, I missed all that, so maybe college is the route you should take to be successful."

I saw four long years ahead of me at FSU and getting nowhere. I was not focused on a specific career, although, as I mentioned earlier, Criminology interested me at first. I got into learning about truth and deception and the lie detector test – polygraphs.

I never aspired to be a polygraph expert, but I wanted to learn all I could about criminal behavior. I visited the adult prisons for men at Raiford and Apalachicola, the women's prison in Lowell, Florida, all the boys' and girls' reform schools, and took other field trips. I still have some of my college texts in Criminology, one of which is *Crime Does Pay*. The title meant the field of crime, not criminal activity.

No surprise, my grades were not good. I was on academic probation from the day I got there because I seldom went to class and flunked tests that I shouldn't have.

For example, we had a Physical Education requirement. We didn't have to take the strenuous sports like boxing, weightlifting, or football. It could be anything, so I signed up for two.

Golf was one PE course I took, a nice clean sport. But green time was at 7:30 in the morning. In winter, Tallahassee can get down to 17 degrees. My blood was subtropical Miami-thin. I wasn't about to get up in that weather and play golf. So I flunked golf, when all you needed to do was just show up and you'd pass.

Yet I damn near set the curve in freshman Biology. There were 1,300 students in the class, and my score was amongst the highest on one of the Biology finals.

The other PE course I signed up for was Circus, a cheerleader class, which was basically extra-curricular. It was a college-sponsored circus with no clowns or animals, and traveled throughout the United states and to several foreign countries.

I was able to walk on my hands, having been a gymnast in junior high school, and I thought it would be fun and bring me some glory, which it did. I made the second team as a freshman. Most didn't make first team until their junior year. We performed at FSU's Doak Campbell Stadium and at other schools just before the football games.

I excelled in the adagio acts. I'd catch the girls after they did high flips in the air or leaped down from a pyramid of cheerleaders. I also swung the girl cheerleaders up in the air and caught them. They always felt secure that I'd never drop them.

I most enjoyed performing on the high wire. I had a strong upper torso, powerful arms, and all the necessary balance and agility. As a result, I performed quite well practicing as a catcher in a trapeze act.

In the meantime, my grades were as low as those wires were high.

In 1997, I spoke at FSU (I think it was a year or so after they had Ted Turner.) at the School of Business to the legions of Business students. Dean Melvin Stith said that he had looked up my records, laughed a bit, and added that he would introduce me as a quick learner because I wasn't there very long. I said that I never left with good grades, and asked him not to arrest me when I got up there because I had accumulated plenty of unpaid parking tickets by the time I dropped out of school.

Those unpaid parking tickets never prevented me from renewing my Florida driver license because they had been issued by campus authorities. The only penalty was that I would not be allowed to transfer my grades to another college until the fines were paid. Believe me, those grades were not worth transferring. I like to think that my subsequent support for FSU has more than made up for my youthful parking transgressions; I recently committed to giving a two million dollar donation – to be matched by the State of Florida – to their excellent and effective School of Business still headed by Dean Stith.

SEVEN

Capturing
My Woman's Heart

During the first months of my freshman year and despite my having gone out with several college girls, I thought of Sylvia day and night. I had not seen much of her the previous summer – she'd gone to work for the phone company.

I had written Sylvia in August, 1959, when I arrived in Tallahassee, to give her my mailing address, even though, I thought, I had no chance of ever seeing her again. All throughout her senior year and the summer, she'd been talking about marrying her college man.

As an aside, my postal box number was 694. 69 has been a constant and lucky number for me, and it has nothing to do with those misconceived other connotations. Nor have I ever asked to be assigned those numbers. It all began at my birth. I'm a Cancer with the sign written as 6 and 9. (Astrology as fun and entertainment, not slavish belief). My room number in college was 69. I would successfully manage a Super-X drugstore at 69th and Collins in Miami Beach. I assisted in managing a wholesale drug company with a street address of 6900. 69 is part of my Social

Security number, private phone number, American Express credit card, gate number, bank account, pin number. Numerology – anyone?

As you already know, during my first months at FSU, I paid no attention to my grades. Nothing else was relevant. Not school, business, or family. Only Sylvia was on my mind. And no matter how I tried, I could not come up with a scheme to win the love of my life.

Then one day in November, I went to my mail box and there was a letter from Sylvia. Oh, God! It was wonderful.

Her unexpected letter was, for me, like manna from heaven. As a youngster the intensity of what you feel can never be repeated.

Sylvia left her letter open ended, so I could write her back if I wanted. Had she taken all those months to plan the letter? Sylvia never said so, but I like to think it.

That first letter from Sylvia, which I still have, was about, of all things, the recent World Series: "I'm writing to you about the World Series, about Brooklyn, and some of the team members ..."

She knew zilch about baseball, but it gave her a reason to write me. Although she wasn't a cheerleader, she knew that I'd been a pitcher in high school. Apparently my persistence, and whatever charms Sylvia thought I had, caused her to have second thoughts about marrying her college man.

I immediately replied to her letter, and we began to correspond regularly. That was not enough for me. My grades worsened while I spent my waking hours figuring out the best way to win her.

I finally came up with a plan. I wrote a letter, purportedly to my mother, explaining why I was doing so poorly at college. My GPA was about a 2.1. I said the reason for my low grades was that I was fanatically in love with a young lady in Hialeah, Florida. She was constantly on my mind, and until I settled matters with her, I could not think about going to class or making up my grades. I ended the letter with a typical son's request for his mother to send some socks and underwear, which, I hoped, would give it more believability.

I deliberately mailed that letter to Sylvia. Then I called her at home, and told her I'd made a major blunder. I explained that she was so much on my mind that I may have addressed my mother's letter to her instead. I pleaded with her not to read it if it arrived. Something like telling a person not to think of a blue elephant.

My ploy worked. Sylvia called me back, as I had expected, and she said that I had indeed sent her my mother's letter. I still vividly remember our conversation.

I said, "You didn't read it, did you?"

She said, "Well, I did."

As far as she knew, I had opened up my heart to my mother about the woman I loved.

And I said, "Oh, damn, what am I going to do now?"

Anyway, I went home during the school break. We dated intensely, and two months later, I asked her to marry me. We were wed the following August 1st, 1958.

* * *

After we married, Sylvia and I lived apart for several months. I dropped out of school in the Fall of 1958 to earn some money, and Sylvia returned to Miami to make arrangements for a permanent move to Tallahassee and job transfer with the phone company. She encouraged me to return to school, which I would do the following semester.

By the time Sylvia arrived, she was almost five months

into her pregnancy and it was winter. I'd quit my jobs and was back in school full time. Although, as I've mentioned, Sylvia had the opportunity for a full teacher's scholarship, she saw her role in life as a homemaker and was not all that interested in getting a college degree. She believed that her role in life was to marry and raise children. We did enroll together in a Family Living course at Miami-Jackson, and she once raised her hand to state that she wanted plenty of children and a marriage that would last forever.

Meanwhile, because of bureaucratic snafus, Sylvia's pay from the telephone company where she had worked was held up. She was into her fifth month and showing, and the place where we lived did not allow children. We were told to move.

We'd had no income for a month, and I needed to make money right away. I took a part time job at night as a cashier at a Jitney Jungle, sort of a Seven-Eleven, only larger with four cash register lines. I walked six miles to the job every night but lasted there for only two weeks.

They had a procedure when too many dollars were in the till. They would take out the surplus money, and the person working the register would sign for it. Then you would start afresh with what they called a "bank" of 50 dollars or whatever. However, other employees worked in and out of my cash register drawer when I took a break.

One night, there was a shortage of $20 at my register. Management grilled me, and I explained that several others had worked the register and no readings had been taken. I pleaded with them that I had nothing to do with it. Even after they found out that their assistant manager had robbed the till, they still decided to fire me.

Sylvia and I were now in really bad shape. We had no money, and we were too proud to ask for help from my mother, who was herself struggling to make ends meet, or anyone else we knew. The college advised us to go to our church, but the Catholic Church did not move in a timely fashion.

At the same time, Sylvia and I were heavy smokers back then. We could not afford to buy a pack, so I went around with a paper bag and collected butts. Yes, pregnant women smoked in those days. Apparently it did not negatively impact our daughter Debbie's health or her IQ.

A local Baptist congregation helped us with boxes of canned goods – all lima beans and cranberry sauce. We ate them until we almost retched whenever we opened another can of those delicacies.

Then, David Bates, a great friend who had been best man at our wedding and is a successful attorney today, attempted to rescue us from severe malnourishment, if not starvation. David, who was unaware that he looked and acted like the late actor Lee Marvin, brought us bags filled with groceries. Although we ate some cheese and hot dogs, we were too proud to accept the rest of the food. After much arguing, we convinced him to take the groceries with him when he left.

Finally, I got a job as a short-order cook at a truck stop – hamburgers, bacon and eggs – typical Waffle House stuff. The pace was go-go-go, and I loved the action, although I didn't make much money there. Then, Sylvia's pay finally caught up with her and somehow we survived.

* * *

After we established a regular routine, Sylvia would not go to class for me, but she did help do my term papers at home, and turned them in because I was working several jobs. Then Walgreens hired me full time. The drugstore was located in a new shopping center at 1147 Apalachi Parkway, and I worked as a stock boy for minimum wage of about seventy-five to eighty cents an hour.

Things were looking up for us. Even my grades were improving somewhat for a change. Sylvia had our first child, Debbie.

I started to like working at Walgreens, and during the Spring of 1959, I was promoted from stock boy to Assistant Manager at Walgreens. I also helped out as what is now called a "tech" – one who assists and fills prescriptions with a pharmacist – which took up about seventy-percent of my day. The pharmacist told me that I should go to Pharmacy School, because it was obvious to him that I loved the drug business.

The only School of Pharmacy in Florida was at the University of Florida, with the exception of the black college, Florida A&M – and as I continue to remind you, Florida unfortunately was very much still a segregated state.

By then, Sylvia was asking me **why** I was going to school. My job at Walgreens interested me more than my classes. My GPA had dropped to a 1.6 average. At that rate, I was not going to make it through FSU. What was I doing it for?

She pretty much told me to try the working world and see if we could make it. We could then save enough money in case I wanted to return to school.

I was delighted to hear her say it. I was thinking that I should go for a safe and secure job, the type that my mother insisted I pursue. I was not yet like the other bold entrepreneurial members of my family. I had a wife and daughter to support, and feared getting into another situation where we would so desperately need money to survive.

At that juncture, I told Sylvia that I probably would never go back to school. The only decent paying job available for me with Walgreens was an opening in South Florida. My wife was all for our returning to Miami. Mrs. Chappelear was not well, and Sylvia wanted to be close to her mom.

That wasn't the driving force, however. I wanted to get away from the college scene.

So in 1960, I took a position with Walgreens as Assistant Manager of a store right by LeJune Road, near the Miami Airport. I would be with Walgreens for almost nine years.

EIGHT

Advice For The Family Man

When I went to work at my first Walgreens in South Florida, I thought that I'd finally found a career for myself. Prior to that, my retail experience had been limited to working in grocery stores as I grew up.

I always liked people and working with the public. I also enjoyed the challenge of a new situation every single day. The newness of it was the challenge; there was no redundancy working in retail. We always had new customers, new faces, new products. And I seemed to have the ability to make things happen.

For example, I could take a stack of glasses and move them to one end of the store, move other items around – although there were permanent sections – and bring in men's ties or shirts, then watch how they would sell. I would put up signs that would be aggressive enough to be noticed by consumers who then purchased the items. That was exciting and gave me a real adrenaline rush.

I understood that I had new opportunities to grow, to become store manager, a supervisor too, which also was a great challenge. Back then, about ninety percent of the store managers were pharmacists. Of course there were some very good pharmacist-managers, but they really couldn't be all that effective as retailers while they were tied up behind the counter all day filling as many as three hundred-plus prescriptions daily.

Walgreens believed at that time that even if a stock boy had the ability to rise through the ranks, he would not have the savoir-faire or maturity of a college graduate who was better educated and could speak well. They also saved money by giving a pharmacist-manager a slight increase in salary while paying the non-pharmacist managers less. In any case, the pharmacist-managers generally were not all that savvy about front end merchandise and price points, and they often let the lower paid assistant managers run the front end retail side of the business.

Still, about 5 to 10 percent of Walgreens' managers were not pharmacists, and as long as there was a 1 percent or less chance for me – as long as there was a shot – I was going to go for it. That's how much confidence I had in myself, to see how fast I could make it up the ladder. I believed that if I wasn't **the man**, no one was.

Anyway I worked long and hard hours as Assistant Manager, and I loved it. We all know – if you enjoy it, it can't be work.

I knew how to work only one way – hard. I put in, on the average, about an eleven hour day six days a week. Back then, along with savvy management skills and being honest, much had to do with how long somebody would work in order to be promoted. The bosses wanted to know if their employees were willing to put in a ten hour day and get paid for eight. The people who watched the clock and went home would not get the promotions. If you sat in the back with a sandwich while reading a magazine and no one knew it – and if you were there long enough – management would believe that you were great because you worked ten or eleven hours a day.

I read no magazines while on the job, although some did. I more than just worked at assigned tasks. I totally immersed myself in my job, every part of it from Pharmacy to the cash register, to the safe, to bringing out from the back the on-sale Kleenex, to the incoming orders.

Although it seemed Walgreens truly did expect that for people to succeed they should work longer hours, I didn't do it for that reason. I wanted to work. I wanted to be there. I had total dedication to my job.

Sylvia would later ask me straight out – that was before our divorce: "What was always more important to you? Business or our relationship and the family?"

Because I have always put God, family, and business in that order and say so in all my speeches, my reply to Sylvia may seem hypocritical. I told her if she wanted me to be totally honest, **at that time** the hours I spent at work took priority over the amount of time I shared with my family. If I had told her anything else, I'd have been a damned liar. That didn't mean I wouldn't have taken an arrow for her. It didn't mean I wouldn't go through walls for her, or hurt people who were trying to interfere with my family. But my first duty to my family was to succeed in business.

We can kid each other and use all the verbiage about the subject we want. We can talk about how family comes first. But if you're going to be successful, family does **not** and cannot come first at crucial times, especially if you're struggling to survive, as we did when Sylvia was five months pregnant and we had no money for food or rent.

I never wanted to be placed in that terrible situation again, which is why work came before time spent with my family. Those who tell you differently, I feel, are totally deceiving themselves.

It's interesting how people **always** rationalize whatever they do, as salve for their own souls. They convince themselves that some wonderful end result justifies whatever means they've employed. Unfortunately, as George Orwell wrote: **"There are no ends, only means."**

Those same individuals constantly say, even to their own selves, that the family is more important than the business. That is self-delusional. Yet, people will **never** be completely honest with themselves because they can't accept the truth. If they did, they'd probably jump off a bridge.

Instead, they say, "Wait a minute! My kids **are** more important than the business."

The truth is they probably were not. Today, my children may very well be more important because I've had success in many areas. But during the time when I was trying to reach for the brass ring and rise to the top, everyone had to get out of the way. It was stand beside me or move aside. That's basically it. And I firmly believe it really is true.

Of course I wasn't asked to give up my career. You always want your wife, who is your best friend, to accept those long hours as much as you do. I was so very fortunate to have Sylvia as my partner in building the Sundown business. She was untiring and selfless. Sylvia gave up a lot in her pursuit of **honest success**.

As for time spent with the family. It's not the number of hours, it's the quality. When I hear men speak of quality time with their wives and children, I can assure you that they're fantasizing at best and are only fooling themselves about it. Dillusionary, if you will.

Regrettably, many men do **not** spend quality time with their families. To me, quality time is when you go home, shut off the TV, and go over homework with your children. You don't read the newspaper until you're done looking at their homework and speaking to them about their day. You can and should let them be part of the business, as I did with mine when they were small. To me, that's quality time, and anything less – to sit there and passively watch football with your kids on Sunday – that is not quality time.

Work can be tough, but it doesn't have to be. It should be fun, exhilarating. It's rather sad when you see fellows after-working hours at the lounge of choice talking about the tough day they've had. I often wonder what's hard to them.

Take a thorough look around at people doing their jobs, whether it is physical or mental. I'm not sure, but maybe there's not a hell of a lot of difference between the two. We used to see the sign, Men At Work! Now it just says people working. To me, all those signs are a joke, because very few are working to their fullest capacities.

Yet, they often look to be pitied and mothered when they arrive home late expecting dinner to ready – and it better be. They expect the wife to ask, "Oh, honey, are you all right? Did you have a tough day?" And in the meantime it's the mother who really worked a full day and night in more jobs than most. And few men assist her in those never ending thankless tasks.

Some women can be terribly unfair as well. If a man is not earning what she expects, she demands more; if he works long hours establishing a business to provide financial security for his family, she complains that he does not give her and the children enough time and attention.

Do not place those you love in a no-win situation. Be honest with yourself and those you deal with. But also remember, brutal truth should always be cloaked with charm and kindness, if it must be stated at all.

NINE

My Effective Pricing System

My first Walgreens opportunity or job in South Florida was a beautiful new store, and I was fortunate to work for a great manager, Hal. Because it was off LeJune Road by the airport, traffic was heavy and we were very busy.

I became the assistant manager in only three months, which was a big deal for me because it meant more dollars. At that juncture I bought a home in South Miami Heights, a slightly lower middle class development, which we couldn't afford, but we did it anyway.

In those days you could buy a home with around 1 percent down, and get a refrigerator, washing machine, and everything else thrown in. We paid $11,500 for the home with a down payment of about $150.00. When we eventually sold it, I got back $250.00 and took the refrigerator with us. Since then, I've never made a better deal buying and selling a home.

I traveled 30 miles one way to work in a broken down old car, which took about 40 minutes. I stayed at that particular Walgreens for about two years until they moved me – still an assistant manager – to their second busiest store in the entire state of Florida.

That was in North Miami Beach, which meant for me an hour and fifteen minute ride to work. I had no problem with that. We'd had another child by then, Dean, my oldest son, and I'd have traveled even farther to make a decent life for my expanding family.

It was a tough store. Normally, working there was a platform for going into management. Everybody who was ambitious tried to work their way to that store. The feeling was that if you made it in North Miami Beach, you could make it anywhere for Walgreens as a manager.

Sounds like the lyrics from *New York, New York?* I meant to say that.

Why was the North Miami Beach Walgreens a tough store? First of all you had mostly ex-New Yorkers, a heavy ethnic population of older Jewish people. I used to kid that Condominium was the first Yiddish word I learned. I picked many other colorful words and habitually continue to use them. *Schlepp* and *maven* come to mind.

The North Miami Beach customers were often difficult to work with because they didn't want to pay full retail. They always looked for bargains, whereas the customers at the LeJune store had been predominantly middle class folks, with an abundance of stewardesses and airline personnel who never seemed to question prices.

I learned a great deal about pricing from the North Miami Beach customers. I analyzed their buying habits and found the challenge exciting to convince them that I was giving them the best possible deal – never anything unethical, but almost outwitting them.

I'd always had a penchant for math and numbers. Even at an early age, I had seriously studied price points. I'd also never stopped studying people.

I intensified my observations and solidified my conclusions because much of what I was doing in retail was categorizing brackets of people. I watched how they walked, what they wore, just about all aspects of the human condition, and most especially their buying habits.

I asked myself several questions. What would draw a customer? Was 69 cents better than 77? I worked on formulas to determine which numbers worked best together. My retail environment was the laboratory for me to prove my theory that a price of 77 or 88 cents on non-advertised merchandise would sell more items than the lower price of 67 cents.

The pharmacist-manager was too busy filling prescriptions with his other two pharmacists, and left the pricing to me. It was my show. I had the freedom to test my theory, while every other store in the chain was pricing from a gross profit number and selling products at that number, regardless of which price point really turned people on.

Anyway, I concluded that double numbers were very important. Put a dollar in front of it and those drew more than anything else. 88 cents, $1.11, numbers like that. So what I did at their North Miami Beach store was to prove to the company, management, and myself that I could make more profit for them than they had ever made before.

For example, when the company wanted to sell a product for 73 cents, I'd tell the other employees to watch me. Then I'd mark the item at 77 cents. I was unabashedly pleased when I sold more of the product at my store for 77 cents than the other Walgreens stores selling it at, yes, 69 cents. And I had some of the toughest and, I felt, most astute customers in the entire chain.

That was the major challenge for me, and I loved it. I felt a tremendous sense of accomplishment that my theory consistently succeeded when practiced.

I want to repeat, emphasize and assure you, that my use of double numbers is not instinctive. It is a proven fact.

We still do it at Rexall Sundown, and with double-double numbers. We can often sell more of an item at $11.66 than at a lower price of $10.95 in our relatively small SDV Division, which has now become our testing ground for new products.

I would like at this time to explain the gross profit goals of Walgreens at that time. It was predicated on inventory. They were looking for at least 32 percent overall gross profit in North Miami. Of course bills had to be paid, and after it was all over they anticipated a reasonable net profit. Actually rather meager.

I had become a retail sales *maven,* Yiddish for expert, and the gross profit jumped from 32 to 34 percent. Now 2 percent on four million in sales back then meant about $80,000 more profit for the store, which pleased management.

From that situation I was given the opportunity to become Manager, amongst the youngest non-pharmacist managers Walgreens had ever put in charge of a store. I was twenty-two.

My initial chagrin that the Walgreens I had been given to manage was not in Miami quickly disappeared. Back in those days, you were so pleased and proud to become a store manager you'd work damn near anywhere. If they said Nome, Alaska, you'd go. And so, in 1962, I went to Greensboro, North Carolina.

TEN

A Lesson In Initiative

THE GREAT ICE CREAM MELTDOWN

The Walgreens in Greensboro was a small downtown store at 218 South Elm Street. In the early 1960s, Greensboro seemed very much like the communities portrayed on *The Andy Griffith Show*, and I experienced some culture shock. As an example, a bag of reserve funds in the safe had been labeled **Extry** by my predecessor.

Walgreens had been very aggressive in the 1940s and '50s in the marketplace north of Atlanta and south of Virginia, but in the '60s they were losing business to the up-and-coming Eckerd chain and not putting money into their older stores. Instead, they were changing them from conventional to self-service.

Conventional stores were the old stores from the '40s and '50s where the clerk would hand you something from the display. Self-service is just what the term means. Come in, hunt for the items you want, and pick it up yourself.

So, there were a lot of changeovers in the retail businesses, and about three years earlier, Walgreens had reluctantly changed its Greensboro store from conventional to self-service. It was one of the last. That made it exciting because it was a new venture for them and for me.

Over a period of time, I learned that some of the people I had hired at Central Plaza, the LeJeune store, as assistant managers and stock boys, were also becoming managers. But they had not been sent to places like Greensboro. They became store managers in Miami, and that made me angry. After my success with the North Miami Beach store, I wondered why I had been the one Walgreens sent to Greensboro.

There was one glaring difference between Greensboro and the RFD towns portrayed in those idealized TV sitcoms. I arrived there at the time when the Civil Rights Movement was really heating up. Greensboro was in the heart of the segregated South, and the Grand Dragon of the Ku Klux Klan lived there. They had the sheets, their vile propaganda, whips, and burning crosses.

Remember, it was 1962. Martin Luther King had yet to march in our nation's capital. Forget those amusing, incompetent country sheriffs played by lovable Jackie Gleason you've seen in films like *Smokey and the Bandit*. Real life gave us brutes like Bull Conners and his deputies who behaved like Storm Troopers with truncheons and vicious dogs when they dealt with the demonstrators.

While I worked in Greensboro, Woolworth's, a few stores down the street, had a sit-in – yes, that famous one, when the black protesters sat in the whites-only section of the lunch counter until the good-old-boy cops forcibly removed them.

That did not happen at my Walgreens store. The soda fountain had been removed when they changed the store to self-service.

I wanted out because of the bigotry, and I was angry

that all my buddies were getting stores in Miami while I was stuck in Greensboro. I asked my supervisor, George Fleming, about it.

Fleming was a strong disciplinarian and a good teacher, one of any "chains" finest. In those days, management pretty much ruled through fear, as many parents do. Aside from walking around with a pad and going over all the numbers, we'd go over the monthly figures together.

I asked Fleming if there would ever be an opportunity for me to get into a bigger store. He told me bluntly, "You've only been here for about a year now, Carl. And we don't put an Eddie Arcaro on a jackass."

In the 1960s and before, Arcaro was, and still is regarded by many, as the greatest jockey of all time. Fleming's comment infuriated me. He was telling me that I was so new they had decided that I was not ready for a nice big store. I'd have to work my tail off for them and patiently wait for management to decide – if ever.

In the meantime, I was something of a maverick in Greensboro. Walgreens had made a deal with Borden's and other companies throughout the country, and was known for its fine selection of ice cream. They had forgotten, however, that it was an old downtown store. We had wooden floors. Not even terrazzo.

Walgreens had not taken into account that people could not carry ice cream on a bus because it would melt and leak before they got home. Their so-called freezer bags were a sham. I think they were supplied to us by ice cream vendors. They were simply heavier bags with no special fiber in them.

Because I was seeing stalled sales in ice cream, I decided to take extreme measures to rectify that situation. We were open seven days a week, and on one Saturday or

Sunday, I went in determined to remove the ice cream freezer without telling my bosses.

I had about forty to fifty employees in the store handling the different shifts, and chose the strongest amongst them to help me. Wilbur, the head stock man who would have seemed natural speaking to TV's *Mr. Ed*, was a Samson and led the charge to rip the freezer out of the floor boards. Because I didn't know how to dismantle the thing correctly, our efforts just went to hell in a handbasket, and it was completely demolished. Then I got some linoleum and covered the mess we'd made on the floor.

Of course I'd already had a replacement in mind. I contacted the distributor who had been servicing Woolworth's down the street with 45-rpm records and LPs. I placed the records where the freezer had been, and dolled up the entire display.

I was doing my own thing. I'm a fair artist and can write those double numbers quite well with markers. I had everything priced right and sales zoomed. We sold more records than Woolworth's, which was a much larger store. My 45s and LPs outdid our previous ice cream business by twenty-to-one.

One day Fleming, my supervisor, walked in with Lalar Ballard (love those Southern names), the lady who was in charge of ordering ice cream for Walgreen's in his district. She would drive over a hundred miles one way to check up on the sales at my store, and was extremely distressed by my recent activities.

Fleming demanded to know why we hadn't placed any ice cream ads during the past few weeks. I explained that I'd had a problem with the machine – that the freezer had been giving me trouble right from the start. I still remember our conversation.

I said, "Mr. Fleming, as you know, we haven't sold that much ice cream in the past, and sales were virtually nil."

"What are you trying to tell me?"

"Well, the freezer was problematic. I tried to work on it, but I didn't do too well."

"You knew who to call. We have mechanics and people for service."

"Frankly, I just took it out."

"You did what?" Fleming then got irate and said, "We have contracts and we have to run ice cream ads."

I said, "Well, we don't have the ice cream freezers here anymore."

Fleming was the Atlanta District Manager and his territory went all the way to North Carolina. I will admit I was concerned that he would bring in a new manager. The way they usually operated was that a manager rarely knew if he was going to be axed. Fleming, however, was a gentleman about it after I showed him the sales figures, and he actually became excited about the 45s and LPs. After that day, I never saw Lalar Ballard again regarding ice cream. Her focus was subsequently shifted to tobacco sales.

*   *   *

The most important thing the supervisors of Walgreens were interested in was volume. Profit should come with it. My volume was up and so were profits. Fleming was very pleased because it made him look good in the eyes of the company. I'm sure he told them it was his idea for me to take out the ice cream freezer. Who knows?

There's a term I used while I worked for Walgreens – the final exam. The report card every month was our 32-plus percent gross profit, which they anticipated we should be making. Our final exam came when they took a physical inventory. After that was done, we knew **exactly** how much money we made or didn't make. In every instance, I always made more money than they had expected.

By the time of my ice cream removal, however, I became convinced that I was working in a dead-end job. I continued to hear Fleming's admonition that they wouldn't put Eddie Arcaro on a jackass. That was a real blow to my ego. As you can see, I've never forgotten it.

I have never forgotten another lesson I learned from that experience. Companies and corporations can become so big, that talented employees who succeed outside their methods of operation are often unappreciated and stymied. The credit they deserve for their successes can easily disappear in the paper shuffle created by some myopic management.

ELEVEN

Pharmacist Techie And My Wig Enterprise

I had always enjoyed Pharmacy, and often regretted not finishing college with a degree in that field. I looked up to the pharmacists. They had the full education I had only skirted. Nevertheless, I learned everything I could about pharmaceuticals and the prescriptions we were filling wherever I worked for Walgreens.

Then a bizarre event gave me a wonderful opportunity to further expand my knowledge and experience in that area. Today, anything goes, but in the early 1960s society was considerably less open than it is today, especially in the Bible-Belt South.

The sex, drug, and rock-and-roll culture had not yet begun to transform America. *Playboy* was still banned in many North Carolina communities.

In Greensboro during my four year tenure there, one of our pharmacists was caught buying mail order pornography – magazines and 8mm movies. He had three children and a lovely wife, and the police took him away in handcuffs during a day when we were filling many prescriptions.

I called my supervisor, by then a different man than Fleming, and told him that the police had just arrested our pharmacist. My supervisor told me to close the pharmacy because they didn't have a replacement, and to get an ad running.

Fortunately, Mr. Zimmerman, an eighty-four year old pharmacist-retiree was there to advise me whenever I needed him. Therefore, without the company's complicity, I volunteered to do the work, and filled all prescriptions, about 120 a day. I already knew a great deal about dispensing prescriptions from my days as a techie in Tallahassee and at the LeJeune store, and I could type accurate instructions, which were then affixed on the bottles for the customers: T.I.D. is take three times a day; B.I.D. is twice a day; H.S. is at bedtime. I also knew all the other Latin abbreviations.

I had no assistants, except for Mr. Zimmerman. I eventually advised the home office that we had brought in an interim pharmacist to fill prescriptions until they found a full-timer. I was cautious and never made a mistake. When I couldn't read a prescription or wasn't sure how to fill it, I told the customer we were out of that particular drug. Whenever the prescription called for use of mortar and pestle and making a formula, again I'd say we were out of it.

In more cases than not, I'd tell people that we were very busy, and their prescriptions would be ready in about fifteen minutes. I knew they'd take off and come back later. I didn't want them standing there and watching me while I filled their prescriptions.

If I'd been found out I might have lost my job and been fined, but they could never take away my license. I didn't have one. Nevertheless, I got my chance to be a pharmacist, which I'd always wanted to be, and Mr. Zimmerman sat by me, believing in my abilities, as I did.

You can imagine how proud I was when my daughter Debbie earned her degree in Pharmacy and was **first** in her class. She then went to work for Walgreens – almost a family tradition – and became an area supervisor of pharmacists. About five years ago, Debbie came to work for us at Rexall Sundown; she currently is our Vice President of New Products and works closely in the manufacturing aspects of Q.A. and Q.C. (quality assurance and quality control).

While filling those prescriptions, I learned that I could be totally in control of myself during a crisis. As for the pharmacist, he had trouble finding an attorney to get him out of jail, and he was not able to return to work for about a month. After he posted bond, I allowed him to sign in and fill some prescriptions so he could continue to draw his pay because his family was suffering financially. He would come in at night and go over the prescriptions I had filled. Of course, everything was fine; and as far as the control center in Atlanta knew, we still had an involved, full-time pharmacist. Well, we did, didn't we?

He ended up quitting the store. The Court put him on probation, and he had to take special courses and counseling. I can assure you that what he was caught with was what I strongly feel not as distasteful as some of those "skin" magazines masquerading as literature. But you weren't allowed to mail that stuff in the sixties. Now it's gone way too far, to the point of disgust, and to me is totally reprehensible.

* * *

During my last year with Walgreens in Greensboro, I did

something no other manager thought of. Others might be content to manage and weasel their way upwards in the corporation; I saw outside opportunities everywhere. My entrepreneurial drive, which had been stuck in neutral since the day I entered FSU, now kicked into gear.

The area where I worked was about sixty percent black. I'd observed that wig shops were opening up left and right; yet the majority of black women when wearing wigs had selected those made from synthetic materials.

I felt that the wigs which would sell best should be real hair, not synthetic fibers. I researched in a library, then got in touch with a supplier of wigs at 109 Cane Road in Hong Kong.

I began to import wigs on my own while I was still managing the Walgreens store. I made and put out on consignment in local stores a pony-tail and a rack with tapered ends, over which a woman's hair can be arranged to give the illusion of greater thickness.

Although I bought the wigs on a regular basis, I did not sell them at Walgreens. To my employers, that would have been tantamount to dishonesty.

I was so immersed in managing the store I didn't have as much time as I would have liked to personally run the wig business. But I was desperate to find a way to get out of my seemingly dead end job.

I thought that wigs could do more than augment my income and perhaps become a full time business. I knew it could work. I never had any doubts about that.

And it did work very well, until there was an embargo on hair. I had a major order – major to me at that time – about $3,500 worth of goods coming in. Then I got a letter from the Customs Department. They said my supplier was taking all the hair off cadavers, which was a no-no with our government, and it didn't sound too appetizing to me either.

I pleaded with our government for about three months and called some people who had some pull. They finally released the shipment, and I did get back part of my order. I was virtually out of the wig business by then, and sold only half of my final order. Competitors much larger than I had gone into the business, and the exporters I dealt with had to go elsewhere to find the goods.

By then, I'd been at Greensboro about four years, with a total of almost nine years tenure at Walgreens. Another final exam came in, profits were up, and I was going nowhere. Despite my high gross, they didn't like my independent way of operating. They still saw me as a nonconformist who didn't blindly accept the party line.

Walgreens had their SOP manual, Standard Operating Procedures, the book all managers were supposed to follow. You go to page 27A, and you must not deviate. I looked at the book, and then if it wasn't practical, I went my own way.

That was another reason they didn't want to put me in a bigger store. I was making money for them in Greensboro, and could well imagine what they were saying about me. "Why give DeSantis another store? Let's just keep him there."

Fortunately for me at that time, Kroger Grocery out of Cincinnati was coming out with a chain of drugstores called Super-X. When I came down to Miami on vacation to visit my mother who lived with Aunt Barbara, I interviewed with Super X. They had stores all over the country including Greensboro, Salem, and Durham, but I didn't want to go to any of them. I knew that if I did, I'd once again be stuck there forever. That's why I interviewed in Miami.

They told me that as soon as I could pack my bags and come on down I could be a store manager. But first I'd have to learn their operational procedures. Even though they were hiring many former Walgreens managers like myself, they figured it would take me about six-to-eight months to learn their business methods.

I didn't hesitate. The pay was slightly better than I was getting, and I moved my family back to Miami. By then my third child and second son, Damon, was born.

I had escaped at the right moment. A few months after I left, I was told that either Walgreens had sold the Greensboro store to White Cross, another discount chain, or closed it.

I had gone with my instincts and was right to do so.

TWELVE

Super-X, Super Customers

**Customer: "I told you, I don't want to buy an
elephant. I don't need an elephant."
Salesman: "But today, we have a special. Three
elephants for the price of Two."
Customer: "Three for the price of two? Now
you're talking!"**

I started with Super-X in Hialeah on West 49th Street,
and soon after, they transferred me to a new store at
69th and Collins in Miami Beach, an area which was home
to many Jewish retirees. They felt I was probably best-suit-
ed for that location because of my previous experience
with the Jewish Community in Walgreens' North Miami
Beach store. Super-X had never operated a beach-store
before, and it was their only free-standing store, a complete building in itself.

Now you should know that Super-X designated their
stores A, B, or C. Many other chains like Sears did that.
Super-X made my store a C operation, which meant that
they did not expect all that much out of it.

The Miami Beach store had about 8,500 square feet,

not very big when B stores were around 11,000 and A stores approximately 14,000. Still, I was in a great position. I loved the business. I loved the store. I worked with many good people there.

I especially knew the buying habits of East Coast retirees. We used to call Collins Avenue, "Maalox Boulevard" because heartburn was a common ailment. The pastrami and corned beef they loved were not always lean. I know – I too *luv* them.

Again, those wonderful consumers taught me much about customer needs and demands. I hoped all my customers and friends were still alive and remembered their store manager when in 1995 I was honored to receive the Israel Unity Award from the South Palm Beach County's State of Israel Bonds organization.

The Super-X chain gave me the freedom to put in all kinds of goods and wares that I wanted without approval from the home office. If I so chose, I could buy beach towels or Coconut Patties, Poppycock or playing cards, the kind with large numbers, from Bicycle or Bee. I also sold matzohs and gefülte fish.

Needless to say, in drugstore retail you must retain certain departments. That's axiomatic. You must have dental mouth wash for example, standard items, but the guts of the store – that was my baby. I could do virtually whatever I wanted, and I **did** pretty much just that.

When Christmas came, Christmas lights were not our biggest seller. We had some, but that was the time of year for loading up with sweets, munchies, and all the things tourists from the Northeast and Midwest wanted.

Big souvenir sections lent themselves to high profits. It was not unusual to buy, for example, a souvenir for 50 cents and get $1.44 for it. That's 65 percent gross profit. Very few items can give you that high a return.

I hadn't had so much freedom to operate a business since I was a teenage entrepreneur. What a rush! I had regained control of my destiny to a greater degree.

Because of my background with Walgreens, I was familiar with drugstore retail numbers. I'd always been good with numbers, and, as I mentioned before, I had the good fortune to teach Algebra and Business Math to classmates at Miami-Jackson, the latter for nearly a month with the sub.

I was not only fascinated with numbers, I loved numbers. I still do. I believe that somehow everything in this world is tied to numbers. I think there's yet to be discovered a mathematical formula for our own DNA, which for me is another story.

Super-X gave me the autonomy to do just about anything I wanted. Managing a drugstore had never been more exciting.

The Miami Beach C-size drugstore became an A store in terms of volume. It rewarded Super-X with the highest gross profit, highest sales, highest net, highest everything. Of the eighteen stores in the Miami District, my store ranked first or near first in GPs (gross profits) year after year.

Among my successes, the ice cream sales were huge. The Miami Beach store won the ice cream contest over all seventeen of the other stores. We sold more half gallons of Borden's than anyone else.

As a reward, they put me and my family up at Disney World with five hundred dollars cash. That was a big amount of money then. My name was in the local newspapers along with photos of my wife and children, all because mine was the number one store for selling ice cream. Talk about irony.

Headquarters took greater notice of me, of course, and

I was made advertising manager for their South Florida District. I would get the formats and layouts from Cincinnati, chop it up, and make my own ad in consultation with the supervisors and managers who worked with me. But the advertising work was not always done in the store.

At home, I loved to sit at the table with my children as they cut and pasted the ads to assist me. That was the kind of quality time I loved best.

With my additional responsibilities came more money. Super-X sent many of its new managers over to Miami Beach for me to teach and work with. I always got great joy out of being a teacher. And, I would read the monthly operating statement to the other seventeen local managers. I believe that some of my supervisors didn't know how to interpret them as well as I did. Brazen pride on my part, I suppose.

As good as things were, however, I discovered that I had limits at Super-X as had happened to me with Walgreens. People, whom I felt, were less capable than I became supervisors. They were, however, more organizationally correct.

Unlike Walgreens, the chain was not inclined to make pharmacists managers – that wasn't the problem. It was my unorthodox success. I was not following their book. Headquarters was thinking along these lines: How can he lead if he's never been in a model store that's run normally? Yet, when I opened their Miami Beach store they had told me that I did not necessarily have to follow the book, and to run it the way I felt would best suit the chain's purpose – growth with profit.

THIRTEEN

Sunrise Of Sundown

While at the Miami Beach Super-X, I worked with a number of wonderful pharmacists. Pharmacy then had always represented about 35 percent of the store's business, and around 25 percent of the profits – not as strong as most people believe. Today, because of the exorbitant prescription prices (not profits), pharmacy can represent up to 60 percent of a store's sales.

What happens is, you pay $10.00 for a drug from one of the big pharmaceutical companies like Johnson & Johnson or Merck. You may be able to sell it to a consumer for only $11.75. To make $1.75 on a $10 investment – you can barely pay the overhead on that, as a percent.

Maintenance drugs are very competitive. A diabetic has to take insulin every day, and similarly that and other drugs are items you sell at near cost to keep people coming back to the store. So there's not that big a profit in pharmacy, at least from the store side; manufacturers, on the other hand, gain handsomely.

The drugstore profit comes more often from the front end. You get the customers in the store, and they'll buy the film and all the goodies I had double-number priced throughout the store.

Super-X often switched pharmacists, seldom managers. I was store manager and buyer in Miami Beach for almost eight years and probably had about a dozen pharmacists during my tenure there. Most of them left to go into business for themselves. Today, unfortunately, the independent drugstore is slowly singing the last notes of its swan song, with the exception of the mold breakers.

Some people think pharmacists are frustrated "wannabe" doctors. I don't believe that. They're just frustrated, as are many others who suffer the tedium of repetitive routine in their professions or jobs.

It's a demanding profession, and the customers often are very tough, especially those, it seemed, on Miami Beach. You needed a certain personality to deal with that barrage day in and day out.

Kenneth Bullhach was such a man. He was one of the best pharmacists I ever worked with and perfect for Miami Beach. He was young and Jewish, brilliant, a true people person, and a wonderful human being.

One day in 1975, I discussed something with Kenny that had been bothering me. Every day, people came in with severe cases of sunburn and asked us what to use. In each case we recommended Solarcaine®. I thought that there had to be a better answer.

At that time, we had plenty of suntan products, and other sunburn lotions – Shuttle Lotion® a local product and Bactine®, an astringent – but Solarcaine® was the one product all our customers wanted. I felt that there was a niche among the sunburn and suntan products for us to create a business.

I let the idea gestate for about a week. Then I went into action. Once I make up my mind, I floor the accelerator. No trepidations about if it will work or won't it work.

I spoke with Kenny and suggested we get into the business. He wanted to know how deeply, and I told him pretty deep. Not only would we produce a Solarcaine-type product, but why don't we come out with some suntan lotions too?

My immediate concern was to get enough start-up money, and I really wasn't worried about it all that much. By that time, my three children were in junior high or high school, and I was making a good living at Super-X with bonuses and perks.

I was able to get my hands on about $2,500 without borrowing from my mother, and Kenny came up with another $2,500. We went to the library to do research and scoured the Yellow Pages to find the sources and a manufacturer.

We selected a company in South Florida called Filpak. The name was indicative of the company. It filled and packaged.

We met with Filpak's owner, Al Wilpon, who is still in business in South Florida. Wilpon said that he had talked to many people like us, entrepreneurs, but nothing ever materialized from most of them, and they didn't pay their bills on time. He told us **not** to get involved in this *stuff,* as he put it, because we had good jobs.

We pleaded with him to make us a batch and gave him an off-the-shelf formula of a Solarcaine® product. Although Kenny was a pharmacist and a chemist, he didn't know much more about making a formula than I did.

Al Wilpon did know. He gave us a couple of variations. It all boiled down to this: Anything that contains 3 to 6 ounces costs about 40 cents, even if it's water. So we created basically the Solarcaine® formula with a little magic dust, a touch of this and that to make it different, and we felt better.

Once we had a product, we needed sales people. I knew

a number of them whom we could use because I'd been running essentially an independent drugstore even though it was part of a large chain. They sold their products to me, but not to the typical Super-X. Aside from my drugstore, they mostly serviced the beach and souvenir shops.

We found Harry Foresmith, an eighty-three year old man who had retired from his own business in New York but was a fireball of exuberance. He continued to *schlepp* his wares with ours from door to door, and his products were in all the stores along the beach.

Harry was a first-class gentleman and we loved him dearly. He worked straight commission only, although we paid part of his gas expenses.

We effectively went from South Beach – today the hot and *au courant* art deco district and luscious modeling center – all the way to Sunny Isles Boulevard, which is 167th street, a twelve mile run before you get to Fort Lauderdale.

We had started with about $5,000 and came out with a series of products: Sundown for sunburn relief, Dark Tan, which is self-explanatory, and SuperTan, ditto.

SuperTan was a big bottle with a push\pull nose. Wilpon sold it to us for about 60 cents; we sold it to the stores for 85 cents, making a quarter on each bottle. The stores then priced SuperTan for $1.19, $1.99, or as high as $2.25. It was our biggest selling item and easily outstripped the sales of our other products. [Sundown Product, Inc.]

Then we began to run commercials and advertise heavily on buses. In a very short while we were taking in over $5,000 a month.

We did quite well and were a good team. Kenny pretty much let me do my own thing, which is the way I prefer to run things anyway. To this day, I won't go into business with partners unless I am in charge. If you want to be my partner, I'll be completely honest with you, but understand one thing – I'll make the hard decisions.

I must have the right, if necessary, for the last word. I've always been an in-charge person. I've always wanted to be in complete control of my destiny. I was able to do that with Sundown for many years – until we went public. That's for a later chapter.

* * *

While working for Super-X on "Maalox Boulevard" and establishing Sundown, I continued to observe and listen to my customers as they tried to make up for their bad dietary habits by ingesting pills and vitamins. They frequently badgered us to carry more vitamins at a cheaper price, and confirmed what I had already learned. There was another big niche waiting to be filled. Kenny and I came to realize that we could and should expand our Sundown line to include vitamins.

FOURTEEN

Mail Order Marvel

While I was Advertising Manager for Super-X, I met some layout artists who worked for the *Miami Herald.* Many were eager to moonlight for extra money, so I asked a couple of them to design ads for me, which they did for nominal fees.

At that time, I was looking beyond suntan products to vitamins. I had been seeing a tremendous surge in vitamin sales. Shute University in Canada – the Shute brothers were both chemists and physicians – had been doing studies on vitamin E and its abilities to fight the ravages of age – from male impotence to heart disease to the free radicals that are formed inside our bodies when we inhale pollutants. As we know, many more benefits have since come out about vitamin E.

The vitamin E in the Super-X stores came from Parke-Davis, Squibb, and the other big drug companies. We also had our own Super-X private label vitamins, which encompassed about forty different products including some synthetic vitamin E.

I saw that our customers preferred natural vitamin E to the synthetic, because most of the studies had been done on the naturals. In any case, I started learning more about that particular vitamin.

I looked around. I studied. The same as I do today.

Natural vitamin E comes from soybeans, and only a small amount can be extracted from wheat germ, which is not cost effective. Synthetic vitamin E is a digestible oil derivative.

I had been watching what was happening with vitamin E and other nutrients, especially among the discount stores in the general area of Miami Beach. I wanted to know what they were doing, how they were doing it, and why they were faring so well.

I went to Fedco, one of our competitors, and saw hordes of customers buying vitamins galore, of the kind that Super-X was not selling in my store. At the same time, I read all the articles about vitamins that were coming out in the *National Enquirer* and other publications.

I began to ask myself many questions: What else can I do? Is there a potential profit situation here? Is there a market?

At Super-X, all I saw were the high-priced spreads from the big companies, and thought that all the national brands were way overpriced. I believed that there had to be a niche for a lower-priced quality product.

I got in touch with a local supplier in Miami who packaged private labels for different stores. He offered to package vitamins for us at two-thirds of the retail price – if the cost to a customer was $4.00, we'd be able to sell it at $2.99.

I knew if I could do that, it would be a major accomplishment. But I didn't want to do it in Super-X. I wanted to do it for myself. I believed my best shot was to sell my vitamins by mail order. Although I never had been a mail order *maven,* I thought that the easiest thing in the world would be to put out a mail-order catalog and do business from our home.

I bought eight key products: Vitamin C in two potencies, C 500 mgs and C 1000 mgs; Lecithin in two different potencies; a B-Complex formula; and natural vitamin E in 3 potencies – 200 IU, 400 IU, and 1000 IU.

E was going very strong at Super-X. I knew that E and C were the bellwethers. Those were selling well at the beach, and I wanted to stick with the winners. In those days, I believed that as Miami Beach went so went the world, which is not necessarily true.

I created my advertisement to appeal to Mr. and Mrs. J. Q. Public. I wanted the housewife and the small towns and rural areas, communities that were nowhere near any discounter. The Marts and other chains that bring low prices to the consumers did not yet exist.

I hired free-lancers and moonlighters who put together a small ad for me. My first mail order ad was a 4" x 1" column and emphasized Vitamins E and C, and Lecithin. I ran the ad under the Sundown name in the *National Enquirer.* In large print, I emphasized the popular letter vitamins, E and C. The ad cost $640.00, full circulation. In 1975, the *National Enquirer* had about three to four million readers.

I was very green. I did not know my mail order math. I did not know how many orders I'd get back. My main concern was *if* it was going to sell.

I rented a small PO box in North Miami Beach. I didn't know then that it's a very big no-no in the mail order business to use a PO box when you're selling products, because people have a justifiable tendency to be suspicious of them. More often than not, such businesses are here today and gone tomorrow with their customers' money. Give them a physical address and they're more likely to write the order.

I soon modified my first ad. I discovered that it was not necessary to add a four-line reply box at the bottom for the customer's name, address, and number of bottles ordered. It took up too much space, and space cost money.

Yet, my first ads went against the conventional wisdom in such a way that it inferred and convinced people to stop paying higher prices. When my wife, Sylvia, and I went to the post office to pick up our first responses, there was a single card in our box for us to see the Postmaster. We had no idea why.

The Postmaster told us that we had received too much mail for our box. The postal workers then came out with gunnysacks. **Gunnysacks!**

I later learned how to chart mail order. Once the ad appears, mail in response to it arrives about three days later, peaks in about ten days, and decreases after that.

The first ad drew just under $18,000 in sales. This earned us more dollars than three months worth of pavement peddling our Suntan products.

At that time, we'd been living in a middle class, ranch style older house in North Miami Beach for about a year and a half. I had no place to fill the orders, so Sylvia and I went to Sears and bought metal shelving. We put it in our bedroom and sorted out the vitamins on the shelves from which we could pull the orders. I then learned what it cost to ship each order.

We worked late in the evenings because I didn't get home from Super-X until ten at night. Often, my wife's good friends from church helped us pack. So did our three children.

In bed, we could hear the cracking of the soft gels as

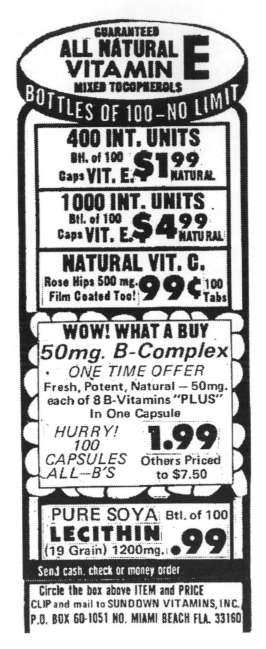

One of my first vitamin ads.

they settled in their jars. The sweet sound of growth at night. That put a smile on my face because I knew that somewhere in the world, while we slept, someone was writing an order and making out a check to us.

UPS used to arrive on a regular basis even though we were not licensed by the city or zoned properly for their trucks to pick up my packages at our house. But the neighbors never complained.

Kenny was still my partner and living in an apartment in Miami Beach, where he met a young lady and fell in love. She was Chilean; he spoke fluent Spanish. Kenny married her, and before he moved to Santiago, Chile, I bought back my share of the business. He was the eternal optimist. A fine young man. I missed him.

I continued to run ads in the *Enquirer*, and was grossing nearly $25,000 a month, which gave me about a $3,000 net profit. This was serious money. Big dollars.

I did not decide to quit my day job at Super-X until I was passed over yet another time to become District Manager. I spoke to Sylvia, and she agreed that we had enough going for us.

I finally believed I could make it on my own, that I could survive, and gave Super-X a month's notice. About the same time, I was in the process of buying a variety store, something like a drugstore without prescriptions.

My District Manager at Super-X, Dick Kaplan, and I had sustained a good relationship. He knew I had established a fledgling mail order business on the side, but I never mentioned my variety store because management might assume that this was a true conflict of interest.

They replaced me in two weeks. Several months later they finally took a physical inventory, which should have been done the week I left. The manager who replaced me had a field day in the meantime. He was an excellent "do it by the company book" manager and changed the inventory to the chain's standard products. The specific needs of the local community be damned. He reduced the prices of my items that were unique to the store such as Poppycock and souvenirs to clear them out. As a result, he destroyed the profits by a nearly 15 percent shrinkage factor, which made it look as if I had been inflating my figures. I was not there to defend myself and am still saddened by that.

I learned or reinforced another lesson from that experience. All people do things differently, but can still get the same job done. If you ask four or five people to paint the ceiling in their stores, one will start in the middle, another in the corner, and so on. They will work at various speeds. And yet that ceiling will be painted.

Contrary to the way I am and the type of people I prefer to manage, many employees are content to work for a patriarch, a strong boss, micromanagers we call them today, and the fellow who replaced me was like that. He hired those needing a parental figure and succeeded in that way – not as profitable as I was, although profitable nevertheless. He got the ceiling painted. He was a good rule-abiding strong and effective manager.

Looking back, of the people I trained during my years as store manager, some 80 percent left Walgreens and Super-X. They were not cut out to be permanent nestlings.

I received one other benefit from leaving retail. I had gone through three holdups, and I don't have to describe how frightening it can be when someone points a loaded gun at you. That was when, despite cries of **don't!**, I started to chase one armed robber down the street.

After I left Super-X and purchased my Five and Ten, I opened a T-shirt appliqué store and was hired as a vice president for another mail order drug business. Everything was coming together.

FIFTEEN

My Little Variety Store

I purchased Jean's Five and Ten from a lady named Jean McDermott – no relation to my friend Corney McDermott, whom I'll mention later – for between $11,000 and $12,000 after taking out a second mortgage on our home. I left the sign up. I didn't think the DeSantis name was so very important then. Nor do I today, even though it now appears on my ties, which is another business story I'll tell you about later.

Although I operated my variety store under its original name for about two and a half years, it was basically a part-time business for me. I was usually there for approximately four hours a day, six days a week; hired help worked there the hours I was away. And my oldest son, Dean, who was about twelve years old and a budding numbers genius, operated the cash register on Sundays.

The store was small and had been doing less than $150,000 a year. It was close to a school and sold plenty of party favors, school supplies, and other high profit products. I thought I could use my retail background and management acumen to move products around, and have a more effective sell-through.

I had a long list of sources by then, so I was able to add

to the variety of goods in the store. Although I didn't have much clout yet, at least I knew where to go to get the items that were selling best in the drugstore chains.

I immediately moved the vitamins out of my bedroom and into the back of the store. In its first year, my part-time variety store netted myself and family almost $25,000. That was about 20 percent more than I had made as a manager for Super-X, which is a good way to measure its value to me and my family.

I planned to create a chain of variety stores, but not like Woolworth's and the other dinosaurs that are almost past tense and truly yesterday's news. I wanted to have a Ben Franklin type of operation, small and compact, which I could either franchise or open three or four of them myself with my profits after I had more successes under my belt. I was going to call my chain DDD'S, the initials of my three children, Debbie, Dean, and Damon.

I had envisioned my family working with me in all my endeavors, as I had been having success working side-by-side with Sylvia and our children from day one in my nutritional business. And they continued to be so very helpful in the variety store. I could see the second generation being more deeply involved. The kids liked what I was doing, so I thought it part of the natural course of events to involve them in the business.

About the same time I purchased the variety store, I started up a T-Shirt appliqué business. The customer picked out the design he or she wanted, and it could be steam-ironed on the shirt.

I rented an 800 square foot store next to a convenience store in the neighborhood where my house was. I bought a heat appliqué machine from a place called Roach Distributors out of Daytona Beach. They had all the transfer pictures from Harley Davidson designs to surfer scenes.

I bought the best T-shirts direct from Haines, Fruit of the Loom, and Stedman's at different price levels. I knew how to do that because of my drugstore background. When I'd get home from work, I'd go over to the store. I hired young people to do the work and paid them very well. I was in that business for about two years.

Then, a wholesaler of generic pharmaceuticals who thought I was indeed a mail order whiz kid asked me to help put him in the business. We came out with a catalogue selling not just generic pharmaceuticals but vitamins too. I eventually worked with him in that situation for about eighteen months as vice president of his company at $35,000 a year. He was an excellent businessman and very fair to me.

Was I still thinking about cans of lima beans and cranberry sauce?

* * *

I did not end up with a chain of variety stores. We had trouble getting the leases I wanted. Ninety percent of the time, retail success is dependent on three factors: Location, location, location – and good locations were simply too costly.

The main reason I never established my chain of variety stores, however, was the success of my mail order vitamin business. Once I saw the mother lode coming in the mail, I thought that I might be on to something grander than the chain of variety stores I was thinking of building. Although my background was in retail, I could see that I was in complete control of my destiny through mail – far beyond what it would be with a chain of stores.

My vitamin business grew quickly because I expanded my inventory and left virtually all the profits in the business for growth. After the first month, I had thirty-three items and then it grew to everything the generic whole-saler had plus some other items I wanted in my line. That brought my list to about one hundred and fifty items.

Mail order gave me an opportunity to write and direct-ly communicate my ideas to the people. I could project my personality through my writing even though I was selling vitamin E and the verbiage that accompanied it would not win any literary contest.

I relentlessly studied the competition. I became con-vinced that I could do it better. I had to. The thought of winning consumed my every fiber – winning against all odds, winning against all competitors. And during those years, there were ten times the number in mail order than the vitamin business today.

I have always felt very comfortable being conversant with people, having the ability not so much to win them over, but to let them know what I'm about, and to under-stand and learn from them. But it can be difficult to do that from a window banner on a store. You have to wait for someone to come in, then you either have to confront them or lead them down the aisles and work with them.

Also, when I write, I can pen ideas that I often cannot express verbally at the moment they're required. That includes ads.

The typical ads from my competitors in the nutritional business were imperfect. They were cut and pasted. They lacked embellishment, those enticing adjectives. I put pos-itive adjectives in my ads, which gave the consumer a rea-son to buy.

I have always used double adjectives when I'm writing - - like my double numbers – two not one. And I think there's a place for it in all writing. Anyway, my competi-tors' ads were dry – vanilla, without luster – and their words didn't flow.

I think conversationally. When you're writing ad copy, it should be the same as conversation.

One might very well say that my competitors' ads were clinical. The consumers were looking for more than that. They had already read the clinical reports of this and that trial. They had heard all the news. Now they wanted something to wrap 'em up – put their arms around them – give them the warm and fuzzies – which is what I attempted to do. They were consumers, not patients.

And did my ads work! A little over half a year later, I was doing almost $200,000 a month. Wheelbarrows full of money. As the saying goes, we couldn't fold it.

Many people believe that mail order is a cash cow, that real green dollars come in. From my experience, I can tell you that probably less than 1 percent of the orders were cash, which was fine with me; when employees open up the envelopes of those orders, they have an opportunity to pocket cash – although I believe that our loyal employees never took advantage of that opportunity.

During those first days of my mail order business, I did not accept American Express, Visa, and Master Card even though they were popular. Ninety-five percent of our customers paid by check or money orders.

I made sure that my advertising in the *National Enquirer* went to "Rural Route 2", small town America. That's where the bulk of the customers came from, because they obviously couldn't get their nutritional supplements at such a low price in their communities.

To my delight, bad checks averaged only about $35 a month. We did not hold the checks and took the orders as large as $500 without waiting for clearance. We trusted the people we were dealing with, and, consequently, that never seemed to hurt us. When I say we, I'm talking about myself and my family, specifically my wife, Sylvia, who handled the books while still holding down a minimum wage job in the Customer Service Department of Burdines Department Store in North Miami Beach, Florida.

* * *

Although I never finished college, I knew how to research. After I listened to the evening news, checked my kids' homework or report cards, I read two to three hours every night to keep current about vitamins. I especially concentrated on business publications relating to the nutritional field.

Now completely on my own, I discovered that my competitors were not aware of many things, nor taking advantage of what they may have known. For example, I read in a credible publication that vitamin E works symbiotically with the B-complex and has a better effect on the capillaries and vascular system if taken with B vitamins.

Thus, I'd put together a formula or ask to have one made and manufactured, and then refer to the article or majority of articles – scientific data – which virtually proved that vitamin E was more effective than the B-complex as a stand alone.

One scientific research project also established, after many trials, that once you mixed the B-complexes with vitamin E, the formula would become as much as eight times more potent in fighting the onset of arteriosclerosis – hardening of the arteries. Yes, that was only one study, be assured, but the evidence kept mounting. My competitors obviously were not keeping abreast of the latest findings; nor was the general public always familiar with the information I gleaned.

I read the JAMA, Journal of the American Medical Association publication. I went to the library and learned everything the scientists knew about selenium and many other key minerals. I would then give out that information to the consumers and let them make up their own minds as I came to them with formulas which were different from the letter vitamins – A, B, C, D, and E.

I mixed nutritional supplement products with the letter vitamins, and created repeat customers because no one else had those particular consumer viable combinations. That gave me a major leg-up on the competition. To this day, 70 percent of the company's products are indigenous to us, different from the competition.

We are not different just to be different for commercial reasons. We do our homework here at Rexall Sundown – I still work closely with R&D – and they've been a big part of our success. We continue to come up with new concordant formulations based on solid scientific data, which, I feel, few other companies in our industry do.

Again, not to overstate it, I am doing what I have always done. It was true with T-shirts, the variety store, and definitely with vitamins and nutritional supplements. I have always wanted to build a better mouse trap, not for the sake of being different, but to actually bring to consumers a viable alternative. Consequently, I think that is why we succeeded and will continue to flourish because of the ineptness and often shortcomings of our competitors, and our passion to win against all odds. Overachieving has been our corporate constant.

There is another reason for our corporate success. We love our work. Of course, it is true that merely selling alphabet vitamins could be boring, the same as being a passive storekeeper. Nevertheless, I found the vitamin business to be interesting for two reasons: I had the acumen to come up with new combinations of vitamins and other nutrients that consumers would accept; and I knew how to work closely with the manufacturers so that they would produce those products at an advantageous cost to us, the benefits of which we could then pass on to our customers.

I was not concerned with dollars and profits as our mainstay, however. That was nearly the last thing I thought about. I sensed that if we could successfully handle the plethora of small problems that bedevil any business, those often neglected profits would be sure to follow. I cared more about what I or the company could do to induce customers to purchase from us and not our competitors. How would we be able to give them something no one else had? It was the competitive thing, the same as when I wrestled with John Guerin all day. He was a tough adversary who won more than his share; thankfully, he didn't enter the vitamin field.

* * *

Had I stayed in retail and eventually moved into a drugstore chain's corporate mahogany penthouse, I don't think I could have fared as well as I did, from a standpoint of wanting to improve my life, being inventive, and sustaining a desire to beat the competition. Going out on my own also brought me praise from one who mattered greatly in my life.

Because I had opened my variety store, the mail order business was growing, and the T-shirt shop was doing well, my mother realized that I had finally grown up. I was no longer her Onion Boy.

She had been the great moral teacher in my life and was generous with us whenever she could afford it. She had loaned us $1,800 from her meager savings to fix the roof on our first house and would not accept repayment.

After Aunt Barbara died, we built an addition to our house, and she lived with us.

My mother was great with her grandchildren who all loved her, and she continued to work until she became ill with cancer. After fighting it for eight months, she passed away. I was on the edge of substantive success when I lost my mother. At least I had her longer than many, and her influence, which had always brought me up front and center, continued as an essential part of my being, and surfaced often.

SIXTEEN

My Incomplete Multiple

Early in my mail order nutritional business, I recognized that most people were taking a single multiple vitamin – "One a Day"® as insurance against a poor diet and the life they led. It might be Centrum®. It was often Myadec® or Squibbs® because the doctor wrote a prescription for them. Or someone would come in with an ad that said take Theragran®. And there were others. Geritol®. Unicaps®. A whole.host of single entity multiples taken once daily.

While I studied those formulas, I observed that people who took their multiples were also taking vitamin E separately every single day. Typically 400 IUs of E is about 400 milligrams in weight. All you could get into a typical one-a-day multiple was 30 to 60 IUs of E, which was less than the consumer wanted. They took vitamin C separately as well, minimally 500 to 1000 mgs each day.

There was no way I could put 500 mg of C and 400 IU of E into one tablet with the other vitamins and minerals -- unless the consumer could swallow a capsule or pill the size of a golf ball.

Sometime in 1977, I decided to do it differently and remove the E and C from the multiple because the overwhelming majority of people were taking them separately. That also reduced the cost of our multiple. C is an expensive entity to produce, and E is even more costly. We replaced C and E with zinc and other less expensive but needed minerals, and increased the potencies of the other nutrients.

We called it Ultramax®, Our Most "Incomplete Multiple" because by law you cannot call a product a multiple unless you include all the letter vitamins. It was immediately embraced by our customers, who continued to purchase our E and C separately.

Our Most Incomplete Multiple cost us around $3.50 to manufacture, and by 1978-79 we were selling a bottle of 100 tablets at about $9.88 in the Mail Order Division. Our profits on the Incomplete Multiple were substantially greater after we removed the E and C. In the third year of our mail order business, that particular multiple did close to a million dollars in sales. As for my competitors, they continued to make their one-dailys with C and E; and, therefore, their products cost them more, and, I know, provided substantially less profitability.

The typical consumer doesn't know the cost of ingredients to a company like ours – that E and C are more expensive than copper, zinc, and calcium. So they thought they had a bargain on their hands, which was somewhat true, because our Incomplete Multiple was a better product due to its nearly 40 nutritional ingredients.

We also began to look at bone meal, dolomite, and other non-vitamin but still nutritional supplements. We knew that our consumers preferred to use those products because they were natural and gave off substantial amounts of nutrients such as calcium and phosphorous.

Back in the 1970s, people were taking brewers yeast and other ancillary products to vitamins. My competition was giving them a 7½ grain product. 7½ grain is a weight measurement, one grain being 65 mg. Although typical consumers didn't understand the metric system, they did know that 7½ grains was what everybody in the industry was offering.

After I took a long look at the entire nutritional industry, I asked a couple of manufacturers if they could make me a supplement consisting of 10 grain bone meal, 10 grain brewers yeast, 10 grain alfalfa, 10 grain this or that. And that's all it was. A slightly larger tablet. But from a marketing ploy, we could legitimately say we had a tablet that was 40 percent more potent at virtually the same price. Of the aforementioned products, consumers were ingesting multiple amounts daily.

If a person was taking 10 bone meal tablets a day, he or she could take 6 or 7 of mine, which was consumer desirable. They would still get higher potency at a lower cost.

In doing so, we added 40 percent more than our competitors to the potency and size of the tablets. Our cost was only pennies above theirs.

Again, we beat the competition because they were not paying attention. And they were following the leader. Funny thing – there were no leaders in the industry. Only followers. Wait for Joe Blow to do it, then follow. The bland leading the bland.

Another fact I discovered early in the vitamin business was that amongst those who took vitamins and nutritional supplements, about seventy percent took in excess of fifteen tablets a day – not fifteen different products – but about six of their favorites two or three times each day. Even in the late 1990s among serious vitamin users, a typical consumer averages about seven products purchased and ingested daily.

At the time our Most Incomplete Multiple Vitamin

made its debut, we had a number of other multiples. They were similar to Centrum®, Theragran M®, and others. Our formulas were more complete and often more potent.

When I say *more complete*, I mean that we had formulas the consumer would respond to, which were perceived to be better than the nationally advertised brands, because we used – and continue to use – many more natural ingredients wherever possible. The major drug companies continue to use basically all synthetic vitamins. Nothing wrong with that. The body truly does not notice the difference – in most cases. But if the consumer wants natural, then we will continue to supply what the consumer wants if the product is credible and efficacious.

SEVENTEEN

Expanding My Business, Expanding My Family

During the last years of the 1970s and into the 1980s, the mail order business expanded. Each time we moved from warehouse to larger warehouse, we began to ask for help from outside the family. As I mentioned in an earlier chapter, many wonderful women from our church helped us fill the orders when we were overwhelmed by our gunnysacks.

One Sunday at Church, I asked Ann Breitfelder, who was my son Damon's den mother, to help out at the warehouse, and she has been with Sundown ever since – for twenty years. Ann loves to tell stories how she used to work straight through from nine in the morning until three in the afternoon at our Hialeah warehouse, pick up our mail on the way home, and have her kids sort it out through the evening hours. Ann became head of SDV's Customer Service, and after twenty-plus years with us, she is planning to take her overdue retirement in the very near future.

We had no telemarketing at that time. Soon we needed more space and additional employees, and we moved to a larger warehouse in Hollywood. By then Ann was in charge of twenty-five people in the mail order section. The main office was at the front door. Everyone was typing on cards. That was before we went with computers.

The lady who owned the house next door let the employees have lunch outside on her picnic table. I would join them. Everybody got to know everybody. We knew the names of everyone's spouse, children, and parents. We truly were one big family.

Today, we almost suffer from our success. Different buildings, many cubicles, and fifteen hundred or so employees make it more difficult to have that same close feeling. But believe me, we try, and for the most part we have sustained our warmth and camaraderie.

We had some excitement when a ferret got loose in our warehouse back then. The ladies were running and screaming all over the place until the little fellow was caught. He did not get into any of our vitamin bottles. Imagine if he had – he might have sired a mutated breed of super-ferrets.

It has been said that there are different types of ESP. Some may be gifted with precognition, others with psychic powers. I believe that I have been gifted with the ability to do a relatively quick and accurate read on people. I will decide to hire someone in an instant and rarely regret it. That is why so many of the employees have worked out so well and thrived with our company's growth. It's a knack that can't be taught, I suppose.

I had a philosophy in dealing with employees. Once I hired them, I spent time sharing my business philosophy with them. Then I'd turn them loose to do their thing – the same way I had liked being treated when I worked for Walgreens and Super-X. I never overly micro-managed. Sure, I'd oversee and occasionally check in and admonish them when necessary for blatant waste of time, general misuse of products, or if they needed attitude adjustments. We all can be expected to make honest mistakes now and then. Who hasn't? I tried and succeeded, I believe, in creating an atmosphere where employees can admit to an error without fear of retribution to any harsh degree.

In a typical business today, if you were to remove the roof of a corporate headquarters or plant, fly over, and take an aerial view, it would appear to be working effectively. But let's take a closer look. You will see that the company has many problems together with an inordinate amount of waste because **the process is being followed but the substance is lost.**

If I've learned anything in my years of management, it is **Empower! Empower!** Review and reward for meaningful accomplishments. Remember, management by committee, plain and simple, does not work. You must always insist upon accountability and maintain **passion for the substance.**

* * *

Later when the various departments converted to computers, I hired the senior outside programmer virtually on the spot. I paid out less and in turn I brought in a tremendous valuable asset who eventually ascended to Vice President.

Not all my early recruits were women. I had known a wonderful gentleman who became my friend, Cornelius McDermott, Jr. known as Corney to his friends. I'd been acquainted longer with his father, whose godfather incidentally had been the legendary Connie Mack, hence their same first names. Mr. McDermott, Sr., had made many visits to my Super-X store as a Maybelline salesman. In those days, there was no way I could have known that his son would end up being a major overall player in our success.

Corney and I both had small businesses. We had other mutual interests, our sons were the same age, and we often got together to speak of cabbages and kings.

After Corney sold his business in 1981, I invited him to hang out at my office. In a short while, he saw there was a big future in mail order, joined us at Sundown, and became a member of my social group of pals and business partners.

Soon Corney was laying out ads, initially under my tutelage and dealing with the printers. He likes to tell one story about himself. We were arguing over the layout and wording of one particular ad. I knew I was right; he thought he was. I suggested that we divide the country and see how each of our ads would do. Mine did better, as I expected. But, let me assure you, his was awfully close.

When Corney helped start up our graphics department, that usually most frugal of men had to endure our repeated interrogations about the large amount of money he was spending on computers. He held his ground, and his vision gave us a state-of-the-art graphics department far beyond those of our competition.

Today, Corney is Department Manager of Print Purchasing. He is wonderfully cost conscious, as I am, and we will spend money only where and when it is necessary. We needed a good person in print purchasing to make sure our suppliers send us their products timely and priced fairly. We're often given a short time-line by our customers – they want our products yesterday. How and what is not their problem. Corney makes sure our suppliers are conscious of our needs and will act accordingly.

We operate the same way with our vendors. Invoices are

paid on time, all the time, not 45, 60, or 90 days later. We want their loyalty; we give them the same.

Another important member of my extended family is Nickolas Palin, whom I met in a delicatessen some fifteen-plus years ago. We hit it off immediately, and we became good friends. Although, I did not have a place for him at Sundown that day, I did offer him a job a few months later. Nick has been a major player in all our successes. Currently, he is our President of the Sundown Division, including all the divisions which deal directly with the retailers, and virtually all divisions of distribution. I think of him as my Third Son, even though he's oh so close to my own age. His genius for business and his people skills have no peer.

In 1979, I contacted Barbara Garcia, another wonderful lady whom I had known for several years, and asked her to work for me at the smaller Hayes Street warehouse in Hollywood. Barbara wore many hats. She used to take orders over the phone and was my credit, wholesale, and operations manager. She also took her work home and phoned customers at night because of the different time zones.

Then an unexpected benefit arose out of our hiring Barbara. She is of Cuban descent, and along with Maria Sanchez, another loyal, long term saleslady, began selling our products part time to the Spanish-speaking chain stores in South Florida like Navarros®, which had twenty linear feet of vitamins filling seven shelves, and to another first-class growing operation, Sedanos®, which also had large and prominent departments and displays of Sundown vitamins.

Our name became familiar in the Spanish-speaking communities, and we advertised in the Spanish yellow pages. Visitors from the Caribbean and all the Central and Latin American nations began taking our products home.

Because of that, by 1985 Barbara's part time work in the Spanish-speaking community had become a substantial full time open division for our Sundown products. Since then, we have learned how to register with a foreign nation and to associate ourselves with distribution companies of good reputation. We have kept our Sundown label in virtually every South American country; a number of our products are labeled bilingually.

We acquire new markets in foreign countries sometimes by word of mouth, but most recently through aggressive advertising and attendance at trade shows. We always check out the people we deal with.

As an American, I am proud that people all over the world prefer U.S. products to their own and look up to us. Presently, we are about to enter Saudi Arabia and the United Arab Emirates. Our products are pure enough to meet their religion's requirements.

Sundown Vitamins are now in more than sixty foreign countries. That is an unintended blessing thanks to Barbara's initiative and the fact that Miami became the Gateway of the Americas. She currently holds an important management position in our Sundown International Department. Her department's goal is the world map.

It wasn't luck. We were prepared when opportunity knocked. We made our own breaks. All successful businesses do. Those who fail, however, often continue to whine and tell you it was all luck!

* * *

Near the end of 1980, I decided to sell our products to independent drugstores. South Florida had plenty of them. Today, that's not the case. The chains are now dominating.

The independents were looking for a line of vitamins which they could sell aggressively and would enable them to compete against the chains. I was doing so well with my mail order vitamins, I believed that if I could hire some sales people to place my products in those stores, I could do as well with the retailers and wholesalers too.

It wasn't as if the drugstores were shy of vitamins. At least four or five local companies were selling to our independents. Nevertheless, I hired a young man, Ron Barnhart. As I mentioned, I'd met him early in my career with Super-X. We have had a thirty year relationship, and he still works with me to this day in other endeavors.

In a little over a year, Ron placed our Sundown brand of vitamins in about three hundred South Florida stores. We then talked about the fact that I really did not want to change the label for mail order. I didn't have the money, and I thought it would be too confusing and costly for us – a double inventory, one for retail and one for mail order. We overcame that by announcing that we were a nationally advertised brand of vitamins, which was true; that advertising, however, came from our mail order business, which primarily targeted the rural areas. We never had a problem with it, however, and Ron continued to expand the business.

Here was the typical situation. Let's say my competitor sold vitamin A to a store at a cost of $1.50 less 10% discount, less this or that at 5%; and the cost to the store would come down to $1.20 with a suggested retail price of $2.95.

I went in with a different method. I gave them one price, no discounts, and let the store mark it up with no additional discounts at their end. I figured out the price I wanted the store to sell my product to the customer. I was always thinking of the end result, the customer. What are they going to pay for the product?

I sold vitamin A at 85 cents and told the retailers that if they bought one or a hundred, it would still cost them 85 cents. Anyway, I'd give them a net price of 85 cents, assuming that most of the stores Ron and I sold to – I was also doing plenty of selling then – could double their money at $1.69. Some stores would get $1.49 or $1.39; but nobody was charging the high price of $2.95 suggested by my competitors.

That was the premise on which I went into retail. Sell low and aggressively pursue the stores which would reflect the lower price to the consumer. I avoided the store that would pay 85 cents and charge the consumer $2.95. I knew that the customer would balk at those charges, hurt our reputation for low prices, and stymie growth.

Because we still had so many fine independent drugstores in the early 1980s, Sundown continued to grow. By 1985, before we acquired Rexall, we were doing about $20 million in sales and still moving from warehouse to larger warehouse.

EIGHTEEN

Sizing Up
The Nutritional Market

Sundown Sells to its First Deep Discount Chain

In the late 1970s and early 1980s, at the time I developed my own line of vitamins, Walgreens and Super-X had their house brands. Walgreens' product, which they still sell and is similar to the old Rexall's Plenamins, is called Aytinal. It really means eight-in-all, because by 1925, the year Aytinal came out, only eight vitamins had been discovered.

Aytinal was a contrived name to make the eight-vitamin multiple seem more pharmaceutical, similar to Robitussin with dextromethorphan. If it sounds or reads pharmaceutical, people are going to buy it.

Although the big chains had their house lines, they were burdened with substantive overhead, which had caused profit pressures. Empires, with their often inherent excesses, are built, and certain gross profits have to be made in order to continue growth. My background is not in accounting, but while managing Walgreens and Super-

X, I learned their operational "bibles" – even if I ignored a good portion of their premises – and voraciously read their operating statements. I saw that they had to make nearly 35 percent gross profit in order to make a meager 3 to 5 percent net profit.

I had done around $150,000-plus-or-minus a year in my little variety store whereas the big drugstores I managed had been doing multi-millions of dollars a year. Regardless, I realized that in a number of cases I was able to buy cheaper than some of the big boys.

I then recognized what I had instinctively known all along. They had been charging me and all of their stores substantially more for a product than what it initially cost them.

Walgreens and Super-X – as most successful chains at that time – added an extra cost to an item at the warehouse level. For example, when I worked for them, they shipped me playing cards from their own warehouses. Those decks of cards, let's say, cost them $4.50 a dozen, and they would charge my drugstore around $5.40 a dozen. That gave the chains a guaranteed overhead absorption of 90 cents after the decks left the warehouse and before I sold the cards to the consumer. Those dollars charged, remember, were needed to cover their warehouse support and a portion of corporate overhead.

Meanwhile, as a manager, I was supposed to make 35 to 40 percent gross profit for the company *above* their already 90 cents overhead charge on my now $5.40 per dozen card decks. They had similar lines of add-ons for virtually every commodity that was shipped through the warehouse.

How did that affect the sale of vitamins? In other words, the chain stores might be buying E and C for less than I was paying to put them in my variety store, but I didn't have their costly layers of doing business, of which, I'm sure, most was justified. That's why they had to charge a higher price for many of their own items than I would for mine. I figured out that in my variety store I would have the room to lower the price if I could keep my own overhead down and maintain staunch disciplines.

Bear in mind, the chains I'd worked for had charged my managed store $5.40 or thereabouts for a dozen decks of playing cards. If I bought them for my little variety store at $5.25 a dozen, I could thus compete effectively against all the monoliths, at least on some items.

Now, use those playing cards as an example for vitamins and other items. That helps to explain why a number of less than savvy smaller chain drugstores were not able to compete effectively "price-wise" with marts and the depot stores when they came on the scene. Those new companies kept themselves lean and mean from the start.

It's a lot easier to do that from the day you open your doors than to change operating procedures in mid-stride. If you're out there earning a 30 percent gross profit and your expenses are running 30 percent, you'll have to turn the entire corporation upside down to make it work. Ninety-nine percent of the time, you cannot straighten out a congenital retail philosophy, one which has been ingrained from the start. Many deep-discounters, however, can work on a smaller percent gross profit and still have a star-studded bottom line because of the initial start-up controls they employ, insist upon, and manage.

Of course, there's a portion of mid-level management people, who work in those burgeoning bureaucratic layers wherever they exist, which cannot accede to lower prices, and are covering their behinds by making themselves seem indispensable in order to keep their jobs. That is still the sad story of too much of corporate America. That is why I ensured that Sundown was to be a lean operation from its very inception. Yet, I'm certain we too have some featherbedders in our operation.

Surprisingly, without a formal strategic plan, we wound up with some stellar accounts. We began to bring aboard the large national accounts as a result of being ready when the opportunity arose. We were selling to independents and local chains in South Florida.

Hordes of people would visit Florida for winter vacation, which was when they got their first exposure to Sundown. Many were in various aspects of the growing vitamin business. They would check out the South Florida retail stores, on sort of a busman's holiday, and what certain individuals saw prompted Phar-Mor, the great deep discount chain, to call us and want to be part of our business.

South Florida was one of the first areas in the country where deep discount really got started. It was a local phenomenon that we had a large selection of quality products available to the deep discounters who could sell at aggressively low prices. And Sundown, because it was our home territory, we happened to be in most of those places. That is how and why Phar-Mor sought us out, and in turn we then began to do business with our first national deep-discount chain.

NINETEEN

Executive Management Seminars

While Sundown Vitamins continued to grow, my little fraternity of closest friends would meet after official working hours at a local upscale restaurant with a club type atmosphere where we would have a bite to eat, drink, and seriously kick around business ideas. I don't socialize with many outsiders, and I've always needed a place to break bread with my friends and have a cocktail or two.

There would be five to seven of us every evening. Lots of camaraderie.

Some people hang out and talk baseball or golf. Business was always the main topic of our discussions. How to improve, how to innovate. Part of my business MO is that casual conversation about our work after official working hours in a comfortable environment improves the product and often leads to innovation through fellowship and effective communication.

Much could be said for those sessions, except that some of us lost our wives over it – if not totally, we certainly lost their confidence – and, I'm sure, if it hadn't been for taking our vitamins to make up for occasional excesses, we might have lost part of our livers as well.

It was not work. It was not labor or a job. It was about what we were. We focused on Sundown twenty-four hours a day.

We are the business. The business is us. We survive and prosper, live or die because of it.

Others work at a job or pursue careers they can't stand because they need or want the money. For us it was more like a cause. That attitude and vision contributed dramatically to the success and growth of Sundown.

How could it be otherwise? We had no choice. Our reputations, our individualities were all on the line because, as I stated above, Sundown was us. That truth remains valid for many of the important and original employees still working here.

And I always believed in getting the job done ethically. Fine people would never have come to work for us and spend years of enjoyable toil if we were not a class organization. Nothing short of the pursuit of excellence could be accepted.

Then about ten years ago in 1987, from fifteen to eighteen men regularly attended what we called Executive Management Seminars, or EMS. We were putting in sixteen to eighteen hour days and had been reading about the positive aspects of Japanese management. The people who worked in those organizations were close emotionally as well as in business.

The EMS group included our top executives, some outsiders too – important suppliers like Jerry Kay, owner of Manhattan Drugs in Hillside, New Jersey – and others who fit in, but did not have to be top level officers in our company. The latter were people who meshed with our psyche

– or psycho, if you will. We always supplied a written agenda for our seminars, which made it easy for the vendor companies to pick up all our expenses. We were still a private company doing millions of dollars, and they were integral to our business. The vendors also sent key sales people to our seminars for a more personal relationship with our management.

As it often turned out, little was done to maintain the agenda as outlined. The trips were designed to be mostly fun with plenty of hell-raising, but clean fun. We'd leave on a Wednesday and return the following Sunday or Monday. We would go to places like St. Martin, take over the island, drive jeeps backwards, and act more like kids away from home for the first time. We did that sort of thing once a year for about six years.

We even sent scouting parties to check out new islands as they pulled the red carpet from under us for boyish pranks. One of the fellows, Bill Hannon, a major supplier's VP of Sales, carried himself like a Senator or politician of sorts, and we'd introduce him as such to get preferential treatment on planes and at hotels, all in jest, however. During another excursion, we convinced the people on one of the islands that another of our "lead" outside vendors was a legitimate presidential candidate.

After a while, the women at our company were getting frustrated, especially when they saw some of the T-shirts we'd had made that were all too indicative of what we had been doing. By then, my wife was referring to our group as the Boys Club.

Then while we were away, the women went to the fish market to let us know that they knew what we really had gone fishing for – to do some general goofing off. They purchased five or six pounders of the ugliest sea creatures they could find and placed them among our desks and chairs. By the time we returned, the offices stank and the fish were close to becoming maggot colonies.

Sylvia had been behind it of course. So we created a Girls Club, and sent about fifteen women to New York and Costa Rica. While the women were away, we then realized that they had been doing a lot of the real work we executives were taking credit for.

Perhaps those EMS trips had much to do with so-called male menopause. At the same time, several of us were swept up by the Harley-Davidson craze of the 1980s. I had owned motorcycles at different times many years before, until I got a little more sense and sold them.

My son, Dean, was the first to buy a big Harley. Then Nick Palin succumbed to the fad. Other friends were riding. So was one of my all-time entrepreneurial heroes, Malcolm Forbes, who was photographed often on his bike. I read and watched everything he did and accomplished, and tried to emulate his positives – except that I've yet to commit myself to ballooning.

I suppose I also needed to relearn why I'd gotten rid of my earlier motorcycles in the first place. And the boy in me felt a need to give in to peer pressure one more time. I bought my Harley and proved to myself that I could indeed do the bike thing one more time. I know that I could survive one of those big international runs from Denver to Panama. *But why????*

I still often fantasize about leaving all my responsibilities behind, changing my Social Security number, zooming away on a Harley, and disappearing into the sunset. Dream on!

TWENTY

Tyrannosaurus Rexall

As we were on the threshold of expanding our business, I began to suffer a life-threatening malady, which no doctor or alternative medicine could cure. The symptoms would intensify, worsen, and last for over ten years. That story will come later in this book.

In the mid-1980s, I was dealing with Jerry Kay, that very special supplier in Hillside, New Jersey. He spent much time in New York City meeting with people from Wall Street and knew many bankers. His tentacles reached far and wide. He threw a very wide net.

Jerry Kay is a very warm and wonderful gentleman. I have the deepest respect for him. He was always fair in all his dealings with me and our company. He helped me in the days when I needed help. He always went the extra mile.

I was a Floridian and had never really gotten into the New York loop. Jerry opened doors for me. I met those bankers and Wall Street friends of his while I was still neophytic about expanding my business, which was bringing in close to twenty million a year. At that time, we were not making our own vitamins. We simply bottled, labeled, stocked, sold, shipped, and billed.

Jerry was manufacturing about 70 percent of all our tablets. He saw that I was a good person to partner with, strong both in mail order and retail sales, which was why he introduced me to those bankers and Wall Streeters. I was, however, already thinking ahead about manufacturing my own products and even possibly going public one day, although there were certainly no hints in that direction. At that time, they were the premature and "out of reach dreams" of an entrepreneur.

Jerry had gotten wind through certain individuals he knew that Rexall would soon be going into the throes of Chapter 7 bankruptcy. He asked me what I thought about purchasing Rexall and what we could do with the name. I told him that I wanted to know what we could buy it for.

A week later, we flew to St. Louis, Missouri, where their plant was located. We got into a limo and went directly to the plant to meet with the principals. Rexall's headquarters had originally been located in Boston, then in Los Angeles, and finally in St. Louis during the 1950s.

The plant was a monster. The warehouse had been there since the 1930s. The cavernous building was about 340,000 square feet and twelve stories high off the King's Highway. The significance that I was about to purchase a meaningful part of Americana struck me with awe and some pride.

* * *

As I mentioned in the first pages of this book, Rexall's story began on a train en route to Seattle one afternoon in 1903. That day Louis K. Liggett conceived of a plan which ultimately impacted the lives of nearly every American in the twentieth-century, and many nations throughout the world. Liggett had already organized a powerful druggist's trade union before he came up with the idea which would become Rexall Drugs, and with it the first truly American concept of franchising.

That same year, 1903, Rexall Drugs was established by Liggett in Boston. He essentially laid the foundation for a chain of independent drugstores to use the Rexall name if they sold his products. That gave them buying power under the broad umbrella of his United Drug Company.

Small town America benefited. Rexall expanded rapidly and thrived, even in 1931 when the country was reeling from the great Crash of 1929 and descending to the depths of the Great Depression. That year, while other merchants were on the verge of ruin, Rexallites, as the franchisees were called, made an ever-increasing profit despite nationwide adverse economic conditions. The credit for their survival and success belonged to Liggett's United Drug Company and quality of goods they produced.

Liggett also manufactured under his United Drug banner nationally respected brand names such as Life Savers®, Pepto Bismol®, Milk of Magnesia®, Bayer Aspirin®, and many other famous products until an antitrust suit forced him to divest.

During its heyday, Rexall manufactured overseas with around 2,400 Rexallites in England and approximately another 1,000 in Canada. Rexall drugstores could be found as far away as Uganda and the Cape of Good Hope. Everywhere in the world and throughout the United States, a high percentage of new customers always said, when asked, that they had been attracted by the name Rexall and all it stood for.

In 1936, Rexall featured in its monthly magazine, *Rexall Ad-Vantages,* a map of the United States with nearly 8,000 dots representing each agency. It took six people more than a week just to stick pins in those dots on a map measuring 5 by 7 feet. They hung it on the corporate Sales Manager's wall for all visitors to see. Eventually, Rexall reached Liggett's goal of a store in every county seat in each state.

1936 was a significant year in Rexall's history for another reason, the debut of the Rexall Train. In this age of instant communication and life in the fast lane, we ought to reflect on the marvels of a more leisurely time.

The wonderful Rexall Train was a twelve-car streamliner that first toured the United States in 1936 in place of the company's traditional drugstore conventions. That year a souvenir folder described the Rexall Train as a Streamlined Convention – twelve cars and an oil burning engine – 1,080 feet from tip to tip in blue and white.

Hudson class locomotive No. 5344 had been art-deco stream-styled in 1934 for *20th Century Limited* service before it was modified for the Rexallites. There was a power car for lights and air conditioning. Each of the other cars had its own astonishing name and function.

Kantleek was named after Rexall's sturdy Two-In-One Stopperless Water Bottle. It served as the train's workroom, storage area, and unofficial "gaming" room.

First Aid was a 16-section sleeping car.

Ad-Vantage (the name of Rexall's in-house magazine) came next. As the name suggests, it was the display car. It had been stripped of its original parlor furnishings and remodeled with art deco streamlined interiors and showcases to display thousands of Rexall products– chocolate laxatives (remember Ex-Lax®, the Candy Cleanser?), real candy, vitamins, cosmetics. And something we may all long to sit at one more time, a 1936 state-of-the-art soda fountain.

Research was another converted parlor car. It housed a half inch scale model of Rexall's new 18,000 square foot research department located at the home offices in Boston.

Bisma-Rex, named for a stomach powder, contained a large map of the USA on which illuminated bottles of the antacid flashed in succession to form a line from coast-to-coast.

Cara Nome, named after Rexall's line of cosmetics and beauty aids, was similarly stocked with drug products and a ceiling-high spectacle. The display showed the perpetual squeezing of juice from a bunch of grapes into a gigantic bottle. And there was the famous $50,000 "Chocolate Boy" that invited the visitor to peer into the can and see all seven steps in the making of the chocolate.

Those cars were open to the public. The remaining cars were off limits and reserved for Pullman and Rexall employees.

The first of those cars was *Klenzo,* named for Rexall's bathroom products – toothbrush, antiseptics, shower bath sprayers. It was an eighty-eight seat loudspeaker-equipped lecture car with a capacity for 300 when cleared for dancing to the Rexall Train Orchestra.

Adrienne was a second lecture car.

Symphony was the buffet car, which was open for lunch and dinner. The train had truly outstanding Pullman trained chefs who prepared French and Louisiana cuisine such as pheasant on toast and lobster in all forms for the Rexallites.

Mi-31, named for a Rexall antiseptic, was the lounge car and contained service bar and dancing floor.

A ten-bed sleeper, *Joan Manning,* came next. It was named after a brand of chocolates.

Bringing up the rear was a private observation car, *Puretest,* named for Rexall's famous line of vitamins – Multamins and Plenamins – and its cod liver and halibut liver oils. It was the residence of the corporate head Louis K. Liggett.

The plan was for the Rexall Train to travel 29,000 miles in eight months, visiting and stopping at 144 cities in the United States. About 10,000 Rexall druggists and 20,000 Rexall salespeople were expected to attend the meetings.

The Rexall Train began its journey from Boston in March, 1936. It went through the Midwest to the West Coast; returned by Northwest and Canada to Chicago; then after a month of refurbishing, on to New England, down to Florida and back to Atlanta.

The Rexall Train was welcomed fiesta style everywhere by bands, cheering throngs, celebrities, and mayoral speeches. Each local newspaper featured its arrival with banner headlines and photos.

The train reached San Francisco May 23, 1936, where Mr. Liggett's car was filled with flowers. The same happened in Fresno.

In Los Angeles aside from speeches, the train was greeted by marching bands, blaring trumpets, Mariachis, Spanish guitars, dancing señoritas and their caballeros, and a Zeppelin dirigible overhead. In Texas, Liggett was given flags made of flowers for each country that had ruled the state.

By November, the Rexall Train had attracted more than two million viewers, twenty-five thousand alone on a last day walk-through in Atlanta.

Apparently all had a grand time on the Rexall Train, including its staff. One porter said he averaged $100 a week from tips – big money in the middle of the depression.

Wouldn't it be a hoot to take another ride on the Rexall Train?

Through World War II and into the 1950s, Rexall was

still going strong with nearly 25,000 stores. The company continued its aggressive marketing with one cent sales – buy a product at its regular price of 49 cents and pay only a penny more if you purchase two. And there were Lucky Seven sales, when all items sold for a number ending in seven – 47 cents, $1.17, and so on. Price points. Yes!

In 1978 Rexall dissolved its traditional relationship with its drugstores and sold out to managers who may have had a percentage of the business. Rexall products were then sold on the open market.

Rexall was eventually taken over by a holding company – an investment firm, I was told, that had invested virtually no money – and a good number of management groups that missed the mark consistently. At the time we came in, the banks were on Rexall's case.

* * *

While we were in St. Louis, Lenny Stowe, a banker from the Northeast and a genuine winner and leader in his own right, told us that the numbers were quite large to start with. We assured him and the Rexall principals that we had the wherewithal and the collateral to do the deal. We were confident that our negotiating skills would give us the best possible deal.

At that time, Jerry Kay's financial record with the banks was not quite as strong as mine. They required me to put my name on everything alongside his, and used virtually all our assets as collateral.

It wasn't all that big a problem. We had money in the bank and assets, real assets in Florida, which enabled me to borrow the necessary funds from the bank. I don't like to carry debt, and paid them back in a much shorter time than the three year loan they'd put in place.

We ended up paying a paltry $2 million-plus. What had we bought? Rexall had raw chemicals as part of its assets, which Jerry received to make more vitamins. There was machinery that I could use to pack my vitamins, and others that Jerry needed to manufacture his vitamins. Those were the hard assets. Tangibles. I shipped what I could use to Florida. Jerry sent the rest to his plant in Hillside, New Jersey.

I also came away with around $3 million worth of vitamins already manufactured, in the bottles – C, E, and other letter vitamins – and over a million dollars worth of Pacman, for which I'd paid a ridiculously low sum. Pacman was a chewable vitamin for children licensed from a Japanese firm that had bought its name.

Most significantly, we had bought the Rexall trademark and name for **only** another $75,000 – a grand old name that was registered in almost 90 countries, and which seemed like one terrific bargain along with all the other assets Jerry and I purchased as a partnership. I have always believed that we acquired more than a name. We became caretakers of a great tradition – a tradition of excellence, quality, and of value.

That tradition is as important to us today as it was to Louis K. Liggett when he founded Rexall nearly a hundred years ago, and as it continues to be amongst the American and international public. Rexall represented what I had built Sundown on – **Integrity**.

Rexall had been, at its roots, an entrepreneurial company, and our firm is and always will be a team of inborn entrepreneurs – intrepreneurs, they're now called. So, in my opinion, we were uniquely situated to be in the same marketing business with the tradition that comes with the Rexall name, the stability that comes from our successful family of companies, and an omnipresent spirit of individualism.

The Rexall name is still very strong among consumers, and it has saved us hundreds of millions of dollars in advertising among the 40-plus generations. I believe to this day that our value would be somewhat less without Rexall's name. About 3,000 stores still carry the Rexall sign to this day.

I had to stop and remember that only ten years earlier, I had been working for Super-X when we sent out our first get-to-know-us mailers. Until it happened, I never in my wildest dreams imagined that Rexall would be mine to safeguard and build on. Yet, when opportunity knocked, I was already at the front door.

Liggett was a great communicator. Perhaps he is still communicating from beyond. I often feel his spirit in name, and see myself as a keeper of the keys.

I've been asked more than a few times why didn't someone else buy Rexall. I can't wonder about things like that. I just do it. Maybe those someones are still talking about acquiring Rexall, not aware that it is already too late. **Once again, too much analysis leads to paralysis. So can boardroom posturing.**

* * *

I continued to be partners with Jerry Kay and Manhattan Drug with the understanding that I could eventually buy him out at a mutually agreeable fair value. He had no problem with that, and initially he became President of the Rexall Division.

I did not immediately put the Rexall Sundown name on our vitamins and nutritional supplements. I continued to use the Rexall name specifically for the Rexall products we were making and buying – vitamins, over-the-counter drugs, aspirin, and the like. We sold them as a division of our Sundown Company. We billed them separately as

Rexall; then at a later juncture we billed them with Sundown products so the order made more sense, especially when we shipped other items with the vitamins.

So, we put all our orders that went out under one invoice, under one roof in South Florida and consolidated. Later, as we prepared to go public, we decided that the Rexall name had such credence and nostalgia value we ought to attach it to our name, give it top billing, first place.

As I said earlier, I never had an ego about names. You don't see the DeSantis this or DeSantis that corporation. My mail order necktie venture would become an exception for reasons I shall explain later.

In any case, Rexall was known for its drugstores, and it was confusing for a consumer to understand how a Rexall product could be sold in an independent store that was not part of the Rexall chain.

We then created the Rexall Consumer Products Division, so the consumer could understand that while the store may not be part of the Rexall chain, it was a Rexall Division product. That broke the ice and enabled us to get into many independent stores whose owners had been reluctant to carry the Rexall brand because many Rexall drugstores were still functioning in blighted old downtown areas.

Few Rexalls had opened in the shopping centers proliferating throughout the country. We had to guarantee the retailers that we would not be opening any new stores either.

I knew, however, that if we went public or were in the process of doing our IPO – Initial Public Offering – people would recognize the Rexall name and show a lot more interest. They have, and the grand old name has indeed proven itself to be very strong.

Our purchase of Rexall had come at the right time. I wanted my own manufacturing plant because we were having problems with deliveries from our many and varied suppliers. Our growth was outstripping how much and how fast Jerry and the others could ship to us. Their inability to keep up with our demands and deliver on time were major factors in our decision to establish our own in-house manufacturing division.

Quality was another problem. Although Manhattan Drug had very good quality in all its products, its tools, punches, and dyes that made the tablets were not always state-of-the-art. Sometimes the tablets came out mottled and did not have the necessary aesthetic quality to entice a customer. They did not look beautiful, and a consumer likes to see a beautiful tablet. If it's mottled or has a crack, they think that the potency has been impaired. As we all know, **perception is reality.**

TWENTY-ONE

The Grand Acquisitor

My Vitamin Basket Stores and Thompson

I had never lost my zest for retailing, and after we acquired Rexall, I felt we could offer a product that was unique. My concept was to put assorted vitamin bottles in baskets, which gave me the name for my next foray into the retail world. In 1985, we opened Vitamin Basket stores in California, Texas, Las Vegas, St. Louis, and the Chesapeake area of Virginia. We put them in discount malls and the like to compete against the General Nutrition stores.

Some did very well. We supplied the stores with a cornucopia of information about our products, and the customers responded favorably.

I paid special attention to our operation in Las Vegas. I had seen the potential in that rapidly growing retirement community segment because we had already attended a number of conventions out there relevant to our industry. As an example, the NARD, National Association of Retail Druggists, often held their conventions in that adult Disneyland.

With Corney McDermott's immersion in the project, I

had selected a shopping center for our first Las Vegas Vitamin Basket, which quickly became one of our best stores, and then tried to get a second location. At the same time, I met Joe Fopiano. He had been with the local newspaper and wanted to meet me. A fast-talking Italian-American, Joe was in his late forties, robust, cheerful, spiritual, and an over-all first class guy. He looked more Irish than Italian, a real cherub.

Joe did more than we required to arrange the necessary publicity to get Vitamin Basket up and started in Las Vegas. Consequently, I built a solid relationship with Joe, and we got together whenever I'd make periodic visits to the Las Vegas store.

Unfortunately, the Vitamin Basket stores did not meet my expectations, and it had just become too much for us to go up another avenue of distribution because we simply did not have enough management people available. We'd get a call from a mall center informing us that Mary or John was not able to open that store in Texas at 9:00 AM. And we'd have no one to send in their place.

Also, we had trouble finding the right locations. We just did not have enough clout to get them.

We ended up selling the Vitamin Baskets to Jerry Kay at Manhattan Drug. He wanted to get into the retail business.

Despite the Vitamin Basket setback, at the end of the 1980s, we were selling mail order, to retail stores, a deep discount chain, and to health food stores. We then further diversified.

* * *

Immediately after we acquired Rexall, I regularly attended a number of what they call DCAT gatherings – Drug Chemical Allied Trade Group. It was something like a trade show, where you meet many pharmaceutical and drug people. Once again through my friend, Jerry Kay, I was introduced to a group of investment bankers at the Waldorf in New York City.

The investment bankers had a list of companies they were evaluating and said that Thompson Vitamins out in California was having major problems, and was gasping its final breath of existence. They felt it was not a big enough company for Wall Street to get involved in, but maybe an organization my size would want to go out there, talk to the owners, and see if it could be saved before it became yesterday's news.

Thompson Nutritional had been founded in California in 1935. By the 1980s, its product line was being sold mostly to health food store retailers.

The difficulties had not been caused by poor quality. To the contrary, Thompson consistently delivered the *créme de la créme* of vitamin and nutritional products. Its problems were strictly the result of poor management.

Thompson's son, a brilliant man, had aspired to be a poet, a writer, an artist, but after his father's death, he inherited the business. Unfortunately Thompson's management and the team he assembled had not been savvy enough to save this once great winner.

Outside management, it seemed, had taken Thompson for a ride. The company became known for its big parties and generous donations. On July 4th, the company would have a big fireworks show and barbecue; on Washington's birthday it distributed thousands of cherry pies. It threw lavish parties in Las Vegas, and in Nashville at a big southern mansion complete with horseback riding.

I flew out with Jerry Kay to Carson, California, just to the south of Los Angeles. I purchased Thompson Vitamins for a very nominal fee and acquired a company, which, at one time, had been doing about $20 million annually in the health food arena. By then, however, its sales had shrunk to a third of that.

We wanted Bill Thompson, the son of the founder, to continue working with us. He was very important in my strategy to maintain continuity and reassure the company's customers that we would not lower the quality and integrity of Thompson Vitamins. The people who own health food stores and the independent proprietors do not always feel comfortable buying products from low priced vitamin suppliers who also sell outside their retail niche. They want something to justify their often perceived higher prices of top quality products, and be able to say to their customers that Thompson has been around since 1935 and is available only through them. Today, it is a premier line available only through **us** to them.

At that time, they didn't need to know it was owned by Sundown. We were still sort of a black sheep in the industry because of our consistently lower prices and negative comments from our competitors, so people did not know truly how high our quality was.

Therefore, we bailed out Thompson and let the company rise Phoenix-like from the ashes of bankruptcy, with increased sales and a corresponding acceptable profit once again. We gave Bill a multi-year contract, and he still represents our company as titular head of our continually rising Thompson Division. We did, however, move the Thompson operation from Carson, California, to our facilities here in South Florida for convenience and efficiency.

I have always covered myself with channel diversification. If mail order started sliding, we were selling to drugstores. If that slowed, we had the health food stores, and so on.

My ego bellows that if I went bust today I could start up

something else tomorrow. That's where my psyche was and is. Sure, I like the action of starting up something new, but diversification is not solely for my gain. I am not being a self-serving, pseudo-altruistic B'S'er when I say that the fifteen-hundred people who work here depend first on me, then the company. Call it paternalism if you want. I want to have it all ways: To grow; to profit for all our employees and shareholders; and to benefit our employees in every good and possible way.

In a way, I feel we initiated a new beginning against our seemingly inept competitors, who, I feel, had the field to themselves far too long. It's like someone saying you can't play bridge, or you're a lousy chess player, and you want to do everything in your power to prove them wrong. Like this Onion Boy proving his mother wrong. That's my driving force.

*   *   *

The eternal search to improve the way we do business also drives me. Sometime in 1987, I was brainstorming with myself about what else we could do to be different and more profitable. I observed that in the mass merchandise stores the non-identifying side of many vitamin bottle labels, faced out to the customer; and those stores, which had gone to self-service, did not have enough employees walking the aisles to make the necessary corrections.

I came up with the idea for a single wrap-around label with two front panels, front and back, so that no matter how the bottle sat on the shelf, the consumer had a better shot to see the label and identify our product. Only a small percentage of our nutritional supplements, the multiples for example, required too much information about their ingredients for a wrap-around double label.

We took out a patent and later prevented one other large competitor from placing a wrap-around on their bottles. Did it work, you ask? It increased our label exposure about 50 percent, and sales of our mass merchandise Sundown line grew by almost 20 percent.

Why hadn't any other vitamin manufacturers thought of it before me? Most prefer, it seems, to wallow in the throes of their status quos, or are merely followers.

TWENTY-TWO

Rexall Showcase
International

Our foray into major multilevel marketing came about when Joe Fopiano contacted me in person during one of our after-hours brainstorming sessions. That night, we spoke of a number of companies that were looking at multilevel or network marketing like NuSkin, Herbalife, and Shaklee, and were all very successful.

I'm not certain who initiated it, but soon we were discussing similar possibilities for a new division over which we could fly the Rexall name and banner. We didn't have the number of stores Liggett had during the golden days of his United Drugs, yet we could be selling quality products with the name Rexall on them through multilevel marketing.

Joe, our West Coast connection, had wind of a new product that was going to be extolled in a major story in the *National Enquirer.* The article described how it lowered cholesterol, naturally and drug free, by up to 40 percent, and induced safe weight loss without harmful side effects.

I told him to come to my office and we'd talk. He brought the inventor who had the patent, and I quickly concluded that it appeared indeed efficacious and could work well through the network marketing channel.

BIOS LIFE® was the name of that product, and we soon launched a multilevel marketing company after the story was featured in the *National Enquirer*. We made one unforgivable mistake. We didn't think we had the right leader; or, we may very well have had, but our timing was wrong.

We didn't know enough yet about multilevel marketing – structuring of the different levels, arrangement of commissions, and the like. Even though this fellow knew how to structure the commissions, we didn't feel totally comfortable. He almost seemed to know too much, and we were novices. He did not have an unscrupulous past – in fact, he was quite honorable – but I felt he was not what we were all about or truly needed. He appeared to be more of a motivator than a manager.

Nevertheless, he stayed with us and launched BIOS LIFE and Rexall Showcase International. The decision to open the flood gates early was made at my behest because I believed that we could handle the legions of excited wannabe distributors.

He brought in teams, actually busloads of people. In total, as many as five thousand people came to our plant. They were all looking to see who owned Rexall and wondering if they should leave Amway, Herbalife, and the other independent multilevel marketing companies to carry our banner.

We did not have all our ducks in a row, which caused a major false start. We were still a private company, and after a year or so I assessed the damage. I had spent about five million dollars of my corporate money in the premature launching of our multilevel marketing division. I call it my money because at that point there were no other shareholders of the company except myself and my family.

I was ready to toss in the towel. I told myself I'd been defeated, and it was time to move on. Then another savvy gentleman who had given me good advice in the past said that he knew someone who could make it all work. He made a phone call, and this fellow came down. We broke bread and liked what we heard.

We put him in charge, and he reinvigorated us. He brought in some exceptional distributor-motivators who assessed us with their "due diligence" and liked what they saw. Later, however, he moved on. A personality thing. He was and is a fine gentleman. We just didn't see eye-to-eye on a number of issues.

He was, nevertheless, instrumental in getting us off the ground on our second try with our new division, which we called Rexall Showcase International, or RSI. We honored the contract, paid him well, and today he's very successful in another company.

Unfortunately, I felt, both men had lacked the ability to run a corporation from the inside with all its ramifications. As a distributor, you have the freedom to run your business the way you want. But we have expectations, controls, and guidelines for each division. You must hire and manage people inside while you're taking care of customers and distributors.

We lost money those years because the bar for breaking even continued to rise. We looked upon RSI as a failure with a dismal future, taking away capital from our other divisions.

Then through many frustrating days and conversations at our Boys Club meetings, a suggestion was made by a very astute and sharp business buddy to put my son Damon in charge of RSI because it **was** going to be a major contributor to both the top and bottom line growth of the company. Damon had been interested in multilevel marketing because it was the only distribution channel he had not been involved with. He was already in charge of our SDV line of vitamins, including our phone marketing direct division that had matured from our original mail order business. This is the same Damon who had to stand on a box years ago to reach the table when we first began to package our orders.

So Damon took over as President of RSI in 1993. It wasn't nepotism. He was the best qualified person for the position, and from the time he took over in 1993, RSI's net sales went from $20.5 million to now exceeding $175 million, an almost 900 percent increase in four years. And still growing. He has become his own shining star, an effectual businessman who has contributed greatly in all divisions.

For multilevel marketing, we would have to sell a different type of product, something unique that we wouldn't have on the drugstore shelves. And, it would be one-on-one where Mary would tell her girlfriend or John tells his buddy about it.

The best definition of multilevel marketing is relationship selling, person-to-person selling. For example, if you eat at a fine restaurant or see a good movie, what do you do afterwards? You recommend it to your friends.

That's the premise of multilevel marketing – to show something you feel good about and share it with the same friends by selling it to them. I'm talking about bringing along distributors, having people sign up to speak about and recommend your product, and to emphasize the wonderful associated opportunities for success.

What made us different from Amway, Herbalife, and the others was the grand old corporate name, Rexall and all it has stood for over the years. That we are now a public company allows even more credibility for those who might consider joining us. Our financial status is never a mystery; consumers and distributors always have access to the company's financial position. Rexall Sundown's stock – RXSD on the NASDAQ National Market – has appreciated well over 1,000 percent since the company's initial public offering in 1993. Individuals who invested $5,000 those first days would see their shares become worth well over $75,000 today.

Most recently, we were chosen as one of NASDAQ's 100 index stocks, a barometer, if you would, of all the multithousands of listed non-financial corporations. And we did not apply to be on that list. What an achievement!

Additionally, our distributors and consumers all know that we manufacture our products for each division with the highest FDA and H. V. Shuster evaluations, which are explained in subsequent chapters. We are a class act having garnered the dietary supplement industry's highest compliance score in multiple audits by H. V. Shuster, an independent laboratory and quality assurance audit firm out of Cambridge, Massachusetts. That quality is another core reason for our success along with consumer friendly pricing.

Today, the Direct Selling Association looks towards firms like RSI to help set industry standards and to provide a model of integrity in the operation of viable networking companies. Our attorneys work diligently with several states' attorneys general to assure that the RSI opportunity is not simply the best in the industry, but it is also one that won't crumble in an avalanche of regulations and red tape.

With our unique tradition and position of leadership come certain responsibilities and challenges in multilevel marketing. You have but to pick up any supermarket tabloid or turn on a TV infomercial to see products touted as cures for hair loss, weight gain – even cancer. These so-called "magic bullet" products will always be around and unfortunately, at best, have limited credibility and staying power.

Other multilevel companies have risen and fallen on those kinds of products. That is not what RSI is about.

We have a rigorous consideration process for any RSI product. Once we identify product categories that deserve our focus, we look for two qualities – uniqueness and efficacy. We put whatever it takes in research time and money into developing the finest products, and we put those prospective products through one final test: Can we offer them at a value price to the consumer?

RSI products are unique within the Rexall Sundown family. Our BIOS LIFE 2® – advanced second generation BIOS LIFE – is under two U.S. patents for the "method and composition for reducing serum cholesterol." BIOS LIFE 2 actually starts working for an individual if it is taken at a minimum of two times a day for thirty days. As much as ninety-percent of those who ingest its supplemental benefits see a reduction in their serum cholesterol and triglycerides. BIOS LIFE 2 also assists in balancing out blood sugars because of the fibers, Niacin, and the patented Chromium together with a nutritional matrix of ingredients.

If you like BIOS LIFE 2 and see positive results, then you'll want to share that product with your friends. Why not make money doing it? You make *bupkas* – as they used to say on "Maalox Boulevard" – when you recommend someone else's restaurant or film to those same friends.

Multilevel selling is essentially building your own business. It's a wonderful structure for one to become an independent business person with an opportunity to attain monetary goals. It works on this premise: We, the company, will pay you a commission, an override, or a bonus based on your successfully sharing that information, which eventuates into a sale.

Among other categories of effective RSI products we offer: Weight Management; Cellular Essentials® for cardiovascular health; Natural Health formulations of vitamins, minerals, nutrients, and amino acids to optimize the healthy function of blood vessels; formulations based on the science of homeopathy – a safe effective method of correcting illness and disease symptoms without drugs and harsh chemicals that can have side effects; Aestivál® Skin Care, skin enhancement therapy, body care, and outdoor body protection – all based on the research and science of glycolic and lactic acids known as Alpha-hydroxy acids; Nutritionals – women's products for bone and blood and men's health products for their unique problems; and Clear Source® water purifiers.

Distinct from other multilevel marketing companies, our RSI will not sell a $20.00 or $30.00 bottle of anything when the consumer can purchase a like item off the drugstore shelf at $4.99 or $5.99. We do not enter a product category for the sake of being in it unless we can offer something unique, effective, and value priced.

We are different from our competitors and others in multilevel marketing in one other important area – the quality of human being who sells or distributes our product. We have one logical requirement. It's called **fill out an application**.

Without sounding as if we're trying to recruit the reader, we do want to emphasize that we do not coerce our people to purchase huge amounts of product they cannot afford. All they need to do is purchase a starter kit for $49.50, which currently is an initial investment. The rest depends upon their drive and entrepreneurial skills, as in life.

We have gone many steps beyond those of most other companies. We make sure we dot each i and cross every t. We are always mindful of the person who is going into business. We feel, in the long run, that this is the correct way to handle both the distributor and the shareholder out there who might be concerned about multilevel marketing and the negative myths often surrounding it caused by the misdeeds of others.

We really want our people to share the Rexall product, because that meaningful, healthful product line is unique to us and can truly impact someone's life for the better. The Rexall name has, we feel, great credibility.

On the other hand, as in any enterprise, if you're in business for yourself, we know that serious financial success comes only to a select few. To be included amongst this pinnacle group, you have to be in the top 5 percent. If you follow the rules and leadership training, and if you do things in an honorable way, you can succeed beyond your wildest dreams.

We are delighted that a very important division of our company successfully carries the Rexall name – Rexall Showcase International. RSI belongs to the DSA, Direct Selling Association. Ninety-five percent of all the revenue generated through this industry comes through companies that are members, and I am a very proud father because Damon DeSantis is now on its Board of Directors and sits beside Dick DeVos, President of Amway, and Christina Gold, executive vice president of Avon Products, Inc., and other luminaries.

Today, RSI is in the business of selling health and wellness products, which adds to overall company profits. We will strategically venture out in other areas through RSI to develop new categories of products and service. Amway now distributes Rubbermaid® products and has formed a strategic alliance to do the same with Waterford crystal. The multi-billion dollar giant, AT&T, has made its own strategic alliance for multilevel Shaklee to distribute some of its products and services.

We can and will do the same. We know how to create a base of consumers, distributors, and ultimately can put a multitude of high quality products through this exciting and upscale channel of distribution. Who knows what tomorrow will bring?

Two factors drive people in the business. Product and opportunity. Each drives the other.

RSI is also expanding internationally, and that can create additional growth opportunities. Multilevel, aka Network Marketing, lends itself to international expansion because of the nature of people having relationships regardless of boundaries. As with our Sundown products, people from many nations have come to Rexall Showcase International.

International marketing gives us a greater ability to grow. We can leverage relationships here and abroad. It's all the same.

People!

RSI is doing especially well in Los Angeles amongst the Korean-Americans and Korean immigrants. They and their families, friends, and associates took our product line and nutritionals to Korea, which created a great demand for our products, and we have now opened up RSI distributorships there. The same has happened in Mexico.

As I complete this book, RSI is establishing a corporate office and opening for business in Hong Kong and soon in Taiwan.

By temperament and culture, the Asians of the Pacific Rim have a unique and aggressive entrepreneurial spirit.

Throughout the entire network marketing industry, as this book goes to print, the annual gross volume is $80 billion worldwide – $18 billion in the United States alone, with around 10 million people involved in selling. Asia represents 44 percent of that total volume of dollars.

Mainland China is now a major goal for RSI to reach out to. Selling vitamins and nutritional supplements there will not be a cakewalk. We'll have to educate the Chinese because of their traditional reliance, often solely, on herbal home remedies. As mentioned above, the Chinese have a natural entrepreneurial bent, which is why we feel confident about our eventual success.

Avon, Amway, and several others are there in China and are marketing diverse products including Barbie® dolls. The PRC currently government allows people to sell virtually all types of goods and services and make up to $50,000 a year, as a ceiling. The main obstacle to establishing RSI or any network marketing company in China appears to be very political. The power elite seems to worry about a company having the "ears" of thousands of people and conducting meetings to large groups of people who will then follow the corporate leader. The current communist government tends to resist any loss of political control, although they have been relaxing certain restrictions within their economy.

Only about fifty foreign companies are currently doing business in China. Let the big boys pave the way. We prefer to wait until consistently applied laws and rules, which we can feel comfortable with, are in place for us to operate under.

Europe is a potential market for us where RSI expects to do well.

Network marketing affords a wonderful opportunity to inspire thousands of entrepreneurial avatars. I believe

An early win
at age 10.
First place in
the Quizdown.

If only *Grease* had been
written when I was 16...

Early Days at
Walgreens.

Managing my
Greensborough
Walgreens
drugstore at
age 24 with
my senior
pharmacist,
Mr. Forman.

Jerry Kay, Nick Palin, Barbara Eden and Carl DeSantis
at a vitamin industry trade show.

Honored with a Fabergé Egg by Edward Villella and
Theo Fabergé for underwriting the Miami City Ballet Company.

Honored by FAU for contributions. From left to right:
Arthur Hiller, Anthony Catanese, Carl DeSantis, Bruce Mallen
and Robert Wise.

Carl DeSantis in the manufacturing facility at Rexall Sundown.

Part of the Rexall Sundown Campus.

Carl DeSantis in the Rexall Sundown Sales Display Room.

this: By following my principles of people power, you can achieve phenomenal financial successes on your own. It's being done day in and day out by individuals who prepare and employ those necessary skills which will put them into that select group of major achievers.

TWENTY-THREE

Going Public, Part One

FAR *MORE* THAN WE *BARGAINED* FOR

About the time we purchased Rexall, I came to a major decision. We would have to hire seasoned outside management people for the first time. I had to consider the possibility that we might take the company public one day, and we would be wise to have qualified individuals with wide corporate experience guiding us through the mine fields laid by Wall Street and investment bankers.

It all came about through a mutual friend who introduced me to Geary Cotton. Geary had worked for an international CPA firm, opened his own firm, and had been treasurer of his largest client's company. Our company was doing around $12 million annually back then, and I wasn't sure if we really needed a staff accountant.

Of course before we decided to hire Geary, we had to interview him. It was a typically casual gathering of our officers. First we asked Geary if he ever had occasion to imbibe a *cold one.* He said he did. Next we asked if he smoked. He said cigars, and we offered him our finest. Then I asked if he could spell CPA. When Geary said he couldn't, we knew that he would fit in with the rest of us, and I hired him. Oh, yes, I think we asked a few other equally poignant questions, but these stand out in my memory. Despite our playful tomfoolery, we recognized that Geary's CV was stellar indeed.

Geary had already convinced me that we did require on site financial guidance. Although we had purchased Rex-all, we were still essentially a family business, a mom and pop operation, if you will. At that time, my wife was doing all the books with two helpers for payroll and cash flow – three people in all.

Geary likes to tell about the day we met for his orientation. Over coffee, I told him three things. "One, use that bathroom. It's the executive bathroom. It's everyone else's too. Two, there's a space outside for you to park your car. Three, I don't know what you're supposed to do, so I really can't help you. I thought that as a CPA you'd know your functions."

He did. When Geary asked to see the payroll journal after his first few days on the job, Sylvia said he couldn't because that was confidential. As is obvious, we were still a young home-spun business, and like any set of parents, we found it difficult to allow our "offspring" to grow up. I then told Geary to start doing his work in other areas. Payroll, we could handle.

In a short while, Geary summarized the situation for me. We were a typical entrepreneurial company with loyal employees. Controls and flow of information were poor. Our systems were manual. We had a lot of work to do.

Geary laid out a plan for us to position ourselves to go public – if we so chose. I allowed him to do the necessary things – develop management systems, advise me to bring in for the first time senior level people from outside. Although we could have continued to be successful in our status quo situation, I believed that we could do even better with additional expertise.

As expected, it took time to get the management systems in place. We had our first full-fledged internal audit about two years after Geary came aboard. Then we started our balance sheet audit as we prepared to position ourselves to go public.

The Securities and Exchange Commission have very specific regulations: If you want to do a Registration to go public, you must have three consecutive years of full audits. In fiscal 1993, we met those requirements.

Before we went public, I researched further and read books that described all the nightmares of taking a private company public. I wanted to go in fully prepared. I brought on board Rick Werber, a former SEC attorney. He did not work for the Security and Exchange Commission. He was a partner in a highly respected law firm, Holland and Knight, but his background was primarily SEC work and he had spent a good deal of his time as a partner assisting in taking companies public and working with public companies. My thinking was that if I truly wanted to go public, I'd need someone with that kind of background. Rick had another plus – plenty of experience in corporate litigation – and he easily "fit in" with our after-hours brainstorming group. He has since become a dear friend and respected colleague.

I already had a superior CPA in Geary Cotton, who is now our CFO, Chief Financial Officer and was familiar with the routine of going public. He had worked for one of the "then" Big Eights and had a strong background working in concert with Coopers, Lybrand, and as an accountant auditor with Laventhal and Horwith. He'd also had his own private practice.

What probably helped us the most was what we learned

through conversations with the likes of Thompson McKinnon, Merrill Lynch, Dean Witter Reynolds among other heavy hitters, and the smaller boutique houses like Raymond James that talked to us about taking Rexall Sundown public. Many of our devoted employees also pitched in and worked long hours helping us to go public. More than a few of them currently head various divisions of our company.

Now, I'm not big on the word *team* as such. To me, it conjures up "sports" and I'm in business. We're all employees who work for a communal purpose. Anyway, they all made it very easy for me. They did some strong homework and got us ready to go public once we turned on the burners, all in a little more than seven months.

While we were in the throes of all this in 1992, the Phar-Mor debacle occurred. Some less than scrupulous activities had been going on there with certain individuals at that time. Essentially, the main man, it appeared, was caught with his hands in their till, and, from what I understand, had the proverbial two sets of books. He had been, it seems, borrowing money from GE Credit and other big boys out there, based upon false claims of profits and inflated inventories that did not exist. It was reported that Phar-Mor was also funding many of the owner's private interests.

In the meantime the Phar-Mor stores were growing at the fastest rate of any chain that had ever hit the retail scene. We had started out with them when they had only four to six stores, and as we grew together, they eventually represented about 60-plus percent of our retail-to-consumer volume. Therefore, we were understandably concerned about their future and ours.

It came as no surprise that all of the people we'd been talking to about going public suddenly became timid.

They wanted to hold off since Phar-Mor represented such a large percentage of our sales and profit. Remember, it was the first major chain we'd gone national with.

Despite the shenanigans of a "few", however, Phar-Mor had been paying all its bills to us on time. We were a very important vendor, a key supplier. Our vitamins played a major role in their sales program, and it is good and normal business practice to take care of those you need most. We do.

They needed us. And we certainly needed them. We represented a meaningful percent of Phar-Mor's profitable volume, and it wasn't as if we had suddenly gotten a deal with a three hundred store chain. We had grown together, which made the relationship comfortable for the both of us.

Because our growth had been so dependent on Phar-Mor, we became cautious before that chain's "time of troubles". We calculated that if we ever lost the Phar-Mor account, we could survive; but if we were caught with no cash flow from receivables, it might very well be near-lights-out for our company.

Since then, Phar-Mor has reduced the number of its stores from three hundred to about one hundred. That, in turn, caused us to reorganize our own company through personnel changes, cuts in all executive pay, and even tighter controls on our already disciplined spending.

During this period, Nick Palin went to Phar-Mor to ensure that we would continue to be a meaningful part of their hundred-store chain. He was successful. We preserved our base of business with them, and through all this adversity we had been made more efficient and profitable because we had gone through a more detailed analysis of our own business – leaner and meaner, if you would.

I want to emphasize that as a result of our own corporate foresight, we anticipated that if a potential problem arose, which might become a terrible reality, we wanted to be ahead of the curve and be in a proactive mode. I also wish to make it very clear to the reader that we had not been aware of any improprieties whatsoever. To the contrary, Phar-Mor had looked very strong to us; remember, up to then, it had been in essence an exemplary organization that had virtually created a new era in discount retailing.

We understood, however, that we were a small company, a private company, and the accounts receivables – money owed to us – was swelling. Even though Phar-Mor was paying us on time, they were selling so many goods that it was not unusual for them to owe us a substantial amount – several million dollars – on any given day.

Remember, Phar-Mor was a most integral part of our business. And although large, our profits had been whittled away in ongoing price negotiations. We did not want to factor their account. The cost would have been prohibitive. Although our company was profitable, we had a logical concern. What if anything should happen to them? Ever.

What had alerted us to potential danger? Phar-Mor's receivables had been increasing because they were opening more and more stores, and as a result had arranged new terms to pay us somewhat later than stipulated in our original agreement.

We called in some major insurance companies to go over our growing accounts receivable. One of them saw the substantive size of our business with Phar-Mor and recognized how much stronger their chain had become. That company gave us a receivable insurance policy at a comfortable premium. The decision was unanimous. We would insure our accounts receivable, **all** of our accounts receivable, in the event of any down-turn.

When Phar-Mor went Chapter 11 and the unscrupulous dealings of a very few were exposed, causing havoc with many suppliers, a major portion of our money was collected through our insurance. Of all the other companies dealing with Phar-Mor, we believe that we were one of the very few to have credit insurance. And who says no one is watching over us?

Our competitors had expected us to collapse like a house of cards; instead, we came back stronger than ever, which really interested Wall Street. They saw that we were savvy enough to have credit insurance and were impressed by our comeback with a tremendous rebound. We thank you, Geary Cotton and staff, for that foresight.

We aggressively went after new accounts. Where Phar-Mor had been a plus for us, it also was a minus to some extent while we were doing business with them. Phar-Mor had been so strong a competitor – meaning they were extremely low priced – few others, especially the newer deep discount chains, wanted to carry the Sundown brand of vitamins.

Because Phar-Mor was then in Chapter 11, as a result of the above-mentioned improprieties, and the number of its outlets reduced by two-thirds, we needed to expand our sales to recoup the lost market of some two hundred stores. We had been talking with K-Mart for some time with limited success. Now we told them the bitter truth that we were losing many millions of dollars in the Florida marketplace alone after the run with Phar-Mor, and no one retailer had picked off our "plus" business at home which had existed prior to the scandal.

K-Mart decided to test us, and very soon after, we were

in their stores throughout the nation. As a side note, that same year, serious flooding in Georgia and northern Florida drove thousands of people from their homes. When K-Mart's regional manager called us and asked if we could help, we sent out free vitamins to those displaced families. It's wonderful when businesses pull together to help people in distress.

Shortly after K-Mart took our products and after several years of perseverance, we began doing business with that stalwart of the retail world, Wal-Mart. Timing is everything. It's doing a good job and being in the right place when they want you. We have always grown from adversity. That is how we turned a veritable calamity into a positive selling situation and expanded the market for all of our products.

Today everything is more sophisticated. It's a highly technical business now, and we're on-line with computer systems. Like everything else in life, the toughest part is getting started, although, to be honest, every day in business can be as difficult – but the wins are indeed rewarding.

I am truly delighted that Phar-Mor has handled its recovery well and is growing again. They are a very good account with us. We still work closely with Phar-Mor, and, hopefully, will continue to be their Number One brand.

Despite Phar-Mor's problems, our delay in going public was virtually unnoticed. If there is a lesson to be learned here, it is this: **If all or most of your eggs are in one basket, you'd be wise to insure that basket.**

TWENTY-FOUR

Going Public, Part Two

I did not want to do a total ESOP, Employee Stock Ownership Plan. And, frankly, I was losing my zest to grow. I knew that if we had to go to the banks for expansion or acquisition loans, the interest could devour valuable, hard-to-find profits. We had no debt, but I felt that in order to grow to where I wanted to grow, when I wanted to grow, and in what way, we had to have the talent pool to make it happen. There were many smart people at Rexall Sundown who had plenty to offer. We needed more.

As we were about to go public, twelve to fifteen companies were making our vitamins and nutrient products, and Manhattan Drug under Jerry Kay's leadership was still supplying more than 70 percent of our nutritionals. I felt uneasy that I was not completely in charge of my own destiny. We wanted to make our own particular product, be it vitamin C or whatever, and we didn't want to have to wait one extra day.

Furthermore, the manufacturers were earning profits from us, so why shouldn't we be making the products and reinvesting those profits? Then we could bring down our cost or bring down the price level to the stores, which would make us more competitive and allow us to sell substantially more goods. Consequently, I strongly believed that we had to make our own tablets and capsules and become as completely self-sufficient as possible.

We had some concerns, however. South Florida, unfortunately, is not the beacon for the pharmaceutical industry. The humidity is only one negative. Hoffman-LaRoche and the other pharmaceutical companies that supplied us with the raw materials we used were headquartered in the Northeast. To them, it's the same as shipping to South America, climate and all. Also, we didn't have the personnel in South Florida who were familiar with manufacturing; whereas the Northeast and the Pacific Coast had an enormous pool of the kind of talent we required.

The only suppliers of raw materials working in geographic proximity to us were in Puerto Rico. That is where the large drug companies had been given, I feel, sinful tax breaks by the government. It went something like this: They could charge themselves outrageous prices, which included their behemoth profits for making a product, pay no tax on it, then ship it to us on the mainland for infinitesimal profits. And the result? Virtually no taxes were paid by their continental U.S. corporations. In return for this special treatment, they agreed to hire the local populace to fill their personnel needs.

The public offering also appealed to me and the rest of my management staff because it gave them and our employees a wonderful opportunity that was due them for their loyalty and hard work year in and year out. They would become part of the company's ownership, understand how and why Rexall Sundown was profiting, and share in its rich bounty which they helped create.

Our going public would bring more discipline and even higher morale to the company because there would be no secrets. We'd be living in a glass house. I had no skeletons anyway so it made no difference to me if we went public. I saw only the positive side.

I used to have fireside chats with my employees every two weeks on a Saturday to go over operating statements and show them how we were doing. Once we went public, they could read the quarterly reports like other share-holders out there and know the exact status of the company as co-owners now with an even stronger feeling of pride.

At the time we went public, we had about 350 employ-ees. More than a handful would become millionaires, and another hundred or so would make multi-thousands in bonus options. I am very proud to have played a role in creating those equitable rewards for so many deserving loyal individuals. Today, we are working with 1,500-plus full-time employees, and that does not include all the legions of wonderful folks who are part of the Rexall Showcase International Division.

I had one other reason for going public. We were out-growing our facilities. During our humble beginnings, we'd had to make do with a 16,000 square footer. Then we moved our headquarters to Oakland Park, adjacent to Ft. Lauderdale, and took over an approximately 70,000 square foot building. The first time I saw that building, it looked like a monolith, and I said we'd never be able to fill it. Within two-plus years, it was so inadequate that we were on the verge of filling containers in the parking lot.

Yes, we had run out of room yet again, and needed a larger facility. Because IBM was downsizing and undergo-ing other negative financial situations, the availability of prime property at less than market price in Boca Raton made sense to us. We'd either have to go to the bank and borrow, or we could do a public offering for our necessary expansion. Why should we debate further and stymie our growth? It was time to make hay in the sunshine, as the rustic saying goes.

After we overcame the Phar-Mor hurdle, we went back to the investment bankers. Although they said we lacked a product manufacturing facility, they decided to underwrite us just the same.

To establish our Initial Value, we had to do the usual dog-and-pony road show and talk to the major investors. In one instance, I was reminded that to succeed in life one should, of necessity, be fluent in several levels of conversation: Tribal and class jargon to convince family and old neighborhood buddies that you have not forgotten your origins; locker room and saloon banter to get along with the guys, or gals as the case may be; multi-syllable words you may never use in real life but need in order to get through school; American Standard English to handle day-to-day situations and make yourself employable; technical language for whatever job or profession you may have; and a spiritual vocabulary to communicate with whichever Supreme Being you may believe in.

I also knew the difference between bioflavonoid and a 1940s Brooklynese double-talk word like *cravnoid*. I was not, however, prepared for a specific example of Wall Street terminology during a meeting with the humorless head of a large investment fund. It didn't help that she reminded me of an old-fashioned schoolmarm or nun who wielded a wicked ruler.

When she asked what our "Street coverage" was, I heard **street** with a small **s** and assumed that she wanted to know about our sales force. I recited how many sales people we had in Los Angeles, South Florida, and other major market areas, and went on to assure her that we were planning to hire more, until she interrupted and coldly corrected me.

Street, capital **S,** was Wall Street, and she had wanted to know which prominent Street analysts were covering, a.k.a. following, the growth of our company. Although she did not crease her face with the slightest smile at my blunder, we managed to survive the interview. And so, I learned that in one narrow geographic area a "Street person" was not one of the homeless or a *wise guy* from the neighborhood, but instead, one who works in stocks, bonds, or commodities.

Context is the soul of communication.

* * *

A company never knows until the day before it goes public what its initial share value will be. So many factors can cause a change. Then a wonderful, and yes, beneficial coincidence occurred a few days before we went public. While we were performing our grueling road-show, *Newsweek* came out with an article extolling vitamins and possible cures for circulatory disorders and other similarly debilitating diseases. The only vitamin bottles in the accompanying photographs came from our company, and the Sundown label was there boldly and prominently displayed for all the world to see. To this day, many people believe that I had an **in** with the publisher. Sorry to disappoint them, but it just wasn't so. If anything, some "Angels in the Outfield" were looking out for us, again.

That serendipity caused our corporate image to soar. Our initial public offering was a great success. We offered 2-plus million shares, about 23 percent of the company, and were over-subscribed by nearly 30 million. The book - - amount of shares they wanted – went way outside our initial offering and price range.

In 1996, we made a second public offering of about

another 8 percent of our shares to raise additional money for the company. By then, I had been advised to diversify my portfolio. As an officer of the company I had founded, virtually all my assets were in one stock. Ours. And a great one it is.

My concept of diversification may very well differ from that of the typical investor. I wanted to **create**, after diligent research of course, new ventures from some of my inspirations, and a second offering would give me the capital to go full bore into those projects. I find it immoral to passively collect interest on great sums of money. Those dollars should be used to capitalize new businesses and create jobs.

Our second offering was very successful, and I sold some of my personal shares. It enabled me to involve myself in other ventures and help others realize their dreams, which I'll mention in a later chapter. I want to emphasize, however, that I have not shirked my responsibilities with Rexall Sundown. Nor would I ever. Because of my enduring love affair with marketing, I continue to be very much involved in all aspects of the business, particularly my love of marketing, the creative challenge of new product development, and most especially, dealing with people.

There are many small players in our industry, and that second offering put us in the best situation to consolidate and grow. It positioned us to become the unquestioned leader in our industry with our financial strength, resources, and diversified channels of distribution. Acquisition had become our newest pursuit.

I will admit that I had some reservations about taking Rexall Sundown public, which had nothing to do with finances. I was essentially a private man. Very few people knew or cared who I was. Now we were playing with the big boys, and my name would appear in print.

But, as I've said many times, I wanted to share our good fortune with our loyal employees and continue to provide substantive bonus incentives. After we did the champagne and self-congratulatory thing, we had to look to the future.

First, we wanted to sustain our ability to balance corporate discipline with the entrepreneurial spirit. We also intended to continue to nurture the feeling of family among our employees which we had established from the start more than twenty years ago, and continue to have some fun at our meetings as well.

I want to emphasize that without an entrepreneurial spirit, a company can really go downhill. At one point, about 25,000 drugstores carried the Rexall name. That is a monumental number when you consider that a giant successful and prosperous chain like Walgreen's has yet to reach 3,000 stores, albeit their volume surpasses any and all drug chains past and present. And let's not forget, the United States has a much larger population than it did during Rexall's final days of glory, perhaps 100 million more people.

After Liggett died and Justin Dart left, only corporate blue-suiter types ran the company, and they eventually wound up in Chapter 11. We think that the entrepreneurial founders and what they instill, together with some necessary corporate discipline, offer the best possible situation for a company heading into the twenty-first century. That is where we are at, what we are about, and will continue to be.

TWENTY-FIVE

Rexall Sundown Campus

Before we went public, our coffers were full of needed cash, so we went ahead and purchased the property for our new complex. We borrowed minimally from the bank because we knew we could pay it off with the offering.

We could not pass up an opportunity to buy a choice piece of property below replacement value. When something like that comes along and a need exists, you have to strike quickly.

Just do it! I cannot say it too often. Avoid ongoing corporate discussions, committee indecisions, and opinion polls. **Analysis to paralysis.** That MO just doesn't cut it. You must get off the dime! Decisively!

We felt that if the offering was not successful – although we believed it would be – it was still the right move to make. The property had belonged in part to a Scottish owned company called Rodime, which had gone bankrupt. They had made the hard drive for some IBM computers and still owned the rights to the 3½ inch floppies.

What would become our headquarters building had been Office Depot's home plate in that company's early days. Without going into all the financial details, within thirty days of closing the deal, our purchase cost was reduced substantively because we signed a lease to add almost a million dollars in rent before we took occupancy.

What a buy! And now it would become another shareholder asset below replacement cost.

Rexall Sundown's main campus in its present configuration now sits on 22-plus acres, on which we have a 58,000 square foot office complex, and an 83,000 square foot manufacturing plant for our nutritional products made and packaged there.

Breaking news: We have just completed the purchase of another 160,000 square foot facility a few miles to the south of our campus, a necessary addition because of continued phenomenal growth. And, in 1998 we will be moving our corporate headquarters yet again within the same industrial park. We have purchased the almost 100,000 square foot former headquarters building of Levitz, the nation's second largest furniture manufacturer, and contiguous, adjacent property for an additional build-out when necessary.

We currently do about 75 percent of our own manufacturing. We go outside for the rest because we do not make certain powders and the soft gel vitamin E type of products – yet!

Soon after we moved onto our campus, we added another division and continued to grow. We acquired a 100,000-plus square foot building, which had been an IBM asset. It is one of our distribution plants and warehouses a mile and a half north of our Boca Raton complex, which we purchased at another terrific price.

In Sparks, Nevada, we have leased an approximately 65,000 square foot warehouse where we keep bottled and packaged products for distribution so that we can turn over orders west of the Rockies in less than a day. We also lease another 60,000 square foot facility solely for RSI distribution.

I'm going to wave my own flag and pat myself on the back. We have always been disciplined about buying the best for the least, and we have not changed our ways just because we are a public company. In fact, the balance sheet shows the value of our buildings, less depreciation, at, I feel, unrealistically low numbers, and yet they are worth so much more. Frequently, there is substantial hidden value that you cannot bring out in the asset column. Our shareholders have done well indeed.

In June of 1994, we opened our new plant in Boca Raton. Dick Clark, famed producer of TV shows and host of *American Bandstand* and the *$100,000 Pyramid,* was there as our company spokesperson for the flag raising ceremonies.

The beautiful and charming Barbara Eden had been the first celebrity we worked with through our then soft gel manufacturer. That happened at a show in the late 1980s. Her presence had been necessary to get us noticed because we were still a small South Florida company at that time.

Then we went looking for a more permanent celebrity to help publicize our company. We found Shirley Jones to be the right kind of person. She was well known from her singing and successful movie and TV career, and she had won an Academy Award for her role in *Elmer Gantry.*

We shared the same values and found we had a chemistry with Shirley and her husband. In other words, we hit it off. Shirley understood that we were not doing big advertising for TV. It was strictly POS, point-of-sale, advertising at store level and at our trade shows. She helped us get a leg up on the competition because a recognized national figure was using our products. Shirley Jones was indeed a plus for all of us.

Then we decided that we wanted to expand our image further. Who else was better qualified than Dick Clark, America's oldest living teenager – in physical appearance? He is considerably more mature and exceptionally wise in all areas of business. We flew out to Los Angeles, and as we conferred, we saw that we shared the same values. We liked him as a person; he liked us as a company.

Although in his sixties, Dick Clark still works many hours and is a thoroughly professional businessman, courteous and kind to all. He became our spokesperson in 1991 and is an ideal representative for our products. He is a pleasure to know and work with, and he has participated in helping raise money for many of our charities.

One night on *The Tonight Show*, Jay Leno asked Dick Clark how he managed to look so young although he had entered his sixties. Dick Clark told Leno that aside from some genetic blessings, he simply keeps taking vitamins, something he had been doing since his mother started giving them to him at age five. He has said in subsequent interviews that he had been using Sundown products before he ever became our spokesperson.

Our newest stellar representative is none other than the host of *Jeopardy,* Mr. "Intellectual" himself, Alex Trebek. What a fine win and gentleman he is. Welcome Alex!

We had gone public. We had new facilities. We were nationally recognized. Now it was time to deal once and for all with the canard spread by our competitors because we were selling our vitamins to the consumer at a lower cost than theirs. They were telling the retailers and everyone else who would listen that they were getting from us only what they paid for. We intended to silence them once and for all by earning the highest evaluations from the industry watchdogs.

TWENTY-SIX

Government
Industry Standards

Ohhhh, Mr. Donderbeck,
How could you be so mean?
As to have invented
Such a wonderful machine.
The pussycats and long-tail rats
No longer will be seen.
They grind 'em up to sausage meat
In Donderbeck's machine.

I learned the above ditty from a delightful elderly "Maalox Boulevard" gentleman customer. That, along with the writings of muckrakers like Upton Sinclair, who exposed the meat packing industry in *The Jungle*, explains why we needed a Food and Drug Administration in the first decade of the 1900s, as well as the last.

Among its varied functions, the FDA regulates pharmaceuticals, dietary food, and cosmetics. The FDA arrives unannounced and inspects our plant at will. They could care less what industry evaluators like H. V. Shuster have to say. They want to investigate companies on their own. A negative report can affect the timing of a company's plan to go public and seriously damage its credibility.

There are different regulatory requirements for each category we produce; and we manufacture products considered food, not dietary supplements, and we offer OTCs – over the counter drug products – to a number of accounts.

When we first opened our manufacturing facilities, the FDA people came often to evaluate our R&D and Good Manufacturing Practices. They will not return as frequently unless a problem is brought to them, and for another reason, which I shall explain.

The October 1994 Dietary Supplement Health Education Act (DSHEA) affected our industry for the better. It clarified the categorizing of our industry's supplemental products, which really helped us. Everyone is now regulated more stringently.

We have had excellent relations with the FDA, and I believe that their random inspections can bring out the best in a company. Their people are thorough. During their interviews, they ask good questions and write detailed reports on a company; whereas the Shuster report is more industry driven.

After doing a number of checks on our plant, an FDA representative said at one juncture that they wanted to use Rexall Sundown as something of a standard for excellence. They brought in their people and used our employees as examples as if to say: "This is how it should be done."

That's why we're recognized as tops in our field. And for another reason: We do not settle for the minimum, go for the gentlemen's grade of C, the single, if you will. We go for the home run. **We look beyond the fence.**

* * *

I believe that the government's daily requirements for a person's nutritional intake are still too low. The Good Manufacturing Practices Acts passed by Congress, which regulates vitamins and nutritionals, although not as stringently as food and drugs, say that in order to live normally, you should have a daily minimum amount. It used to be a minimum daily requirement, MDR. They've gone through more changes – recommended daily allowance, or RDA, and now RDI for intake.

RDA and RDI are misnomers because what each person does is so different from the other. Still, you're better off having some standard saying the RDI for anyone is X. Those criteria were set for *normal* people. Unfortunately that's like saying the average family has 2.1 children.

For example, B vitamins are generally used for problems often connected with mental well-being. Those who are under stress on a regular basis are going to need more than the small recommendation that the government suggests.

Unfortunately, about 25 percent of the population still smokes. The depletion of their vitamin C and other nutrients just from smoking is enormous. But the FDA does not take smokers into account. You have to augment your diet and misbehavior with your own doses of nutritional supplements.

What they're learning now is that the RDIs should be disregarded. Some products have therapeutic value in them from about three-hundred to more than a thousand times the RDI.

A current example is Folic Acid, which was traditionally prescribed for a type of megaloblastic anemia. We could not sell more than 1 mg of Folic Acid in a tablet because it might mask a different disease called pernicious anemia, and a doctor might miss it in the examination. Yet, recent studies have documented and proven that the lack of Folic Acid causes neural tubular defects in children before they are born – defects in the brain and spinal cord; in adults, especially males, its lack can cause homocysteine levels to be higher in the blood, which may also contribute to heart attacks. That was brought to the attention of the general viewing public by ABC TV's 20/20 in December, 1997. Unquestionably, these ongoing scientific studies prove that Folic Acid is one of the most important and essential vitamins after all. We came to market promptly and aggressively with our now fast selling Homocysteine Defense Formula. It's now part of my daily regimine.

Another example is Beta Carotene, a precursor of vitamin A. The industry found out that fat soluble vitamins – especially vitamins A and D – are stored in the body and can be toxic when taken at very high levels.

But the FDA suggested in the case of Beta Carotene, which is found naturally in plants, that when you ingest it, it turns into vitamin A only as required by the body, and, therefore, is non-toxic at virtually any intake level.

Yet, if you take vitamin A from fish liver oil or ergo-calcipherol in very high doses over an extended period of time, it can build up in the liver and may cause side effects. That's why they say there may be some problems if you take highly excessive amounts of fat-soluble vitamins.

The FDA is also looking at vitamin C. The recommended daily allowance is 60 mg; originally the minimum daily requirement was 30 mg. Now the government is talking about raising it to 150 or 200 mg. From 30 to 200 mg is a seven-fold change in thinking in less than two years. And they're still at odds with the scientific community. What is a lowly citizen to do?

TWENTY-SEVEN

Quality Control And The H. V. Shuster Evaluation

A t Rexall Sundown, we operate at the highest possible level to ensure quality control. To begin with, one must buy chemicals and raw materials to make vitamins and ancillary nutritionals, *and* bring in the very best people to make them. We hired several chemists who had gone to the best universities and later worked for major ethical pharmaceutical drug firms before they came with us. We have also brought in and still employ people who have been in the QA/QC business – Quality Assurance and Quality Control of chemicals and operations.

We spend substantial time and money to hire the right people with solid backgrounds from firms and companies where quality is the major issue. Although we have the low-priced spread in the marketplace by offering the lower priced vitamins, we recognized that in order for us to grow we would have to send the glad tidings out to the industry that our quality was second to none.

At this level we were not concerned what the consumer might be thinking. That is not said to disparage our valued customers. We knew we had quality. Most people are trusting. They believe that if it says 500 mg of C on the label, then there is 500 mg of C in the tablet. Otherwise, the store, no matter which, would not be carrying it – or the FDA would have shut down the company that made the vitamin if it's not correct.

It's different when it comes to how our competitors deal with the trade – the stores we sell to. I call it their shameless self-justifiable falsehood. They were running out of justification for their higher prices.

The distributors, chains, and stores who sold our product, were being led astray by a number of our competitors who disparaged our products and essentially told them that they were getting what they paid for. Simply said: Sundown was selling an inferior product because the price was less.

That's why we hired the very best people for quality control, and why we continue to do so.

To validate what we are about to our vendors and the public, we brought in H. V. Shuster, that independent analyzing laboratory and quality assurance audit firm. Shuster works with our entire industry, all the major drug and discount chains. If you think of it as a Better Business Bureau for our industry, you would be wrong only in one major area. Shuster does not merely tell you what it has heard; it goes to the companies and carries out some extremely intense auditing itself before it issues a report and certification of their good/bad practices.

Shuster is the number one company in its field with the highest rating. Because the large national chains buy their products from manufacturers and other companies and often put their name on those products, they will send Shuster in to evaluate them, whether they be purveyors of vitamins or salad dressing. Shuster audits every aspect of inventory and raw material, manufactured and packaged, and reports back to that company in about four weeks. A basic scenario would have a chain drugstore calling up Shuster and asking what they knew about Sundown.

So, to negate what our competitors were saying – you get what you pay for – we brought in the Shuster experts. Because of their rigorous testing and evaluations, only a few ever qualify with high enough marks to become a Shuster-approved company.

The Shuster experts first evaluated what we were doing, then told us where we could improve. They worked with us over a period of at least six months at a great cost. They had us bring in new state-of-the-art equipment, and with their guidance raised our quality to the very highest standard in the industry. They also helped write our SOPs – Standard Operating Procedures – made audit recommendations, and set up stringent guidelines for the manufacture and packaging of all our dietary supplements.

Not barely the highest recommendation would suffice for us. We wanted to be head and shoulders above the competition. We believed it was the right thing to do, the correct course to take. The only way.

Our people were then trained, and they in turn trained their fledglings. I'm happy to say that for the past two years, we've ranked number one in quality as a nutritional company, through the assistance of the H. V. Shuster Laboratory Group out of Massachusetts.

Our Sundown products have received from Shuster the *highest* rating they have ever given to a vitamin and nutritional products manufacturer. Our facility was rated 96 on a scale of 100.

Let me emphasize, that by opening our facilities to Shuster, we successfully prevented our competitors from damaging us with their oft-repeated and tired cliché, "You get what you pay for." From a marketing standpoint, our prices were and are overall at least 20-plus percent lower than the competition while our products were certified to be of the finest possible quality in the industry. That enabled us to inform and assure our retailers and individual consumers that they did not need to pay high prices to get the best quality. End of question. End of that battle – for now.

The Shuster Certificate of Excellence was a phenomenal achievement for us and continues to be a **major** major accomplishment. No longer would the retailers be the least bit concerned about the potential validations of our products and company. If they wanted the best, we were the best. Period!

* * *

We follow all U.S. Pharmacopeia standards. This includes testing our product for purity, quality, potency, stability and safety through all stages of the manufacturing process, which includes storage, packaging, and labeling. And we comply with Current Good Manufacturing Practices issued by the Food and Drug Administration and any applicable state regulatory requirement. CGMPs encompasses all aspects of the manufacturing process including personnel operations, facilities and controls, equipment, and production and process controls. Sundown meets or exceeds CGMPs for all of its dietary supplements.

* * *

Our meeting and exceeding the standards set by the FDA, CGMPs, and Shuster paid off handsomely for Rexall Sundown and its shareholders. We received that exhilarating news from gross receipts and reports from IRI, Information Resources, Inc., an independent marketing information group that validated our #1 status in the industry.

IRI and other companies like it are used by our competitors too. IRI tallies computer-generated sales records from the retailers and in turn resells that information to manufacturers such as us.

Those records enable us to track sales of each item in every possible measuring category – regionally, by nationality, classes of merchandise, individual stores, or chains.

IRI reports are a tool for us to measure our ability to sell off the store shelf. We can say we have the best quality and pricing; this affords us the ability to accurately pinpoint our marketing successes and challenges in any retail outlet.

Over the past several years, we have seen our retail distribution expand considerably. At the same time, our consumer take-away has grown to the point where we now continually outsell our competition.

Our Sundown Vitamins brand became the number one seller as reported by IRI at the end of March, 1997, and has not relinquished that position. Sundown's first-ever achievement in capturing the top ranking within the entire vitamin category is even more important when you consider that the Sundown brand is sold in significantly fewer stores than its major competitors. More amazing, also to us, in the past three years, Sundown has risen from an almost zero ranking to become the nation's **number one seller** of herbs as well.

That is the result again of our untiring staff, at all levels, aggressively marketing new products as well as our broad array of vitamins and nutritional supplements. That is how and why Sundown Vitamins, the flagship brand of Rexall Sundown Inc. has taken over the number one ranking among national vitamin makers as this book goes to the printer.

TWENTY-EIGHT

A Truly Wonderful Machine

Beyond FDA, Shuster, and CGMPs, much of our lab work, which ensures the highest possible quality and efficacy for our products, has to do with property characteristics. Computers have changed many of our procedures. They can verify that our suppliers are sending us pure materials.

In ancient times, Greeks and Romans complained that the powdered mummy and powdered crocodile dung they had ordered from Egypt for their curative properties were being adulterated with fillers and substitutes by their suppliers. How they would have envied our truly wonderful machine.

We have purchased for nearly $100,000 one of only a few dozen near infrared – NIR – spectroscopes in existence. The machine itself is only about the size of a standard ream of 8½" x 11" paper and can evaluate a product to sixty-four levels of composition.

NIR spectroscopy works in this way. First, we place a small sample of an ingredient – powder, tablet, or gel – in a bottle or on a piece of paper. Next we lay the sample on the machine's elevator. It goes down, and the machine sends infrared rays through the sample, creating a fingerprint of the product, so to speak. We get the results within seconds – as a graph on the screen or a printout.

We do that twenty times to set a standard of purity for the product. Then the next time a sample is inserted, the machine can recognize or see the item qualitatively and creates a graph measuring it against the test standard.

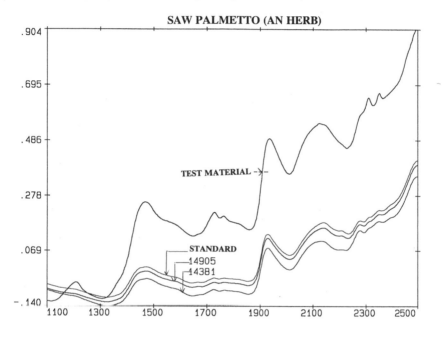

NIR can also quantitatively measure multiple items at once. With plants and herbs which may have hundreds of markers, it can create a distinctive profile for each, instead of looking for each marker. NIR can identify deviations, omissions, additions, contaminations from various vendor samples.

Raw material identification is the most common application of NIR in the pharmaceutical industry and the production process, formulation, to final quality control. We can use NIR to verify packaging materials and samples such as powders, slurries, pastes, tablets and any solid materials using diffuse reflective measurements.

Liquids are easily analyzed. Measurements may be performed directly at the NIR spectrophotometer, or remotely with a fiber optic probe.

The speed of measurement and simplicity of NIR are key benefits. Results are obtained in about three seconds. It is non-invasive, non-destructive analysis, which leaves the sample available for further testing.

Once a material has been positively identified, its quality can be assessed by NIR to determine if its chemical or physical properties – levels of purity, grade of the material, moisture content, or whatever else we may want to know – are within the acceptable range.

The value of NIR to the food supplement industry is becoming more apparent as new applications are developed. NIR affects our cost of doing business in a positive way. Testing time is reduced significantly. It improves inventory control. It reduces quarantine time. It helps meet just-in-time goals. Other benefits in production are greater yields and better quality products. NIR helps build quality into the process rather than only testing it for an end product.

As I said above, we use the machine to build a standard for our products. We can use it for a vitamin C or an herbal. That's its real value. When a product like Saw Palmetto comes in, we can look at the spectrophotometer and it will go sixty-four levels deep to give us the exact make up of that product. Because we had already set the standard in the system with twenty pure samples, we'll know if it really is the Saw Palmetto quality we must have or if the supplier brought in something below our standards, an adulterated or sub-potent product.

Although we manufacture most of our products, we

must buy certain raw materials. Some are what might be called alternative. A good percentage of these products are new.

Many companies jump on the bandwagon when a new product is touted. Shark cartilage is a prime example. I could put cartilage samples in front of you. One might be shark, the other pork cartilage. You wouldn't know the difference. Cartilage is cartilage.

Shark cartilage, with its proven benefits, brings in substantially large sales. As you might expect, there are people out there who will sell you cartilage without verifiable source in its place. Unfortunately, deceptive and dishonest business practices have indeed existed since the days of ancient Egypt, Greece, and Rome. That is one more cogent reason why our NIR is so useful. It is essential for our reputation and the quality we deliver that we purchase only from suppliers who have been proven to be honest day-in and day-out.

TWENTY-NINE

Costly Mistake, Valuable Lesson

We went public, raised more than 30 million dollars in our initial offering, and were in the throes of building our own plant in Boca Raton. Despite that full plate, we, nevertheless, continued to be on full alert for new acquisitions.

Jerry Kay and I were always meeting people at industry trade shows. Through our trade relationships, we heard that Pennex, an over-the-counter drug manufacturer, was in trouble.

I remembered Pennex from my Walgreens and Super-X days because they had supplied the chains with a number of OTC products. I wanted to know their current status, and sent out a scouting party. I learned that Pennex had one major competitor, the Perrigo Company out of Michigan.

Perrigo had been around longer than Pennex and its business was nearing the billion dollar level. Perrigo had OTC drugs. About 90 percent of its business came from aspirin, ibuprofen, antacids, everything that did not require a pharmaceutical NDA – New Drug Application.

Pennex was a competitor of Perrigo and at one time had been doing over 100 million dollars a year. It had been taken over by a holding company from the Netherlands and had a facility of about 300,000 square feet outside of Verona, Pennsylvania, with about three hundred employees. It made over a hundred different items including analgesics, cold and cough remedies, antacids, and laxatives. Nevertheless, Pennex was in a situation where the banks were ready to call in their loans, give it away to the highest bidder, or flip them and sell off the assets.

We moved quickly. We stayed there a full week and worked at breakneck speed with outside attorneys we didn't know until we made our deal and prevented Pennex from going into insolvent bankruptcy. We let the company meet its payroll and continued to employ its then limited work force.

We knew very little about making over-the-counter drugs, but I thought we could get a nice chunk of the business because Perrigo was doing, we felt, about 65 percent of the private label OTC business in the entire country. We thought we could use Pennex to get the lion's share of the rest.

We had made the deal for a few million, and over the next year and a half put in additional millions to get the operation on track. Then I realized that we could not get Pennex moving properly, because along with all the inherent problems of a re-start, Perrigo aggressively lowered their prices substantially. At that point, our equipment was too antiquated to compete properly. These days, you need high-speed manufacturing machinery to make money on anything, especially OTCs, those commodity items where you see the names of your favorite store and the other chains on the labels.

For those customers who chose to pass on their private label, Pennex had a Good Health® label of its own, which represented a small fraction of its business. The rest was private label.

Pennex had the capacity to generate more than $100 million worth of goods annually, but only produced $12.4 million in fiscal 1994. Although Rexall Sundown had record sales in 1994, we had a large percentage of decrease in net income because of our ongoing problems with Pennex. We decided that our other divisions should not have to carry that company. It was time for Pennex to carry Pennex.

Today, I am fully aware of the two mistakes we made with Pennex. Prescription drugs and OTC items have a markedly different set of rules than vitamins. For example, we cannot be creative and add vitamin C to a cold medicine, because the combination has not been specifically reviewed and approved by the FDA, or a fixed recipe or monograph exists for the item with no deviation allowed. Whereas, we can add embellishments to nutritionals without government assessment of every formula - - intelligently based on our knowledge from R&D, our own stringent guidelines, and the FDA's regulations regarding acceptable ingredients.

That being the case, we could not make a raspberry flavored cough syrup cheaper and better than the competition's. And we still had to compete with Perrigo, a company that was extremely price-aggressive at the time. If they offered a product at $6.00 a dozen and we undercut them at $5.50, they would come in with their high-speed equipment, further undercut Pennex, and cause us to lose money at $5.50.

Would we invest additional multi-millions for high-speed equipment? We were very thin on the kind of management we needed. We'd had the word of some key executives at Pennex who promised they would immerse themselves in the acquisition, which, I feel, they failed to do. And my nature is such that I don't take over a business and let it languish too long and cost the company moneys we can ill-afford the way others too often tend to do.

The Pennex affair caused Wall Street to look at us with doom and gloom. They "reprimanded" us by downgrading our stock because they saw no hope for Pennex. You have to give Wall Street guidance. They want to know what you intend to do. When you tell them you're putting multi-millions of dollars into equipment and additional millions for whatever else, and they see us changing management the way you change socks, the word was that we didn't have a handle on our business and shouldn't be in that segment.

After getting clobbered for a couple of quarters on our stock price, we decided to divest ourselves of Pennex. We released management, gave most of the full time employees one to six months severance pay depending upon their time served with the company and closed the plant.

There's been conversation that we could have saved Pennex. Had we been a private company I might have stuck with it a little longer. But Wall Street is not forgiving and the pressure was on for us to get out and move on.

We sold Pennex and took the write-off. We will not be looking at OTC private label manufacturing for a while because it is far too competitive and profits are slim indeed. Perrigo's "market cap" is certainly not enviable, based upon the volume they generate.

Market cap is the number of shares outstanding times the share price. We approached a 3 billion dollar cap in mid-1998. Not too shabby when you remember where and when we started out in our bedroom. **Bedroom to Boardroom** – but a title like that for this book would have been misleading.

We know how to make money. And when we can't, we'll shake the albatross from our neck.

The moment our shedding of Pennex made the news, our stock jumped up sharply. And of course it's been up, up, and away ever since. True, there have been some, I feel, unwarranted lows, but price recovery has always been around the corner.

We learned several lessons as a result of the Pennex affair. First, we have to be more diligent in investigating a company. Next, good management should already be in place. Finally, we should not purchase the hopeless inadequates and try to elevate them, as time is not on our side in such situations.

I am always concerned about people. Experience has taught me this: **When planning to acquire a company, aside from evaluating its cash flow and assets, you must always ask if you're also getting the kind of people who can keep it growing and are malleable to management's way of doing things.**

There are still many companies out there with considerable talent, but they may be underfunded or are not taking what we believe to be the right course of action. We are looking for something appealing to bring to the shareholders that we can be proud of – the kind of company that can throw off top-line sales and bottom-line profits the way we do at Rexall Sundown, or have the potential to.

For more than the last five years, our growth has maintained itself at over 30 percent. Today, our profits are enviable indeed and appear to be a positive aberration in the commodity driven nutritional industry. Vigilance, discipline, and an "I care" attitude at all levels are the major ingredients which have brought about this industry phenomenon.

THIRTY

Managed Care

Having many different product lines has worked well for us. We have eyes and ears in the market place to track what's happening out there in the different niches on a steady basis. For example, we can often utilize the health food stores as a proving ground for a product. It's an environment where people always want to try a new efficacious product and will pay top dollar for it.

If we see a particular nutritional selling well in that market, we may make a variation of it. If we like the formulation, we will produce it and deliver it to the ever expanding mass market.

We also measure how much soft profit is being thrown our way through our other divisions besides the health food store lines. My belief is that we must stay attuned to all those divisions because each one can receive information, which inevitably makes us stronger.

Our move into Managed Care began as a result of my discussions with John Isakson, a tough field commander who had survived combat in the rice paddies of Vietnam. Because John had then spent twenty-five years in Pharmaceuticals, he was familiar with the hospital, nursing, home care, and physicians market.

When I met him some thirteen years ago, John was Director of Sales and Marketing for R. P. Scherer, one of largest manufacturers of soft gel capsules. We developed a good business and personal relationship.

I thought so highly of John that in 1993 I asked him to be on the Board of Rexall Sundown as an Outside Director. We wanted his expertise after we went public and were in the process of acquiring Pennex.

As you already know, if the Pennex acquisition had succeeded, we would have had control of our own destiny manufacturing OTC products. Through John, we saw a big opportunity to jump into a new enormous and growing market that had been essentially untapped by the traditional OTC companies – managed care, nursing homes, HMOs.

We thought that Pennex would give us an opportunity to enter that new market. As a public company, great diversification helps image. When people asked us who were served, we wanted to reply every type – from individual to retailer to hospital.

Of course we all kicked around the idea of entering managed care. Was it going to work? Would it play well in Peoria?

John and I flew out to California and went to Kaiser Permanente, which has no peer in Managed Care, the biggest in country. We wanted to know what they thought, if we should take our products into their bailiwick.

We met with their Northern and Southern California people in contracting and purchasing, and bounced the concept off them. They thought it was a unique opportunity. The name Rexall and our capabilities were unbeatable positives. On the plane back to Florida our new baby was born, Rexall Managed Care.

I asked John to leave the Board of Directors so he could put the new division together. That was at the end of 1993, early 1994.

We started from scratch. We had to hire experienced sales people, administrative staff, telemarketing, customer service, and contract personnel. At the same time, we developed a product line of 150 to 175 vitamin and OTC products that would be meaningful to the managed care market. Our OTCs originally came from Pennex. Currently, they come from several reputable firms, including Perrigo, with our high standard of quality assurance.

We created unique Rexall labels and a brochure with the RMC logo, a mortar and pestle, and made sure they had a non consumer appearance. Then we went after all the big purchasing organizations in the country, and had incredible initial success for two reasons.

The grand old Rexall name was a respected name. Dare we say beloved? All the seasoned pharmacists had at one time or another dispensed Rexall prescriptions. Consequently, we did not have to sell Rexall. It was already perceived as a real brand – not generic or multi-source.

The other reason for our success was basically our manufacturing practices, which had the highest ratings in the industry. All RMC products have the Shuster blessing. Therefore, our quality is a given. The fussiest customers who visit our plant always leave reassured and make pleasant comments about our operation.

Therefore, we secured a number of contracts with the biggest hospitals in the country. We got them through purchasing groups such as Premier Hospital, which has close to 2,200 hospitals under their umbrella; the University Hospital Consortium, which has teaching hospitals underneath its blanket all over country; and others successful in long term care. We have done very well with HMOs – Humana, Harvard Community, Kaiser Permanente, and others.

Managed Care is a more than 1.6 million bed market covering ninety-percent of the nursing home beds in the country – Omnicare, MHA to name a few. To service these members, you need wholesale distribution, the McKessons and the Bergens. They got our products into the distribution centers. When our customers need them, the wholesalers can deliver in 24 hours.

We shipped our first product in September, 1994. At the end of this past fiscal year, we had about $9.5 million in gross sales with a correspondingly acceptable net for a start-up business. That is a very good run in so short a time, much of it due to great recognition of the Rexall name.

Our RMC is growing as we increase the line with new and unique products. One item is a prescription eye drop called Timolol®, which among its capabilities attacks high ocular pressure caused by wide angle glaucoma. It is especially useful in the nursing home care market, as the elderly are prone to ocular problems.

How does the patient pay for our products? Generally, a third party insurance company pays, or it is provided by the HMO. Our HMO products are available in hospital pharmacies at prices competitive with pharmacies across the street.

Hospitals have our products in two places. Those going through surgery – the acute care side – get them when ordered by a physician and dispensed by a nurse while the patient is in bed. A physician may also recommend our product, and on the way out, the patients go to the in-hospital pharmacy with a card proving they belong to the group – and we make sure that our products are included in that claim.

The OTC and vitamin industry is growing because cost containment and preventative maintenance are the catchwords of managed care. Keeping people healthy is a cost savings. How? By taking the proper supplements: Folic Acid to help prevent birth defects and heart disease; Calcium for osteoporosis.

We expect that insurance companies will be looking at selected vitamins and OTCs as a cost-effective first line of defense against illnesses, preventative "medicine", if you will; and include in their medical plans allowances for firms and individuals to purchase those nutritional supplements.

At an average of four dollars, vitamins and OTCs are much cheaper than the typical prescription at twenty-five dollars – and that does not take into account the required visit to the doctor's office which can often cost another substantial amount.

As with our other division, RMC is alert when a prescription product becomes available as an OTC. We evaluate its worth and may then add it to our line and ship it out. One example is Aleve®, which we have produced as a private generic label for Kaiser. We do private labels if HMO membership and quantities purchased are significant.

Those HMOs, led by Kaiser Permanente out in California, are buying substantial numbers of bottles of our pre-natal vitamin each year for their mothers-to-be. They purchase our liquid antacids under the Rexall nomenclature.

As the song says, "We've only just begun."

THIRTY-ONE

Entrepreneur As Chairman Of The Board

When we went public, at first I lost much of my freedom to do as I wished with Rexall Sundown. Quarterly reports are one of my greatest burdens. The instant we finish dealing with one such report, we have to get ready for the next, with only three months between them.

Suddenly we're into the second quarter, and by the time we get through with conference calls and all that non-entrepreneurial stuff, we already are into another month towards our next report – and, be assured, we'd better deliver a more superior report card than we did before.

I truly dislike the institutional purchasing of shares for programmed selling. For example, a teacher's union may buy our stock at the given price we're offering, but they have a little form that says **sell** when it reaches a certain level.

When that happens, our small investor who has minimal, but meaningful shares, panics and sells too. Herd mentality, to a large degree. Of course the sword cuts both ways. When the big boys buy, others follow. That's like the six or eight deck Black Jack tables in Las Vegas. Wall Street stocks have similar artificial big runs that frequently favor the short sellers or the longs.

We want to run this business equally for all shareholders, like we would in any business, not from quarter to quarter where you always have to play catch up.

For anyone in the public arena, maybe there should be a group of people who should be set aside to take into account how Wall Street will react to an X, Y, or Z outside event, rumor, or actual truth concerning a specific company.

If we are spending all our time talking to Wall Street, that's not what our employees nor our institutional investors and shareholders in general want – they want us to be working. They want us to be thinking about what we're going to do next. They want us to be creative. They want to know what will be our next incomplete multi-vitamin or blockbuster nutritional supplement.

Why shouldn't we report twice a year like Japan and other countries, or better yet, once a year? Why not have three different exchanges for a company to choose among? One for quarterly, bi-annual, or annual reports. Then let potential shareholders decide where to invest.

CFOs and corporate "know hows" should handle Wall Street. That's one reason why I brought in Christian Nast to be President and now Chief Executive Officer of our company. He was one of the Vice Presidents of Colgate Palmolive, and is used to dealing with people at the corporate level. I have had very little meaningful conversation with Wall Street since the IPO.

Incidentally, after I relinquished my title of CEO to Chris, the Street thought I had put myself out to pasture, which was not the message I wanted to send. Therefore, I created a unique new title for myself, Chief Corporate

Officer, CCO, to let everyone know that this bull was still in the arena. A side effect of all our titles at Rexall Sundown manifests itself when *Hail to the Chief* is played at our corporate HQ. Several of us walk into the room at the same time.

Chris established a necessary corporate discipline at Rexall Sundown, which, through his varied talents and passion, has taken us to new heights. That gives me the freedom to do what I love the most – to work with people, to create in marketing, and in those ways to continue doing the very best for the company. To be sure, I can stand up in the bully pulpit and talk, but that's not what I'm getting paid to do. I'm getting paid to ensure that Rexall Sundown continues to grow profitably.

Do not misunderstand me. Despite the burden of quarterlies, going public has enhanced and embellished what I can do. It's the best thing I've ever done. For the company. For the employees. For my family, and now the shareholders.

There is, however, a personal downside to our growth and going public. As I feared, we lost our anonymity. The bigger we became, so did our size as targets. We became fair game for the litigious and the media.

THIRTY-TWO

Doing Business In The Nineties

A ll businesses face costs these days that they didn't have to deal with decades ago. Many laws have been passed intended to benefit individuals and society as a whole: Pollution and environmental standards, workplace regulations, and a need to ensure equal opportunities for all employees, all regulated by three-letter state and federal agencies.

Added to the cost of doing business are those contingency fee driven lawsuits from disgruntled nobodys who continue to fail the burning stove test they should have learned by the age of two. How we all wish to see a meaningful change in the tort system.

As mentioned in earlier chapters, we have met and generally exceeded all government standards for our industry. I am proud to say that we have had no more than a handful of employee-driven lawsuits since we began our business more than twenty years ago, and they were trite indeed. That is because we hire the very best and treat them fairly – as family more often than not. We promote based solely on merit, talent, and loyalty.

Currently, we have a diversified group of employees who get along very well with each other. During our first sensitivity training sessions, we asked people to stand when their group was mentioned – African American, Hispanic, over forty, female, various religions, assorted national origins. By the time we were through, no one was seated. Everyone understood.

I am concerned, however, with the bias against businessmen in the news media, Hollywood films, TV shows, and nearly all educational institutions. Often, they can't tell the difference between entrepreneurs – those who create jobs, allow employees to become wealthy, and produce the best product at the lowest cost for the consumer – and the unscrupulous dollar driven lowlifes: The rentier who buys apartments and raises rents beyond the reach of working people; the sharks who take over companies then milk or close them while lining their pockets; lawyers who litigate businesses out of existence with over-zealous time consuming and cost wrenching lawsuits. They contribute significantly to unemployment and create much misery and should be exposed and condemned by the media and the public at large.

Yes, perception truly is reality. Most people have a positive image of the stock and bond profession based on the classy offices they may visit or see on film, or as a result of watching the well-groomed, educated, and articulate men and women such as those who appear on the PBS show *Wall Street Week*. They and most others who work on the Street are usually fine, honorable people.

Unfortunately, a small but visible number of parasitical "no-lifes" also populate the Street. Some hustle customers over the phone with the same tenacity and ruthlessness as any boiler room telemarketer who makes unsolicited calls.

And there are floor runners, money launderers, and other categories of flunkies and hangers-on.

Regrettably, some masquerade as objective writers at certain industry journals that are guised as informational newspapers, newsletters, and magazines. These less than impartial writers unwittingly, in some cases, can do irreparable harm. All large business, especially those that produce products with recognizable brand names, are vulnerable to such journalists who hope to find at least one disgruntled employee or conduit willing to trash the company and maybe get on TV for a between-commercial moment of fame. If they cannot find any of the above, then those media junkyard dogs sniff around for anything that verges on negativity so that they can spin it into their significant story.

Now that we are a public company and our names have appeared in the press, we have had to deal with unfounded accusations, some of them based solely on my Italian name. As an example, one litigant claimed that we defrauded suppliers. Based upon accusations within his lawsuit, the FBI was required to investigate those charges, which they found out to be absolutely false, without basis in fact. Consequently, they dropped that investigation.

When newspapers pick it up, the headlines will read: FBI INVESTIGATES COMPANY. You will not, of course, see the headline: FBI DROPS INVESTIGATION OF COMPANY. CHARGES WITHOUT BASIS IN FACT.

I can handle those problems because I know myself. I do have trouble, however dealing with innuendo, half truths, and biased reporting when stories affect our employees and outside consultants who have given their all. Several caring people have had to pay a steep emotional price for our success and going public.

Although they have confirmed that there is nothing illegal, unethical, or wrong with Rexall Sundown, certain individuals and one specific article in a business publication have attacked, without conscience or an understanding of the consequences, the background of a few of my associates. That has caused great pain and suffering for them and especially their families and accomplished little else in the long run – unless one chooses to interpret as more than coincidence what has happened to our company two years in a row at exactly the same time, after the first quarter reports of earnings.

Because we are now a public company, the origins of one story in 1997 may have a more sinister background than a feeble attempt at mere tabloid exposé. At one point, of our now nearly 75-plus million shares outstanding, only about 400 thousand were in the hands of short-sellers (they are the investors who gamble that a stock will go down in value). Then suddenly, the shorts borrowed to buy almost 4 million more in anticipation of a drop in value of our shares.

Our stock rose instead. Did dishonest individuals then decide that something had to be done to reverse our upward trend so the shorts would not continue to lose millions? Suddenly, it appeared, certain short sellers began to spread negative rumors about our company, which created typically a self-fulfilling prophecy because many investors act on such tales first and think later. Also, some in the media may have let themselves be manipulated by the shorts.

Forbes and *Barron's* decided to investigate our company. *Forbes* sent one of its top senior editors to interview us directly. I prefer to believe that as a result of speaking with us face-to-face, hearing our side, and seeing our operation first hand, *Forbes* decided not to go with a negative story about our company based on those rumors we feel were circulated by the short sellers.

What we got from *Barron's* was merely a phone inquiry. Not surprising, that business publication came out with what I felt was a vile feature article. It questioned our ability to continue selling at a high level, my integrity, and, most offensive of all, emphasized the "unsavory histories" of several key associates, without offering an opportunity for honest refutation.

The title revealed the bias of the article – *Vitamin D-Minus* and implied that our stock had dropped from a high of about $39 per share to about $20 because investors were concerned that we had consorted with some very shady, unscrupulous characters. The truth is that many growth stocks had dropped at the same time because players, those who play the charts and are not true investors, were driving the market.

They had overvalued certain stocks, then when the shares reached a specific high price, they bailed out. There was a liquidity crisis at that time. Anyway, that was my take. The big blue chippers can, on many occasions, divest themselves of a million shares to gain liquidity and the price of their shares will often still rise.

The growth stocks, those capitalized at around 20 million-plus shares, all took a hit around the same time we did when everyone seemed to want more liquidity. And if that was not enough to drive down our stock, remember that those short sellers had a lot to gain from rumors spread about our company. Self-fulfilling prophecy.

Even if the *Barron's* writer had not deliberately composed this story specifically for the hedge funds and short selling enthusiasts, it was, nevertheless, certainly a "short-seller's" dream article. Yet, that article was totally unnecessary and had absolutely no relation to our stellar business ethics.

Filled with innuendos and limited "info" – without any attempt to seek in depth refutation or clarification from us – that feature on our company also included legalistically protective phrases such as: *"Barron's* is aware of no official investigations ...." We could say the same about them. Rexall Sundown is aware of no official investigations of *Barron's.*

I'll concede that some employees and associates may have had pasts that included bad breaks or poor judgment when they were much younger, but all have worked honestly and ethically for Rexall Sundown. I tolerate nothing less. You know from my earlier chapters how I learned that even teenage miscreants can be redeemed and go on to a useful life, and if a Walgreens store manager hadn't wanted to go home, I too might have had blemished recorded past.

Because *Barron's* failed to discover the slightest negative practice at Rexall Sundown, it decided to publish the past history of a few individuals, one of whom was a man who consulted with us and played a meaningful role in the success of one of our divisions. True, he had an unfortunate episode in his past **forty-two years ago** when he was only sixteen. Unfairly tried and incarcerated, he later received a full Governor's Pardon.

This same gentleman, so malevolently maligned in that article, married and raised a wonderful family. Although financially successful, he never forgot his impoverished roots and has led a purposeful and philanthropic life. That tabloid style article succeeded only in bringing unnecessary grief to this exemplary family.

Most of these periodicals do a fine job fulfilling their role as watchdogs; however, there are exceptions amongst the honest and hard working journalists, and they should stop wasting their time digging up the past of employees and consultants who have and continue to work honorably. I suggest that such individuals should do the investor a real service. Investigate the MBAs who have goody-two-shoes backgrounds. You know the kind of people I'm referring to. Those who have opportunities to behave unethically and criminally in government and the business world.

I won't name the biggies who have gone to jail because of their junk bond schemes or insider trading, but I wonder – were they also bumming around with pseudo-gangs as kids, or were they getting good grades and acting like Mr. Clean® while cheating on their exams and research papers?

I look at them and say to myself, "They are not the guys I would have run with as a teenager." But such men and women can be redeemed – as in the case of *Barron's* in March, 1998.

I mentioned earlier an annual coincidence which temporarily affected the value of our stock. After our stock dropped to about $19 in the spring of 1997, it rebounded stronger than ever. We went beyond $40, split, and were approaching $40 again in the spring of 1998. My optimistic nature did not want to see the warning sign when 9 million of our shares were in the hands of the shorts until *Wall Street Journal* ran a negative article about the nutritional supplement industry in general and Rexall Sundown specifically.

Exactly as the year before, our stock dropped, about 8 points, during the week following that article. This time, however, *Barron's* listened to our rebuttal of the *Wall Street Journal* feature and printed its own article that was generally accurate and fair to Rexall Sundown, and which redeemed that publication from my point of view. Yes, our stock rose again.

Was it coincidence or do the shorts have allies at certain publications who guarantee their profits? I have not yet researched if other corporations receive similar annual trashing. But you can be assured that in 1999 – if not sooner – before we issue our first quarter report, I will take a careful look at the number of Rexall Sundown shares held by the shorts and be aggressively proactive.

THIRTY-THREE

Playing Favorites

THE PURSUIT OF CREDIBILITY

After Rexall Sundown successfully went public, I learned yet another lesson, which one might express algebraically: As you grow in business, so does the height of your subsequent hurdles.

In 1994 Congress passed the Dietary Supplement Health and Education Act, under which, the National Institute of Health established the Office of Dietary Supplements. Unfortunately for our industry from that point in time, the ODS had received minimal funding from the NIH, whereas the pharmaceutical companies were the end recipients of much larger sums that had been appropriated by Congress. Consequently, the NIH, I feel, still underfunds the vitamin and nutritional supplemental industry's research arena, while giving seemingly preferential treatment to the large drug companies. That is somewhat understandable, considering the blockbuster drugs that have come to market with their help.

Of course we realize that the vitamin and nutritional supplemental industry's relationship with the NIH is in its infancy. Things are looking up, however, because we now have their ear. Hopefully, we too will receive the benefits of taxpayer funded NIH research and enjoy the respect currently shared mostly by the larger drug firms.

Meanwhile, some of those major household name pharmaceutical companies have use of thousands of acres in Costa Rica's rain forests where they speculatively farm for gawd-only-knows-what plant derivatives. If they get lucky, they can convert their eventual to be patented discovery to a pharmaceutical and charge seemingly unconscionably high prices to the consumer, while they pay a paltry stipend for the rain forest's abundant treasures.

That is fine in itself, but even though they research that bounty of nature, they often send a significant supply of that potentially therapeutic herb back to the NIH, which does a good amount of their homework in concert. The NIH then gives it back to the major pharmaceutical companies to do their Phase I, II, and III studies and then market it, if feasible. Those drug manufacturers then seek out their up to 20 year patent protection, and typically, an expensive prescription results out of any of the efficacious parts. Therefore, rarely do nutritional companies like Rexall Sundown have an opportunity to give that find to the consumer at a realistic price.

Let me cite another example. Acetylsalicylic acid, a derivative of Willow Bark, is aspirin. Aspirin is an over the counter product. If a company like Rexall Sundown had to reintroduce aspirin in the current marketplace, it would be nearly impossible to receive FDA approval. But be assured that any one of the major drug companies most likely could, and then aspirin would become a prescription item and cost substantially more – like AZT. And another low costing, fairly priced beneficial product for the consumer is once again unavailable.

The same, I feel, would be true if they found a meaningful cure for cancer from nature. It would then become an overpriced prescription, because the pharmaceuticals have to answer to their shareholders who are used to earning continually some of the highest profits on Wall Street. They need patented items to thrive and survive.

That is the essence of my major battle. Neither the NIH nor any other agency has jurisdiction over what the drug companies decide to charge. Our industry is rife with stories of investigations that imply a number of companies have often become abusive with their profiteering. Only aggressive competition will change that, and possibly, shorter patent protection time as well.

Of course those companies fail to tell the public that in many cases a substantial amount of the research was done by the NIH in conjunction with them. The NIH – aka the tax payers – once again pays the lion's share, and pays again dearly at the prescription counter.

Furthermore, as an example, the drug companies spent millions of dollars when they invited hundreds of doctors to symposiums in Rome, Paris, and London. Those companies are not spending that kind of money on core R&D no matter how much they say they are. **Nota bene:** That sum was buried in their R&D budget.

In that context, Rexall Sundown is trying to educate the consumer and the buyers. One of our biggest problems out there right now is with certain procurers from some of the large chains. We are aware that they do not recognize what the nutritional business is truly about, and they won't listen to the breakthroughs we're having. Some are, albeit a few, more interested in *what can you do for me* rather than *what can we do for the consumers.*

Much of our growth had been stymied for the two or three years before we became a public company because of my edict: We will not sell to stores that buy a product from us for one dollar and charge the consumer an unjustifiably high mark-up. Instead, I went ahead and looked for the – I don't want to call them discount houses – but the fair-priced stores where our products will be available to consumers at a price they can afford, and reflects fairly a consumer-friendly price.

That was our MO and that is how we have pretty much remained. We are in the marts, other fair and lower priced outlets, and in aggressively priced grocery chains. We monitor as best we can those retailers that seem to overcharge the consumer for our products. We still do our best to refuse to pursue their business whenever they surface. And, if the truth be told, in many cases it's difficult not to sell to them because we also go to wholesalers who in turn may sell to those I believe to be "robber barons" and defeat our overall pursuit of fair and honest business practices.

It is my firm belief that Rexall Sundown products should always be sold at a fair and reasonable price. Hopefully our consumers are becoming better educated. We certainly try to ensure that they will be more demanding in the area of price and availability, with quality.

The reader should be informed about the big pharmaceutical companies that often manufacture the raw materials we use for our vitamins. Because about 70 percent of their profits are reaped out of pharmaceuticals, their salespeople and spokespersons are encouraged to generally poor-mouth the vitamin end of the business. They complain that they are not making profits when they sell us vitamin C at $12 per kilo. That is 2.2 pounds if you are not aware of the metric system conversion.

Their complaints ring hollow. Their real cost of vitamin C is a secret. If we pay $12 a kilo, for all we know it might cost them only a couple of dollars a kilo. We simply do not know. Yet!

Their big profits come at their manufacturing and distribution levels. The major pharmaceutical companies do not have to compete for space on the retailers' shelves. They have no worries about new patents. They already have method patents on the raw materials. Therefore, those divisions make and sell their vitamin E, Beta Carotines, vitamin A, and so on, which represent a substantive portion of their total profit. And we do the compressing, tablet making, bottling, advertising, and marketing of their letter vitamin raw materials. It's as if they condescended to give us permission to do all that.

Some pharmaceutical companies are exceptionally good at publicizing their very profitable vitamin business. They have easy access to the writers at major consumer publications, and promote what has happened in the vitamin industry. Every time those publications report a breakthrough or new study, in about thirty days we often see a price increase by all the raw material and chemical suppliers. I'm not saying there's a cartel out there, but –.

The pharmaceutical companies have manufactured their own vitamins in the past, but failed to market them properly to the consumers, which created no real problem for them in the long run. Because they have a near monopoly on the raw materials, they decided that it is more profitable and considerably less inconvenient to be the suppliers to our industry.

One of the big companies, Archer Daniel Midland, is primarily involved in producing natural vitamins, and opened a major plant at an enormous cost to manufacture vitamin E. E comes from wheat germ too, but the process to extract it is too expensive. Soy beans are the more plentiful source of natural vitamin E – even if people are tired of hearing about tofu derived from soy.

When Eastman Kodak divested its chemical division,

they created a major shortage of natural E. Archer Daniel Midland has the other "lock-on" of that product, along with Henkel, a German based drug company. *Verrry* interesting how natural E has gone up in price substantially in the past couple of years. I'm sure the reasons are many. Consequently, Hoffman-LaRoche, which produces mostly synthetic vitamins, is currently looking into natural E and planning to open a plant for that purpose in the near future, we are told. Competition should make the raw material suppliers price more aggressively.

E is E according to our government, synthetic or natural, but as I said in another chapter, people prefer natural. And in E's case, natural has been proven to be nearly 35 percent more efficacious than the synthetic form.

Why don't we manufacture the raw materials? For us, that would be another level of investment from about 500 million to 1½ billion dollars. Not one of us at our end of the business – the capsule and tablet manufacturers – has ever looked into it. But, perhaps, one day?

Some companies have tried to buy the raw vitamin C from manufacturing plants in China, but the Chinese have yet to figure out how to do the mesh or fineness for the granules with consistency, although their C is pure and very aggressively priced. Also, when a non-pharmaceutical raw material plant is coming along rather well, often the big boys often buy it out, and eliminate the competition. Seems something like a DeBeers cartel to me.

For us, manufacturing raw vitamins may yet be the right route to go at some juncture in our future.

THIRTY-FOUR

My Malady

A business can fail or must be shut down because the successful initiator, who is more often the driving force, suffers from a severe illness or undergoes major incapacitating surgery. It does not always have to be that way if one has the will to persevere. Of that, I can assure you.

One of the great ironies of my life began in my forties. Up to then, I had perfect health, no measles or any other debilitating childhood illness. I can't even remember having a cold until I got one about six months ago.

As I reflect on my past, perhaps it began when I was in high school working in a grocery store in a neighborhood populated by American blacks and immigrants from the Caribbean. I was in the produce department, the back room, when I saw a woman staring at me. She looked like someone Ann Rice would have written about.

Perhaps the woman didn't like what I was doing. I don't really know. She put up her hand – maybe a voodoo thing – said something in a foreign tongue, and gave me a peculiar look. That was all. She walked away, and about a second later, the next thing I remember is that I ended up in a hospital. And whatever that meant – who can say? Was it a curse or a warning?

At the hospital, they gave me all kinds of tests, including somewhat painful spinal taps. Why had I blacked out? They could find no cause. It was the only time I had a problem like that, until I was about forty years old.

I'd always been especially proud of my exceptional balance and agility that had taken me through sports, high diving, and my extracurricular circus acts. Lightheadedness and loss of balance never affected me while I played sports or did my circus act at FSU.

When I still worked for Super-X and opened my variety store, lightheadedness and dizzy spells began to occur. I could be anywhere – on the beach, in a store, on the sidewalk. I'd be going fast, then feel lightheaded, and have to stop. I'd lose my balance and wonder what was happening to me. Because the problem was not pronounced, I wasn't too concerned, but it seemed to worsen once I got out of retail.

It became more serious about five years after I started up the mail order division of the business. The attacks would occur less than 5 percent of the time during waking hours. The only thing I did was slow down. Often times, I had to screech to an abrupt halt.

Then about twelve years ago, I was buying some fishing tackle in a marine store for my son Damon's upcoming birthday when I had a severe attack. People came over to help me because I couldn't walk, and they sat me down. I was not pale, however. Someone called fire-rescue, and they took my blood pressure. It was fine. They could not understand what was going on. Someone from my business had to come and pick me up.

Another time, I was having lunch with Dean, my oldest son, in a shopping center. I'd ordered a sandwich and a Pepsi. I took a hit of the cola, and next thing I knew, I lost total balance and fell off the chair I was sitting on.

Fire-rescue was called again. By then, I thought I had a sugar problem, that my attack had been brought on by sweets from the cola. I thought I might have diabetes. I took tests for sugar problems; the doctors couldn't find anything wrong.

Of course I should confess that I was doing some excessive drinking and smoking from three to four packs of cigarettes each day. I was no different than many of my customers who took nutritional supplements and vitamins to compensate for their often poor habits.

I was like the fellow in this joke told by a priest at a mass I attended:

Mary and John had led a beautiful life. They were in their eighties, healthy and active. She was running every day. He was playing golf. For many decades she has seen to it that they both were on a fat-free diet. Then one day, both are hit by a truck and they die. They are greeted at the pearly gates by St. Peter, and she asks, "What do we do now?"

St. Peter says, "You like this, Mary?" And he shows her all the things she ever admired, wanted, or enjoyed doing. "You like butterflies? You want to see the lion lie down with the lamb? You've got it all."

To John, St. Peter says, "You like golf? Here are all the possible golf courses that have been and ever will be designed. You can play on them throughout eternity."

At that point, John turns to Mary, elbows her in the ribs, and says, "You and your fat-free diet. I could have boozed it up, eaten red meat, desserts, and could have had all this twenty years sooner."

I tried to connect the dots. I was smoking heavily, and they were Camels. I drank more than my share of alcohol from six in the evening until past 11 PM at least three nights a week. That was after my divorce because while still married I was answerable to my wife. After the reins were taken off, I abused myself all too often.

Sometime in 1985 I started getting a bit lightheaded for about ten to fifteen minutes twice a day. I thought little about it and sort of went with the flow.

Then approximately two years later, I was out with the guys very late. I'd had a number of drinks and smoked at least two packs of cigarettes.

The next day I got extremely lightheaded in my office for a significantly longer time, two to three hours. My balance was way off. I could not walk straight.

About a year later while in my office, a sudden tremendous dizziness hit me. Someone called 911. The paramedics checked me out, and found nothing. Then I went to a hospital. No diagnosis.

That was a wake-up call. My problem had exacerbated itself to point where I couldn't walk and had to hire a corporate driver, Jim, who is still with me and today works with all our executives as head of Corporate Services. Jim drove me everywhere and helped me walk. Often he'd hold one of my arms while I balanced my free hand against a wall.

I needed to have oxygen at home and at the office for those sudden attacks. It didn't seem to help much at all.

My mind was not damaged, however. I was alert to some degree and active. I continued to operate my company, at times in name only. Cogent thoughts were often difficult to sustain during my bouts with the unknown malady.

Because of my uncertainty when the attacks would occur, I had anxiety about our first public offering. I feared one could manifest itself at any time, day or night.

I then cut down on my smoking to about five cigarettes a day. I recognized that when I was inhaling all those chemicals, I became more lightheaded. I stopped drinking excessively at night, and, to my surprise, lost fourteen pounds. I also had fewer incidents with lightheadedness.

Once while on a trip to the Islands with about a dozen companions. I was there less than a day and had drunk only part of a beer, when I became extremely lightheaded and dizzy. I went to a local hospital. All my vital signs were fine.

I was still concerned and flew in an air ambulance to NYU Hospital for more tests. I spent eight days there with neurologists and cardiologists while feeling lightheaded and having difficulty walking. I went through all the tests -- CAT scan, MRI, EEG, you name it. The results were the same. Vital signs okay. No diagnosis.

Now remember, all this was going on while we acquired Rexall, Thompson, established the Vitamin Basket Stores, initiated RSI, dealt with the Phar-Mor problem, and planned to take the company public.

I was not confident with those repeated no-diagnosis evaluations, so I consulted an internist in Fort Lauderdale who had a name for my malady – Hypoxia Adoesid. He told me to give up smoking. What else was new? Of course, and meaning no disrespect to the medical profession, every doctor who smokes, drinks, and is overweight will tell you to lose weight, stop smoking, and exercise. I did cut back on my smoking and slowed my drinking to a trickle.

In 1991, I went to a psychiatrist who thought my spells were anxiety driven. He gave me a prescription for Xanax, which I thought I'd never take – 1 mg up to three times daily. 1 mg would have made me catatonic. For a limited time, I took ¼ mg four times a day, which seemed to quell the lightheadedness to some extent and alleviate the problem of anxiety.

But the spells continued to increase in intensity. I often

used wheelchairs at the airports. I needed help walking. My malady shortened my work day and time spent in meetings. I was in the throes of losing confidence in my ability to function properly as President, CEO, and Chairman of the Board. I had to lie down during the day. It frightened or upset many of my employees to see me lying on the couch. I felt that I had to console them. I tried to joke about it.

* * *

Sometime in 1992, I was so desperate to find a cure for my affliction, that I was willing to try anything, see anyone. Over the years, I had sustained a friendship with Al Wilpon, the supplier who had made my suntan lotion in the first days of our business. He knew about my light-headedness and told me about a recent positive experience with a healer.

Al's relative had circulatory problems, and after open heart surgery, the man's condition continued to deteriorate. Then someone told Al about a healer who was well-known locally in DeKalb, Illinois. She had only one requirement for her clients: They had to believe in a higher being, a spiritual being. Because Al and his relative were of the Jewish faith, they first checked with their rabbi, who must have sanctioned his use of the healer because it was not a religious act.

Al described for me how the woman, who was a hairdresser and whose first name was Bonnie, came down, became "Zardonna" during the healing sessions, and essentially cleaned out his valves and heart. He was a new man after a month and a half or so of her treatment.

Shortly thereafter, Al's wife had a cerebral tumor which dissipated 100 percent after she worked with Bonnie. I knew Al to be a rock-solid, rational man. When he said that Bonnie had healed his wife, I believed that she absolutely had.

I asked Al to get hold of the woman, and I spoke to her on the phone. Bonnie was very lovely, warm, and accommodating. She did not sound formally educated, but that didn't matter so long as she had the slightest ability to help me.

Bonnie told me that she would be glad to come down in about six weeks. She did not want to know what my problem was. She preferred not to know.

She asked me to arrange a place to stay for herself and her three assistants. She said she would need to see me about three times a week for a two week period. At that stage, I didn't care if it was going to be seventy-two weeks.

Al arranged for Bonnie to stay in an apartment that he owned in North Hallandale. The only compensation she required was that I pay her expenses, the cost of gasoline for the car and food consumed while here in South Florida.

I went to see Bonnie at night. Nick Palin, our Vice President, also came along as a protective skeptic, caring but dubious. He wanted to evaluate the procedure.

A woman in a white robe of lace and roping out of the Middle Ages greeted us at the door and let us in. I think her name was Tracy. We heard ethereal music played on reeds and other esoteric instruments coming from the stereo. It was very harmonious and spiritually uplifting, and suggested what we might hear in Macchu Picchu.

Then a gentleman in his late twenties and another woman came out from an adjoining room; they were also dressed in white robes. He introduced himself as Brent, and she gave her name, I think, as Theresa. We talked for a while until Bonnie appeared.

I had not known what to expect. She had a very pretty

round face, blue eyes, and looked a tad overweight under her white robes. Bonnie had a perky personality and used many hand motions as she talked. I later learned that she was in her mid-forties, although she looked ten years younger.

After introductions and more small talk, we went into an adjacent bedroom illuminated only by candles, and we could smell incense burning. Bonnie said that Nick could stay in the room with me and watch. She sat me on a table, which suggested a gurney, and told me I should remain fully clothed, but to remove my shoes.

During about a twenty minute prep, Bonnie warned me that she would be talking throughout the session, probably regress me as well, and a combination of unexpected events might occur. I assured her that whatever she needed to do was all right with me. Then she told me that I could keep my eyes open or closed as I wished.

Tracy and her assistant went back into the next room, and Brent prepared to take notes. Bonnie put on what looked to me like a sleeping mask, and explained that sight interfered with her delving into different spiritual levels.

I stretched out on the table, and Bonnie began to chant softly, almost mumbling, in a language I didn't understand. By then, the music was more muted. Suddenly, she said, "I am now Zardonna!"

As Zardonna, she asked for my full name and where I was born. After I responded, she pressed her thumbs together and passed her hands about four to five inches over me, starting with my head. Brent took notes as if he were a disciple learning from his master.

While Zardonna's hands hovered over my head, I felt tremendous heat emanating from her hands. She said that she perceived a problem of oxygen arriving into my head.

Then she continued to move her hands down to my chest. Although the room was cool, wherever her hands passed, I felt warmth; yet they were always four or five inches away from my body.

The music and atmosphere was so restful that I soon closed my eyes. I wanted to figure out if she was the cause of that heat or if something was wrong with me.

When I felt heat on my right leg, I opened my eyes again, and sure enough, her hands were over my right leg. Zardonna stopped again when her hands were over the right side of my body above my appendix area. She lingered there for quite a while. As when she passed her hands over my head, the heat intensified.

Zardonna said that I had a serious problem, a carcinoma somewhere on my right side. I did not hear any alarm bells nor let her warning register that night, because I was concerned only about my lightheadedness.

When Zardonna finished with me and I sat up, she took off her mask. Her eyes had rolled back a bit, and then she came out of it.

Suddenly, Bonnie – or was she still Zardonna? – told me that this was my 980th incarnation. I had been everything from a peasant to royalty, the gamut of human experience. She said that my most previous incarnation was as an anthropologist, and, as such, I left this plane of existence in the 1920s.

Then she said something even more interesting. My soul had already reached the exalted level, the godhead, if you will, so it did not have to return to earth. It had been my choice to come back one more time. Why? To help people.

After Zardonna told me that I had the soul of Julius Caesar, she asked me to understand certain things: There are many souls of Julius Caesar; and many souls enter and leave us at different times. That did not necessarily mean I had been here 980 times, but could have been in 980 different positions or times within people – when they sleep, for example. Anyway, that was her take, as I perceived it.

Then Nick was ready to let Bonnie as Zardonna place her hands over him. He wanted to experience what I claimed to be feeling. First he checked her hands. He had already inspected the room and was convinced that they had no secreted heat-making devices nor had the air been drugged. We were both sober.

So, my "Doubting Thomas" friend went on the gurney, and Zardonna easily discovered where he'd had some injuries. He also felt the heat, and became a believer in her powers, although less so after she told him he had once been Mark Anthony. Ever the cynic, Nick asked what was the likelihood that Caesar and Anthony would both end up in a North Hallandale apartment in 1992?

I went to Bonnie only twice, and she asked me to come back again because she believed that she could eventually help me with my physical problems. I refused because she had not discovered immediately what was causing my lightheadedness. At the end, she gave me some beads and strongly recommended that I hold on to them and carry them with me at all times.

After her two week stay in Florida, Bonnie gave me her bill – $311.38. That is right. No typo. $311.38. She refused to take a penny more.

We kept in touch, but unfortunately, Bonnie became ill while she was here, and she could not heal herself. She had cancer of the breast and was dead in four months.

What had happened? We can't explain. Zardonna was certainly no charlatan, and actually told me more than those doctors who failed to diagnose me properly. Yes, Bonnie as Zardonna never cured my lightheadedness, but as you shall read a bit later in this chapter, I should have listened more closely to something she told me.

I continue to correspond with Brent through the mail and by phone about a dozen times a year. He is a very spiritual and fine gentleman who is always concerned about my health and well being. Few Brents, if any, ever cross our paths.

As for the source of Bonnie's powers, who can say? When we are ill and traditional medicine offers no cure, we will try anything. Unfortunately, for each Zardonna, there are hundreds less scrupulous out there. I believe that Bonnie had special healing abilities. I truly wish she could have helped herself.

*   *   *

Aside from the phenomenal growth of Rexall Sundown during the course of my malady, two major events occurred that affected my personal life. I had divorced Sylvia about six years before the Zardonna episode. It had nothing to do with my lightheadedness. I strongly believed that we were growing apart. Although Sylvia had every right to feel betrayed emotionally and spiritually by me, her financial well being will never be in question. Big deal! This has not done much to assuage my guilt. I'll always regret the hurt I inflicted through no fault of hers. I will always maintain a very special love for her that belies anyone's understanding.

Having been a family man since my late teens, I floundered for a couple of years until I found the courage to ask out Erika, one of our employees, a lovely lady whom I'd recently noticed and admired from afar.

Erika was completely different from anyone I had seen after my divorce: Intelligent, a mature and responsible single mother, loyal, honest, and all that wrapped in an intriguing complex aura of femininity with innocence. Although I still met with my "Boys Club" inner circle of business and social friends, she soon became my confidante, sounding board, and, above all, a best friend. A mutual loving relationship ensued and has grown with the passing years.

She has done her best to keep me on a level path through my current decade of successes and occasional disappointments. She also revived my latent interest in artistic and intellectual pursuits that had either passed me by or I'd forgotten.

I will confess, however, that I have not always been an easy man for her to deal with; at times, I can be unjustifiably contrary. Yet, Erika with her caring love and support was there for me over and over during my repeated bouts with lightheadedness.

Erika has become a major positive influence in my life. I feel and am hopeful I have been reciprocating, at the very least, with the caring, respect, and affection that embraces love's meaning.

*　*　*

In June of 1994, two years after I met "Bonnie-Zardonna" and while still suffering extreme episodes of lightheadedness, I took a trip to Asia for a cultural experience and a search for fine art and artifacts. During those weeks, I drank moderately or not at all. The flight home took twenty-two hours, during which time I smoked but did not drink. I felt okay on the plane, but as I disembarked I became extremely dizzy and couldn't walk. It was my worst occurrence to date. The corridor was spinning. I lost my balance.

Flight nurses and attendees were not far from the scene. I was evaluated. They didn't know what was wrong and told me to go back home and seek treatment. I was truly terrified.

Two days later after some extensive soul-searching, I decided to enter a retreat clinic – no alcohol, no drugs. I thought my problem was alcohol-related and started to go through the 12-step AA program. I continued to feel awful, and they gave me other drugs like Adapin® that kept me "out of it".

We were allowed to smoke, however, and I continued to do so. I was not feeling better. One internist, at the clinic, Dr. Diaz, saw the redness of my hands and observed other symptoms. He told me I had high red cell count – polycythemia – and did not belong at the clinic. He told me to pack my bags and go see a blood doctor, a hematologist.

I left the clinic after ten days. I got fed up asking people for references and getting the very best doctors in the world who couldn't cure me. I said to Jim, our corporate service representative, "Get me a phone book!"

We went through the Yellow Pages and found Dr. Aurea Tomeski in Boca Raton. We made an appointment, and after we got to her building, I could not move in the elevator. That day I had been smoking cigarettes. I took part of a Xanax and the seizure subsided.

I thought I was going to faint. We struggled out of the elevator, and I had to walk slowly step by step into Dr. Tomeski's office – worse than a Tim Conway *shtick* on the old *Carol Burnett Show.* It was a family practice in the real sense of the word. One sister did the blood work, another sister was the receptionist.

Dr. Tomeski gave me some blood tests. She told me that I was still smoking far too much. I had a very high level of red blood cells – 48 to 52 on the scale, with higher levels in the mid forties. She advised me to let blood, undergo a phlebotomy. After doing so, I felt somewhat better.

Dr. Tomeski was not through with me because she thought I might have problems with my spleen. After a CAT scan, she diagnosed that I did not have polycythemia, but saw a spot on my right kidney. She sent me to a radiologist in Boca Raton who confirmed that I had a cancerous tumor in my right kidney. It was removed September 1, 1994.

Zardonna had told me I had a carcinoma on my right side two years earlier.

Because I knew the kidney is the renal gland, I brilliantly figured that I'd had a renal problem and once the kidney was out I would be A-okay, with no further lightheadedness. I thought I could smoke after the operation, which I did in my private room.

I returned to the office about a week later. Although she did not cure the lightheadedness, Dr. Tomeski did save my life because of her thoroughness. She is my internist and friend to this day.

I had stopped drinking, my cancerous kidney had been removed, I'd cut back on my smoking, but, damn it, the lightheadedness continued to plague me and often worsened. The loss of balance continued. By then I was prepared to write an open letter offering a million dollars to anyone who could cure me. I was so frustrated, I was prepared to go to the Internet with the reward.

In November of 1994, I created a seven page summary of my ailments and medical history to save time and energy whenever I visited a new doctor.

1. Showed signs of hypoglycemia on two fasting glucose tests. No advised diet change, etc.

1a. Did blood sugar testing daily for two weeks (up to T.I.D.) – showed no problem.

As of 11-5-94 I started getting a flush like hot flashes, lost my balance, then felt as if a major shot of blood rushed to my head – which was observed by many. It happened three times a week. I had no warning when it would occur. My head and face got very red, legs extremely heavy.

Then I listed my habits:

1. I used to drink heavy, 4 oz. to 6 oz. two to four nights a week, from about 7 PM to around "elevenish" for five to six years.

2. I never drank at home alone. I was rarely there.

3. Previous six months, light to no drinking – approximately three nights a week I'd have two or three glasses of wine from 7:30 PM to 10:30 PM.

4. Last two months I cut down to one drink and a half glass of wine two to three nights per week.

5. I'd been smoking two to three packs a day for years. During the last three months, I cut down to ten to fifteen cigarettes daily. I stopped cold turkey November 24th, 1994.

It appeared that conditions did not change, often somewhat worsened. Symptoms: Balance affected for nine years. Cognitive, thinking problems during lightheadedness. Appears to be lack of blood or oxygen to the brain.

I then listed some statistics. Blood pressure, pulse, height, weight, and the fact that I sleep seven to eight hours. Then I listed my own conclusions for each doctor I went to:

1. T.I.A.s (Transient Ischemic Attacks) could be the problem. I have serious spinal and neck calcification and distortion as seen by two orthopedic surgeons.

2. Adrenal, Insulin, or Endocrine problems.

3. Chiropractor said my brain stem – Atlas he called it – was way out of sync.

5. Absolutely no problems occur while I am drinking at night. Could alcohol act as a vasodilator?

6. This lightheadedness occurs every single day and is now crippling some 70 percent of the day.

Up to two alcohol drinks seem to relax the problem. However, I do not nor do I intend to drink to satisfy this acute problem. I notice, if I do not continue to drink after the first or second, coming off the alcohol, severe light-headedness kicks in. It is worse than ever and requires an additional drink to relieve it.

I have tried Niacin as a vasodilator. It did nothing for me.

I think it's intermittent spasms or arterial "shut downs" in the blood supply to my head. But why.

Then I listed all the tests I had taken for each new doctor:

EKG often, last 12/94 by Cardiologist.
EEG three times, last 7/25/94 by Neurologist.
MRI three times, last 7/10/94 by Neurologist.
CAT scan lower portion 7/12/94 by Hematologist.
CAT scan head twice 6/87 by Neurologist.
Hematology (all blood scans) 6/94 through present.
Heart monitor, twenty-four hours.
Cardiac sonograms twice.
Sleep Apnea Test, oxygen.
Arteriogram (pre-operative).

Then I listed all the visits to doctors I had seen from

March to the end of November 1994, forty three in all: Hematologists, Internists, Cardiologists, Endocrinologists, Neurologists, Psychiatrists, Chiropractors, Orthopedists, and Ear-Nose-Throat specialists.

I emphasized that I had been checked for inner ear disease, vertigo, and took Antivert to no avail.

I concluded with a self-evaluation.

- Taking Xanax for three years intermittently.

- The use of Benzodiazepines this long, even the least potent (¼ mg four times a day) may be causing the reactions. They were good for only two hours or so maximum. It seemed to abate the lightheadedness about 85% of the time. Does not stop flushing, etc.

- Possible use of Oxazepam (Serax) or Buspar to get off Xanax. Supposedly not as addictive. Have looked at addictive drugs as possible magnification of original problem – Xanax, cigarettes, alcohol.

- One neurologist hypothesized that my nerve endings could be totally "shot" due to excessive alcohol use over an extended time and the reaction is like emphysema. It will never get better. He noted that anti-anxiety drugs may be necessary for the rest of my life.

Note an antidote:

When people have the "bends" they are put in an hyperberic chamber. Is this why when consuming alcohol it appeared to regress? That is, if nerves are "totally shot".

I also had on two or three occasions in the past year **serious tremors** in the afternoon. **Not** necessarily after drinking.

Note: In 1987 for approximately six months **I did not drink any type of alcohol at all**, and lightheadness continued though somewhat abated. Not smoking helps some; therefore I've **cut back** recognizing it's a vaso constrictor. Is there a vasodilator drug that is effective? Possibly an herbal we market called Ginkgo Biloba, which I'll discuss later.

That is another lesson I want to share. Although I am not unique, I am certainly not ordinary. It is said that many businesses fail because of the entrepreneur's poor health at a crucial moment. That does not always have to be the case. As I said, during those ten years, we acquired Rexall, Thompson, and Pennex. We initiated the Vitamin Basket stores, RSI, and took our company public.

At some juncture, I plan to take what I have learned about my particular malady and put it in a web site on the Internet. I, and my insurance, paid over $500,000 to doctors and clinics for tests, diagnosis, rehab – and, wouldn't you know it, it was cigarettes all along. Move over John Grisham. *Runaway Jury*, here we come!

Xanax does mitigate the serious effects of my ailment. Today, when I feel uncomfortable I'll take less than ¼ mg twice a day, most days none.

I continue to seek out new medications in the PDR – Physicians Desk Reference. It describes virtually every pill made – what it is used for – what it does – its drawbacks.

I did quit smoking two months after my operation. I finally realized that I felt better not smoking. I've been off cigarettes for nearly three years now. I still drink some, possibly still too much, too often. I don't think so, needless to say.

Although no doctor stated any definite cause for my ten year loss of balance, there is a condition called Thalassemia, or Mediterranean anemia, which is genetic among Italians. In some cases, heavy smoking can cause loss of balance. Not many people have those symptoms, but I believe there are enough sufferers out there who are receiving no help, which is why I plan to start a network to share this information.

I want to emphasize here, that throughout my malady, I was taking vitamins. I believe that they, the prayers of many, and the Almighty contributed to my survival.

I have discontinued my offer of one million dollars to anyone who finds a cure for my malady. By no longer smoking, I have pretty much found my own cure. The symptoms have abated 85 percent, at least. And, I'm sure I've already spent close to that million.

THIRTY-FIVE

My Own Vitamin Intake

Although I exercise, I am no fanatic. Aside from basic calisthenics, my main physical activities are swimming and pushups. I do forty-plus slow pushups three to five times each week. Those who know me will disagree and tell you that my only exercise is looking for ways to improve my business and hunting for new ventures. It's been said my idea of the perfect workout is to think of new ways to sell tried and true vitamins.

Like my former customers at 69th and Collins, I've had some less than perfect habits, which contributed to my adult maladies. I no longer smoke. I've cut down on my drinking. Although red meat is low among my priorities, I enjoy a good steak now and then, especially at the best steak house of all, Don Shula's (aka) *Shula's Steak House.*

I try to avoid the fanaticism common among the promoters and sellers of vitamins, health foods, and alternative nutrition. I've seen people in the health food industry get so terribly immersed in it to the point where their beliefs and claims are so extreme that it affects their business acumen.

Many articles come out with limited information, often based on one person's observation of causes and effect, not clinical studies. Some may be sincere in what they say, but in the good old American tradition from wandering Dr. Quacko, who fleeced the gullible in the days of the Wild West, to TV and Cyberspace, we have had and always will have a number of dubious shamans and snake oil salesmen out there.

Some manufacturers who cater to the more esoteric part of the health and wellness market claim that their products are more pure because their capsules are hand-filled, untouched by unnatural metal. Believe what you will, as you remember that spoons, forks, and knives of "unnatural" metal touch all the food you ingest except, perhaps, fast foods.

I have been cautious and careful to sell and use only proven products. For example, double-blind studies with vitamin E versus placebos have proven that if you take vitamin E at levels substantiated by those studies, you potentially have up to a 75 percent less chance of having a heart attack. And, of those who were taking vitamin E and had heart attacks, very few had a fatal heart attack. I can assure you that those studies made me a believer.

I take E for circulation and to prevent arteriosclerosis, hardening of the arteries.

Twice a day, I take 30 mgs of Co-Q10, an enzyme that the body produces less of as we age. Co-Q10 is actually treated as a drug in Japan; there, prescriptions for it are written by a cardiologist on a regular basis. I take it for a number of benefits – periodontal, circulatory, and vascular. It also improves one's capacity for endurance.

I take two 500 mg time-release vitamin C tablets each day for my immune and circulatory systems. I prefer time-release because vitamin C is water-soluble and the body tends to eliminate it rather quickly.

I take my incomplete multiple because I take my E and

C separately, as do most people who know about vitamins. As you read in an earlier chapter, the incomplete multiple has all the minerals and all the vitamins except C and E.

I take three 30 mg Grape Seed Extract capsules – the word for it is proanthocyanidins – which is an anti-oxidant, one of the best of them all at present. It's a relatively reasonably priced product that helps slow the aging process, brings back elasticity to the skin, and many other benefits.

A recently introduced product may very well be the most potent anti-oxidant available to date. Alpha Lipoic Acid, 50 mg. I personally take three daily to stave off the ravages of aging. There seems to be substantial basis in fact for this breakthrough, now being heralded because of its benefits for diabetics.

I take GLA, gammalinoleic acid, which is the prime ingredient in Primrose Oil. The FDA banned Primrose Oil from the United States about ten years ago. They claimed that it was being used as a therapeutic drug item, which most probably it was. It was given for the immune system and a number of maladies. The FDA said if a product was given therapeutically, we were not allowed to sell nor recommend it. Authors and literature extolling its value, however, are acceptable.

We sought alternatives. The first was colostrum, commonly found in mother's milk, which also has a high level of gammalinoleic acid. After evaluating other sources, we felt vegetable based Borage offered near equal value.

Borage is a vegetable that looks like a tuber but lies on top of the ground. We reviewed the studies on Borage Oil and discovered that it had more GLA than Primrose Oil and GLC. I now take 100 mg capsules of borage oil three times a day. I find that it's good for detoxification, liver dysfunctions, balance problems, lightheadedness, and dizziness. There's plenty of back-up material about it in many scientific journals. The ban on Primrose Oil has since been lifted.

As new products come out that have been clinically tested and are efficacious for my needs, you can be sure that I will be using them: Saw Palmetto for prostate "good health"; Ginkgo Biloba as a cognitive enhancer and good vasodilator; and B-Complex with Folic Acid to lower homocysteine levels, which contribute to heart attacks. All are relatively new, and our sales are ramping up on all these confirmed winners. Our heavily advertised Homocysteine Defense Formula is truly a meaningful success. I believe all adults should be taking it.

* * *

I want to tell you more about the importance of anti-oxidants. They are difficult to understand, but basically as we are exposed to pollutants, sunlight, radiation as well as normal biochemical reactions, molecules called free radicals are generated. The free radicals cause oxidative stress and damage to our cells. Anti-oxidants neutralize free radicals, and the goal is to have enough anti-oxidants to combat them all. Ailments are expedited by free radical damage, so antioxidant therapy's purpose is to protect the body from many diseases. As we age, anti-oxidants play an even more important role.

I have read much about HIV lately, especially the studies made on people who had been exposed totally to the deadly virus. Amongst those who had been taking nutritional supplements on a regular basis and had a proper diet, a meaningful percentage did not pick up the HIV virus versus those who were run-down. Therefore, one cannot emphasize enough that the strengthening of the immune system through nutritional supplements has many benefits indeed. You should not ever assume that good nutrition will make unprotected sex and unsafe needle-sharing risk free.

Vitamin E and Vitamin C are included among the antioxidants. Recently, several studies of selenium have been released. They show that 200 micrograms (remember, 1000 mcg = 1 mg) can prophylactically help prevent certain cancers. Selenium slows the cancer growth rate, the growth rate of tumors themselves, with a very high rate of success among those who take 200 micrograms each day, according to a recent study.

How can one not take this product? I certainly do. It's in my incomplete multiple, so I don't have to worry about it.

The post-World War II babies are moving out of their forties, into their fifties, and approaching their sixties. Chronologically, it seems we're all speeding to our next birthdays. More than previous generations, because they have the benefits of additional knowledge, the boomers all want to be healthy, hold back the aging process, and sustain a high quality of life.

The solution is simple – exercise and proper nutrition. Bottles on the shelves alone are not the answer. We do not have an elixir to guarantee good health forever. You still have to eat well. You should have a couple of pieces of fruit each day, some vegetables, although I personally cannot endorse vegetarianism, yet. As I said earlier, I'm one of those who enjoys a good steak probably more often than most.

I repeat, you must add a little exercise. But concentrate on what you're doing when doing it. Some studies have shown that if you're reading or watching TV while on a stationary bike or on a treadmill your body does not respond properly seventy-five percent of the time. You'd be better off exercising half the time without having your mind distracted.

THIRTY-SIX

Research & Development

AND A POTENTIALLY SIGNIFICANT MOLLUSK

Going public did change my MO a bit. Before that, I primarily used my own moxie; I read and figured out what I could come up with in concert with various suppliers – and not necessarily the tablet manufacturers per se. The raw material suppliers would send me information as to what was going on out there. Keeping abreast of all available "info" was extremely helpful.

Now that we have our own manufacturing plant, about ten-plus employees are doing more R&D and test batching than ever in our labs. We can do many things that we were not in a position to do previously, and we don't always have to rely on outside suppliers, be they tablet manufacturers or producers of certain raw materials.

For example, the natives of the Caribbean have known for some time that conch, a variety of mollusk in a shell, has been used as an aphrodisiac for men, to overcome impotence and return them to the good old days of their youth. After I returned from an executive management meeting in Nassau, we decided to get some conch, have it dehydrated, powdered, and do trial studies on our own.

We are not necessarily looking to manufacture sex-enhancing nutrients, but now that we can test and manufacture on our own, it gives us an opportunity to experiment, which we hadn't been able to do in the past. That's how ideas germinate and products are developed.

I want to emphasize that our R&Ds are not all scientifically based structured clinicals, although we are rapidly moving towards that goal. We still depend on universities and our suppliers of raw materials to do a portion of them at this time. Yet, we also have been looking at the possibility of purchasing a number of science-based R&D companies with in-place ongoing clinicals.

Richardson Labs in Boise, Idaho, which we acquired at the begining of 1998, will soon start to "fit the bill" with its patented products and proprietary ingredient formulations for weight management, women's and children's health, as well as sports nutrition. Nevertheless, while we wait for the results of Richardson's science to mesh with Rexall Sundown's needs, we will continue to formulate the way we used to with vitamins C and E on our campus today rather than wait three or four months for information from the suppliers. One of our big advantages has always been to get our product to the market quickly.

When any of us reads or hears something credible, we get together and decide to give it a try rather than going to a supplier and asking too many questions that may alert competitors. Can you make it? How long will it take to create? How long before it gets into the human body's system? This is just part of the extensive process.

Today, we can prepare a product, put it in a pilot lab, and twenty-four hours later, have a tablet on which we can begin to perform dissolution and disintegration testing. Then when we do have a tried and true nutritional, and we know there is efficacy behind it, that we have done the needed homework and accelerated expiration studies justifying expiration dating.

Let me explain what I mean by accelerated studies. We have mini-labs we set up to duplicate a time of 12 months in only weeks, so that we can learn if a new product is good for a year. Is there any degradation in the tablet? We can find out all these things on our own; whereas in the past we had to rely on the integrity of our suppliers.

We still buy raw materials. Some might very well be called alternative. Many of these products are new on the market, like shark cartilage.

I want to emphasize that our R&D deals mostly with property characteristics and formulation, not the clinicals, although we do have the on-site techies available for validation and development, who also review outside studies and literature on all the available clinicals that have been done both pro and negative on a product. Their research helps to place us in the best position to decide whether or not we want to manufacture and market a new product entry.

One example is Melatonin. In 1995 this nutritional supplement captured the national spotlight as the result of a best-selling book – *The Melatonin Miracle* – which claimed that the product could treat everything from insomnia to who knows what. Not surprising, sales of Melatonin leaped off the store shelves.

Yet, we delayed getting into the Melatonin market because we wanted to make sure which dosage worked best and was safest in our estimation. We also needed to obtain enough supply to meet demand. Currently, we are selling a reduced dosage of Melatonin in the stores that carry our vitamins and nutritionals.

DHEA – dehydroepiandrostherone – is another perfect example of our *cautious approach* to any new product. We learned, despite some positive studies, that this hormone may very well be problematic for people if they did not know how much DHEA was already in their blood. Because DHEA had not been proven completely safe to our satisfaction, we opted as a company not to have the product in our line.

When there's not enough information out there to validate a DHEA as being both safe and effective, we will walk away from it and continue to do so until we have a comfort zone to justify producing it, if ever. Even if most other companies decide to manufacture and sell a DHEA, I'd rather take what we feel is the high road and miss a sale. As additional information about the product comes to our attention, we may once again visit the item and perhaps reconsider taking it on.

THIRTY-SEVEN

From Vitamins To Super Foods

R exall Sundown has been, you might say, the ground-breaker or the cutting edge of the industry. We are aware of a major change in the attitudes amongst many in the medical profession. Today, large numbers of physicians, nurses, and other members of the medical community are personally using many more nutritional products as well as offering or recommending specific nutrients to their patients.

We are looking for ways to prevent rather than wait for problems to occur. We are returning to many of the old herbal remedies. We have been questioning conventional medical wisdom as we have never done before in this century.

If you read the history of medicine, you know that physicians and surgeons (the latter, once known as barbers – really) were held in contempt and generally sought out only as a last ditch resort. Their habits were filthy by modern standards, their cures bordering on the absurd and nightmarish.

People forget or maybe never learned what life was really like in the so-called good old days or golden ages. We complain about automobile pollution; yet, would we prefer to breathe and be covered by the golden dust created by the dried manure droppings – 25 pounds daily from each of the tens of thousands of horses working on the city streets?

So here's a bit of a refresher course in good old medical practices during the many centuries when it was considered un-Christian to bathe or even wash one's hands and face. Bleeding was common from leeches to opening veins and arteries for just about every malady. At one time, the potato was prescribed as a medicine for aging men.

Curative properties were attributed to nearly every substance if it was new, unusual, difficult to obtain, repugnant, but which could be forced into the human system. The more gruesome, disgusting, or bizarre the product, the better.

Dried elimination from maidens was blown into a patient's eyes as a remedy for cataracts. Usnea was an official drug prescribed by the most acclaimed physicians from the Middle Ages to the nineteenth-century. It is a moss, derived from a genus of lichens, and was considered most efficacious if scraped from the skulls of hanged criminals. Even the very first edition of the *Encyclopedia Britannica* had a section extolling usnea's curative properties.

Court physicians, supposedly the finest in the land, often bled and dehydrated their monarchs to death with opened veins, uninterrupted enemas, and forced vomiting. Nearly all patients died from that best of all possible medical care. I know that I have plainly shown enough of the barbaric methods of the past, which were acceptable medical practices.

As a boy, I read the Paul de Kruif books, like *Microbe*

Hunters, which told about the innovators and the incredible difficulties they faced with their medical establishments and academies. In the 1990s, it is difficult to believe the problems Semmelweiss had convincing the established medical profession that if a doctor sterilized his hands before an operation – washing them in hot water – his patient had a better chance of not getting a fatal infection, especially infants as they were being delivered at birth.

Then the pendulum swung the other way, and by the middle of the twentieth-century doctors had become remote deities, so much so, that many of their patients were afraid to ask questions. And they charged high office fees for tasks that could be performed by any well-trained nurse: Giving flu shots, weighing, or checking pulse and blood pressure.

Today we are nearing a middle of the road approach. We are turning – after testing – to old, tried and true remedies, Eastern remedies – alternatives to what physicians recommend as part of preventative medicine.

Believe me, people are not naive. After donating and supporting the Cancer Society for forty years or so, they have seen very little difference in the death rate. They are thinking about life style changes, which includes a modification in dietary habits and the taking of certain nutritional supplements. They can go to the Internet for specific problems and obtain the same information every internist has.

People are asking: "Why shouldn't we take Ginkgo Biloba, which happens to be an herbal leaf from a tree in India and Asia as old as Methuselah?"

Most of the drugs today had herbs as their inspiration. That includes aspirin.

Ginkgo Biloba, which has just hit the marketplace in the last two years, is a vasodilator. It opens the blood vessels and brings oxygen to the brain. It has shown real validity. For years, the medical community has used it for people with tinnitis or ringing in the ears.

Another product for men, which is indigenous to Florida, is called Saw Palmetto. That's where you have pictures of the Seminole Indians standing underneath what looks like small coconut trees. They're really not coconut trees. They're called Saw Palmettos and are everywhere.

They give off a berry that can help prevent the onset of prostatitis. Those berries actually cause the prostate to shrink, often times better than the pharmaceutical products out on the market. Saw Palmetto has saved many men from going under the surgeon's knife, and others from waking up at night with an urge to urinate because the prostate is pressing against the bladder.

Saw Palmetto is truly a wonder of nature.

That does not mean we should all go out into the woods and jungles and feast indiscriminately on nature's bounty. Caution should always be a credo of thinking people. It is a tenet of our firm. Remember, hemlock killed Socrates, and it too is natural.

* * *

The scientific community has long been aware that lack of calcium will bring on osteoporosis. Recently, they found out that most calcium is not absorbed properly, and that there are different forms of calcium. It can come from a number of sources including dolomite, out of the ground, and from leafy green vegetables. The sources for our industry are primarily oyster shell, carbonate and lactate.

Calcium presents problems for many people. So much calcium is needed daily (1250 mg and then some) that the tablets tend to be quite large and very difficult to swallow.

Therefore, we have brought into the company a liquid form of calcium in a soft gel, making it much easier to swallow while complying with the daily doses necessary to prevent bone loss.

We have also moved into iron, which is the number one cause of childhood poisoning. I'm talking about substantial amounts – a situation when a child ingests a bottle of one hundred tablets and they have to pump him out. They can get very ill, and in some rare cases actually die from overdosing.

We worked with a company in Germany and have marketed a product called Carbonyl – carbonyl iron. Based on scientific investigation, we learned that a child could ingest several thousand tablets and still have no ill effects from the Carbonyl. We were the first in the United States to market this completely non-toxic and safe form of iron as a single entity item, which means we did not include it in a multiple.

Until recently, the bottling of iron was regulated by the Consumer Products Safety Commission, which required a childproof safety cap and a warning. Because too many adults inadvertently left the top off of their bottles of non-Carbonyl iron and children continued to become seriously ill from ingesting too much iron, the FDA decided to get involved. They held hearings to determine if iron tablets or capsules should be sold singly in blister packs.

Experts from our own company, a pharmacist and an attorney, went up to Washington and testified before the FDA to convince them we had a non-toxic form of iron that did not require blister packs, child's safety cap, nor even a warning. We argued that the blister pack would raise the cost of iron to the consumer by at least one dollar, which would severely affect the poor, the indigent, and especially the elderly who suffer from iron anemia. Higher prices for Carbonyl would be detrimental to the general health of Americans.

The FDA made its ruling at the end of June, 1997. As of July 15th, any iron product with a single element of 30 mg or more must be sold in a blister pack. However, the FDA did attach an amendment to exempt our Carbonyl product from their ruling for another year.

Once again, Rexall Sundown was the leader, the first company to market this safe form of iron in a single entity dosage. We call it Perfect Iron™. We have introduced it as a singular product, along with having it available in many of our multiples. It can be used safely in households with children, coupled with the fact that it is highly absorbable.

* * *

Currently, I am investigating further a grape seed extract, which I personally take. It has active ingredients called proanthocyanidins which act as potentially one of the most effective anti-oxidants. Proanthocyanidins also help slow the ravages of the aging process. I've been doing a lot of homework on this product, as is our R&D Department.

There are many products like grape seed out there that people are still unaware of, on which continued studies are being done. After I found out that proanthocyanidins are so prevalent in grape seed extract, I told our R&D Department to find out what is active in orange seed. Oranges are plentiful, and an overabundance of seeds are by-products.

We are in the initial planning stages of asking a major university to work in concert with us to find out what is present in orange seeds which may play an important role in our overall health. If the outcome is positive, we will seek a *method patent*, not on the seed, of course, which is

God's work, but a patent on the type of extraction and application of whatever efficacious yield the seed might contain.

If our orange seed project bears fruit, it could very well be a marketable item for our company and a health inducement for consumers. So, we're investigating the possibilities in nature for the properties which any item might have that can be both salable and profitable for us and beneficial to the consumer. It's a very exciting era for all of us.

Research and Development is not only going on with our vitamins but also with what I call complementary items: Nutritional products, plant products, and herbals. I'm referring to a Ginkgo, a Saw Palmetto, or something like a Bilberry that was given to WWII flyers at night to chew on because old wives tales said it helped night blindness. After many studies, nutritionists concluded that Bilberry does indeed help night blindness and sight, and it is now being sold as an effective treatment for macular degeneration.

Many of the old remedies, from an apple a day to what the Indians were chewing are gaining new validity. Kava Kava is a natural product and the herbal counterpart to Valium®. As you know Valium, Xanax, and Diazapams are sedatives. Yet, in the South Pacific the natives have been chewing on Kava Kava for years. They do not get stoned; it merely puts them into a more relaxed non-stressful state.

Another natural product that brings about a positive mental sense of well-being is St. John's Wort, which may become the Prozac of the twenty-first-century. Its preparations are extracted from the leaves and flowers of a perennial common to Europe and North America, *Hyperacum Perforatum*, which has a 2,400 year history of safe and effective use in herbal, folk, and ancient medicine.

Do not let the name put you off. Wort is the harmless Old English word for plant, and it was traditionally harvested on June 24th, St. John the Baptist's Day.

Hypericin is the active ingredient in St. John's Wort. It has been shown to interfere with enzymes in the brain that destroy the "feel good" amines, such as serotonin, epinephrine, and dopamine.

Recently, we have had a sudden instantaneous increase in demand for St. John's Wort because of positive coverage about it in *Newsweek* and ABC's *20/20*. After the latter aired, one of our chain customers asked for a delivery of almost 500,000 bottles. Such is the power of the media! I know – it cuts both ways.

Of late, much research is being done on these products. We are recognizing that there's a plethora of them out there that are going to come to market and have real viability. It's not hocus-pocus or witchcraft. To force a pun, it's getting back to the roots of natural healing and prevention.

I believe that vitamins are moving us towards *improved* whole food. In the twenty-first century, you will see a major move, not just towards extractions of vitamins, but a return to ingesting the entire enhanced fruit or vegetable. Nutraceuticals and photo-nutrients will indeed be the wave of the future.

Fluoride was isolated and put into toothpaste. Yet, some early studies proved that if fluoride is taken in its natural state with other natural occurring components it is even more effective.

The same thing happens if you extract bioflavonoids out of an orange and include it in a supplemental tablet. You're still missing the rutin, hesperidin, and the other integral parts of the fruit.

There will always be those essential vitamins and minerals, but we must never forget that *whole* foods are so very important. When I say *whole,* I'm advising that you are often better off eating an entire orange than extracting its parts.

You must always consider your body's needs. Even if you take bioflavonoids in a tablet, the nutrients which exist in that portion not extracted from an orange may be in a depletive state in your system. The quantities required for substitute amounts of those other parts of the fruit are generally very difficult to obtain in a standard American diet. Therefore, supplementation plus the intake of the whole fruit itself may very well be the only reasonable alternative to nutritive replenishment.

In the future, more foods will be manipulated so that, as an example, an orange in its natural state will contain more rutin and bioflavonoids, which we need, rather than just our ingestion of supplements.

The sale of improved foods will not necessarily have an adverse impact on vitamin manufacturers. We will always have people who regularly choose not to include better or proper foods in their diets. For them, the taking of vitamins and nutritional supplements will always be essential.

As a result, wonderful opportunities continue to abound for forward-looking companies like Rexall Sundown. We can see the future. We expect to work with and acquire or make alliances with the companies that are improving whole foods, or we will end up attempting to create a better orange (aka mousetrap) ourselves. Move over Luther Burbank.

THIRTY-EIGHT

Glucosamine Chondroitin
As An R&D Model

THE CURE FOR ARTHRITIS?

We are often asked how we discover or create our new products. The answer is that we approach our R&D from a number of directions.

Our sales team provides us with feedback from the marketplace. So do computer readouts from the retailers gathered for us by Information Resources, Inc., that independent marketing research company I mentioned earlier. They tell us what people are buying. And yes, to some degree, what they are looking for that is not out there.

We read health publications, medical journals, books, popular magazines, newspapers, and follow university research projects.

We work closely with our raw material suppliers. They frequently offer us products based on their research. They also supply us with information on the latest discoveries – new plant and herb sources that can be used for nutritional enhancements and eventually a more healthful life for our customers.

The Internet has been invaluable and especially useful. Our company maintains a web site at **www.rexallsundown.com**. The Internet provides us with press releases describing the results of university research projects and new nutritional products, which we investigate further by speaking to suppliers and industry related people. We are on the alert for the moment when prescription drugs become OTCs.

We do the same with formulas. We continually look at combinations of vitamins and nutritional supplements that make sense and have meaningful efficacy for the consumer.

To offer new products at everyday value and high quality – the core guideline is in our development – we study the possibilities to see if they are within our strategic parameters.

If we identify a concept that is attractive, has potential, or is an up and coming trend, we look at competition and study how well developed the market is.

We ask ourselves how we can do it better at a lower cost. The market ultimately decides which price level is best for what type of customer. The market is always driven by consumer attitudes.

*　*　*

Glucosamine Chondroitin, a nutritional supplement that has shown to alleviate the symptoms of arthritis through the regeneration of cartilage, is a perfect example of how we decide to send out an **exclusive** new product under one of our banners. Glucosamine Chondroitin made its debut in August, 1997, under the Sundown label.

Glucosamine Chondroitin has been used for years with success in Europe, and here in the United States in veterinary medicine. Horses, the same as humans, also suffer from crippling osteo-arthritis.

Glucosamine Chondroitin was brought to our attention as a consumer-driven product because it was the subject of a book by Dr. Jason Theodosakis, *The Arthritis Cure.* It was not one of those "oil your joints" remedies and seemed to be the kind of item that we could take pride in manufacturing and selling.

We checked out the raw material supply, if this product was viable and could get results. Everything looked good to us, with only one drawback – Glucosamine Chondroitin was covered under a U.S. patent, which precluded us from marketing the product as freely as we do our vitamins.

Rather than go to market in potential violation of a patent, we found the company that had the patent and had researched the natural ingredients, Nutramax in Baltimore, Maryland.

We put our people on the phones. The book about Glucosamine Chondroitin had generated so much interest, "The Arthritis Cure" by Jason Theodosakis, M.D. – over 550,000 hard cover sales – that Nutramax's lines were feverishly busy, and it took us two days and a myriad of calls before we finally got through to their office structure. We spoke with some of their support staff people and found out who was in charge, who was running the company.

We struck up a phone friendship, and Nick Palin boldly went to Baltimore without an appointment. I might add that Nick had a serious personal interest in Glucosamine Chondroitin because he and his family suffer extensively from arthritis; he is still a relatively young fifty year old, and would wake up in bed with his hand deformed like an eagle's talon and in great pain.

Nick let them know he was prepared to stay in Baltimore until he saw someone in charge. He spoke on the phone to one of the principals of the company, who appreciated all of his time and effort, and said to contact him in a week or so.

The following week we scheduled a real meeting. Nutramax sent a team to our headquarters in Boca Raton to check out our manufacturing practices. Of course they found our plant to be exceptional. After Nutramax learned the history of our products and performed their Due Diligence on our company, they awarded us the license and rights to manufacture Glucosamine Chondroitin.

We are the only company licensed to manufacture this near-miraculous product. The parent company holds the patent.

As this book goes to the printer, we are in the throes of heavily advertising Glucosamine Chondroitin as an affordable supplement to all classes of trade. Under our trade name OSTEO-BI-FLEX® early sales results are astoundingly bullish.

What does Glucosamine Chondroitin do? It helps regenerate cartilage. Sixty million-plus Americans suffer from some form of osteo-arthritis. Many have had cortisone shots to the joint. The pain for many can be unbearable.

We also have evidence of Glucosamine Chondroitin's efficacy here at Rexall Sundown aside from the clinicals on which Nutramax had based its patent. Nick Palin has taken it. He says that its success is remarkable. He is now ninety-five percent free of pain and his once-afflicted hand has complete dexterity.

Nick is so strong a believer in Glucosamine Chondroitin that he has given it to his mother, other members of his family, and anyone who will listen – successfully in each case.

What else does Glucosamine Chondroitin do? It regenerates the cartilage cushion between bone and nerves, which in turn alleviates the pain.

Glucosamine Chondroitin may have other benefits, which have not yet been fully realized. It helps to regenerate collagen, and, as a bonus, a side effect tightens the skin and can cause one to look younger.

Glucosamine Chondroitin works, on the average, in about sixty days **if** the high recommended dosages are taken as directed. Although, one may start feeling its beneficial effects as early as two to three weeks.

The raw materials are purchased with strict quality control measures. When the materials arrive, we put them through our NIR machine, then manufacture the Glucosamine Chondroitin into oral tablets here in South Florida. We check it for purity before, during, and after formulation.

The taking of nutritional supplements used to be close to an act of faith, with little proof of efficacy, and yet had its core true believers. Today, they are near-sanctioned by the government, and more so by research universities. Glucosamine Chondroitin, our OSTEO BI-FLEX® is a breakthrough product because it clearly produces dramatic effects in a relatively short time.

Successes like Glucosamine Chondroitin may awaken a dangerous sleeping giant, the pharmaceutical industry. They feed off exclusive patents. If they break into the vitamin and nutritional supplement field and obtain patents for truly wonder products like Glucosamine Chondroitin, they will most assuredly drive up the costs for the consumer due to their monolithic bureaucratic size and layers of, I feel, unnecessary overhead.

Why was Glucosamine Chondroitin patented when vitamins are not? The law states that if two ingredients are combined and give an unexpected result, the resultant product is patentable.

The bottom line is that if we can continue to manufacture products like Glucosamine Chondroitin – aka OSTEO-BI-FLEX® – and sell them at a fair market price, our consumers may live, if not longer, certainly healthier lives. And we'll make money in the true entreprcneurial spirit, hiring more employees as we continue to grow.

THIRTY-NINE

Chairman Of The Board
But Still An Entrepreneur

One might describe me as an addict in one specific area. I cannot resist starting up new entrepreneurial ventures. Presently, I am involved at different levels in several businesses outside of Rexall Sundown.

Starting up new businesses has a lot to do with my basic drive and things I was unable to do in the past because of short funding. Time was never a problem for me. I knew I could squeeze all I required out of each hour.

I have always looked upon work and creating businesses as fun. Work can be hard, to be sure, but as I've said often, what a rush! Without sounding too pompous, it is probably the same as any artist after rehearsing, preparing, then giving a fine performance or executing a fine painting or sculpture.

When I say business is fun, it's because to me business is dealing with people. What has happened, however, is that at my level as Board Chairman, it's amazing and often extremely different from running a start-up company.

When I am in my own corporate mahogany vault, I am not as excited as I was when I initiated my company. To be sure, the tumult I like exists in a different way at the corporate level. And yes, it is wonderful and satisfying to have seen my little acorn grow into the giant oak of Rexall Sundown.

But Rexall Sundown is less of a hands-on operation for me at this juncture. My "off hour" time is now spent to nourish other acorns.

My outside ventures are not guaranteed to be successful initially, but I always believe that the people I choose to run them, along with my input, are the right ones. Because I am able to supply the financing, I know that if we pursue the businesses properly each will succeed in time.

Some of the proceeds from our second public offering brought me a substantial amount of dollars, which freed me to try other ventures without short-changing Rexall Sundown. I had to take care of some personal obligations before I made some investments. I borrowed, using my stock as collateral, to purchase my current home. Although I dislike borrowing, my stock value was growing at 50-plus percent while I'd be paying only around 7 percent interest on the home loan. I preferred to take out that loan and pay minimum interest knowing the company's growth was a sure bet. Today, with a market cap of almost 3 billion dollars, I am indeed proud to say that the DeSantis family has ownership of around 50 percent of the stock.

Then I turned to my new ventures. I saw opportunities coming my way on a regular basis.

I may be investing in a chain of specialized clinics for men and women. The owners, whom I know to be good guys and savvy, are under-capitalized and facing serious local competition. Men's and women's clinics, which deal with problems of the prostate and incontinence, are popular in the aging and aged communities of South Florida, and therefore, overexposed.

We are exploring the possibilities of opening clinics in medium-sized cities throughout the country where we're more likely to have little or no competition. It can be profitable if we approach it correctly. Right now the investment is not nearly as dear as one might believe. On the other hand, we're conscious of what these procedures cost, so we want to be fair both to the insurance companies and for those who have no insurance.

I want to emphasize that if this venture is a go, our clinics will not deal with all that New Age pretense and accouterments. Nor, will they will chart the stars, promise a magic elixir, or even look to put too many folks in MRI "overloads". After you've tried traditional medicine and doctors, then give our physicians and staff an opportunity to help you.

* * *

Now I do not think I am being overly sensitive in an ethnic sense, but it was obvious to me that I might be the first person whose name ended in a vowel (at least it almost does) to move into my current community. Everyone seemed to be named Smith or Wilson, which was later proven to be *incorrect.*

While going through the real estate dance when buying my present abode, they pursued a verbal background check of who I am – where had I been born and more – the usual third degree. When I said, Boston, it was commented further, though diplomatically, about the ethnic groups that lived up there. I knew how to play the game and said my middle name was Angus, which it is, and that my mother's family were Scots from Nova Scotia.

I purchased the home, and all the people have really

been quite nice – a little standoffish, but so be it. I am too. The community is truly a fine one, though. It is a veritable sanctuary and a wonderful place to live, so far. All my neighbors seem to have two or more other homes, so much of the time I'm like the local caretaker, all alone, with the entire beach to use as my big playpen. But my closest friends in the area are in business, and few of us have the time to attend the neighborhood association meetings, which, I am sure, offer opportunities to meet others and network.

After I moved to my hideaway paradise, on the way home from my office I would stop at a restaurant that was reasonably close to my house. It had excellent food and great jazz.

I told a good friend who had a restaurant background of many years experience that it was up for sale. I became sort of his silent partner and loaned him a number of dollars to buy in.

Too many restaurants are marketing to draw the twenty-one to thirty-five year olds with blues, jazz, reggae, and yuppified bar menus of boutique beverages and semi-demitasses of espresso. We plan to cater to a more mature group of active adults and energetic retirees. We want to create an upscale environment where men will feel comfortable wearing jackets and ties, and women their finest dresses and jewelry. Be it Palm Beach or in California, there are many communities where people want to dress up, enjoy a fine meal, and also feel safe.

I'm still doing my homework and working closely with accountants and restaurateurs experienced in the food service and upscale lounge business. If the restaurant and lounge does what I'm anticipating, it can double the current volume with only some minor changes and enhanced management. Once I see my concept in action, we believe it's replicable. It might become the prototype for a chain operation one day.

To be sure, private clubs can fill that void, but I never cared to hobnob with club types. Many are just too damn haughty. They can stay behind their restricted walls. I want to meet all kinds of people, from all backgrounds and experiences – real people who have worked or may have had some bad luck, or both – not trust babies and silver spooners who believe that only money and their blood lines make them special.

I want to say here, as an object lesson, that if I had followed my business instincts, we should have immediately closed the restaurant, redesigned it, created a new menu and wine list, and hired a completely new staff. About the latter, many good people had been working at the restaurant for almost two decades, and I could not in all conscience release them. Unless one has the soul of a pirate, it is never easy or pleasant to downsize a company or massacre the employees to increase profits. So instead, we attempted to make gradual changes and retrain the staff. It hasn't worked totally, but with the application of necessary business disciplines, which were formerly ignored, the future of the club looks bright.

In another similar yet different area of the food service business, I am talking with other people about opening a different chain of restaurants – still on the drawing board – called Sandwich and a Half Shops. Basically they will serve soup and a sandwich-and-a-half. Not soup and half a sandwich. For many people, a typical restaurant sandwich is not enough. I hope no one dribbles on my lovely ties.

* * *

I'm a typical male who does not like to shop. I'll go on a

binge twice a year out of necessity, but as an every day thing, I dislike it. I receive some of the better catalogs because I am as much a mail order shopper as any of our customers. *I do as I say.*

One day, I realized that there was no catalogue devoted solely to men's ties. Although Rexall Sundown, like many other companies, has dress-down Fridays (summertime only), many men out there – the wannabe executives coupled with the boardroom folks, accountants, and attorneys – wear ties regularly. I figured that most had about a dozen ties they preferred.

The origins of my tie collection began when I visited Europe. I saw that men's fashions were marketed on the basis of Italian silks being the best. They were certainly more accepted, the way Paris had the edge on women's fashions. And Italian designers do create magnificent products in all areas, from spiffy cars to dramatic architecture.

I found the suppliers once again using the same operating procedures, as I did with vitamins. I got in touch with some people on my own through the State Department, and pursued those sources when I was in Europe. They were in northern Italy, around the Lake Como area.

Since my background was mail order, I initiated a tie-only catalog. I started it with a small sum, small for a corporation, although it's quite large in the general scheme of things. The initial start-up was relatively nominal.

I did a testing, and in 1996 hired Carmen Knight, a very savvy enthusiastic lady who knows only winning, to head the company. I also used two outside services – one to take the orders on an 800 number and the other to ship them.

The company was named The Hassler Consortium, from the Hassler Hotel in Rome, the one above the Spanish Steps. The lovely Audrey Hepburn gracefully ran down those same steps in *Roman Holiday.*

I thought Hassler was a strong, masculine name for the corporation, and then I needed another name for the collection itself. I played around with several Italian monikers since the ties and accessories all came from Italy. I ended up using my own. It's called the DeSantis Collection, the first time I have put my name on any of my products.

The designs came about as a result of meeting with brokers and one particular company in New York, now close friends of mine. They are working very closely with the people manufacturing in Italy. They brought their swatches and patterns to my headquarters, and I made my selections. I began to learn more and more about ties. There are twills, jacquards, woven prints, satin-silks – so many different materials – woven is king of the cravats.

We tested methods to learn which would pull the best response. We experimented with three mail-order pricing levels. We had a high-priced spread with reasonably large mark-up that we sent to upscale groups. We sent a low-priced mailer to a different pricing market. And then we had a middle of the road price with ten percent off on special offers.

The good thing about mail order – direct marketing – is that you can test, test, test. One danger is that you can test yourself into oblivion, and the poor house. Here again: **Analysis to paralysis.**

At some point you must decide. One thing we found out about upscale customers – the type who will spend a hundred dollars or more on an order – they respond best to an offer rather more readily than to a cut or discounted price.

One offer seemed to work substantially better than all the others: Buy three ties and receive one free, which is, in effect, at least 25-plus percent off, depending on our selling prices of the different ties. All savvy businessmen could recognize that fine a deal in an instant.

We hired a terrific copy writer out of Minnesota whom we found through one of the printers. She has signed a long term agreement to work only for us on copy for cravats as we embellish our line of ties. We have a premier catalogue, as fine as our goods.

Presently I am offering about sixty ties in various designs that appear in six different catalogues a year. The ties are priced from $40 to $65; so at 25 percent off, almost no tie costs more than $35 or thereabouts if the customer orders three, which is really a middle of the road price for premium quality ties.

It's been tremendously satisfying to see the number of orders coming in, and the average order, I'm proud to say, is well over $145. That is far superior to anyone else's mail order list out there for men's softwear accessories, from what I can tell.

One reason for our success is our understanding of the human anatomy. Some men have thicker necks, or are more portly than the average – their gut hangs out. We offer them longer ties and tell them the exact length. These are the choices we provide, which the competition rarely does.

I will normally look at fifteen hundred to two thousand different patterns of fabric for my ties per catalogue. When preparing an upscale catalogue, we play up each design with corresponding copy that grabs the customer and says, "Buy me!". I say we, because we now have fourteen employees working for the firm and we're doing more than $400,000 a month. I anticipate doing 7 million-plus dollars this year, with very little of my time put into it – hopefully, a substantial profit will accompany this after only the second year out. Much of this is due to Carmen Knight, a true superstar, who runs the business.

Recently, I went to a weekend show in New York in

search of more accessories to add to the mailer – from cummerbunds and bow ties to men's belts of alligator, crocodile, and lizard – the highest quality.

For the time being, I won't go beyond that because I want items that we can have in stock. We carry an inventory of approximately 60 to 75 different ties at all times, and if there's any overstock, we can sell it locally at cost or a little above with the DeSantis tag removed. So there's no appreciable loss. We take those slow dollars and put them back to use. A new item – men's socks – was added to our ties and other accessories in our recent catalogues and is making a major additional dollar impact.

The key to direct marketing success is to get the right list so that you mail to the right people. And we've been beating the list percentages substantially. An average decent list will return about 6/10ths of one percent from the mailing, and most of our competitors sell shirts and general clothing, and assorted goodies with their ties. What an unmanageable inventory!

We are averaging nearly 20 percent more on our mailings, a very high return. Our in-house list has a return of almost 5 percent. As I have learned from being a member of the DMA, Direct Marketing Association, most of the direct houses do not receive a higher percent of return on their own lists, unless it's commodity products.

So we're doing things right with our DeSantis ties – and with our belts. Men often have difficulty deciding if they have a thirty-four or thirty-six inch waist. Therefore, we created simpler ads. We made a better mousetrap, which means we first identified the problem.

In our mailers we essentially tell our customers: *If you feel your waist is between 34 and 36½, order "A"; if you think you're 37 to 39½ order "B"*. No longer will our customer have to worry what his size is on a given day.

* * *

I have included one other men's product in my tie catalogue. At one time, a fragrance from Paris called *Jacomo®*
was on the market. I don't know the reason why it became
unavailable in this country. Perhaps it was no longer being
made, or management decided to stop exporting it.

Jacomo was indeed a very elegant, smart fragrance. Men
who used it, including myself, received many compli-
ments. That is why I decided to create a product, which I
feel, is superior to *Jacomo.*

The last thing I wanted to do, however, was to make a
me-too copy of somebody else's fragrance. There are
already far too many knock-offs out there.

I'm well-grounded in the chemical business, so I went
to a gentleman in New York whom I'd known for some
time and who sells Rexall Sundown some raw materials.
Prior to that he was in perfumes and oils. I gave him a couple of bottles of *Jacomo* that I'd been hoarding, and told
him I wanted a similar product but with a little more vanilla, and more woodsy, if you will.

He conjured several variations of my concept, all of
which I thought were wonderful, and I then contacted a
Florida firm for sample scents. After official business
hours, I called an informal meeting of employees in the
office – from secretaries to executives – and let them
determine which one we liked. A kitchen focus group, if
you would.

We put out some samples. *Ecco!* We now have a fragrance in my tie catalogue I've named *Forza Vagante,* Force
of the Vagabonds. My kind of guys. It's a high gross profit
product at $45 a 3.5 oz bottle, and sold over 4,000 bottles
in only six months. Its headquarters, I'm proud to say, is in
Como, Italy. The best part is they can get it only from us.

That's very important in marketing. Customer re-ordering is now becoming a flourishing part of the business.

I am presently considering adding a custom-order shirts-by-mail catalogue. I know how it can be done. Nick Palin came up with the name for that new catalogue one Saturday afternoon when we were *kibitzing* about it – Perfect Fit™.

* * *

Investing in the restaurant-lounge was only the start of my plans for other ventures. I recently bought with one of my sons and a dear friend a large commercial property, a plaza, from which I am expecting a decent NOI, net on investment, not an ROI, return on investment. That is what I'll pocket after all the overhead and the like.

It's a large commercial plaza on multi-acres. On it are a nationally recognized bank and a couple of fine rental producing buildings.

We paid a little over $7.5 million for the property, which throws off a rent of S1.4 million, and an NOI of about one million. I can't think of any other investment of $7.5 million that will earn the team a virtual guaranteed million annually. (Well, okay, other than Rexall Sundown.) Plus, there is the real estate depreciation factor with all those tax advantages. At the same time, the property is appreciating in value with 90-plus percent occupancy. I have a first class rental agent running it for a nominal fee, so for me it's a well-paying hands-off situation. A win-win-win-win!

Others may have already seen potential for a great future in the All-American city of Delray Beach. A large hotel addition and small convention center will be built. The plaza, with its current great tenant roster, includes vacant waterfront property, which is a good place for my partners and me to open another restaurant near the ocean in Delray or where I have adjacent property. At least that's my current intent.

I have also purchased a shop near the restaurant, and my current plan is to put in an upscale international gourmet market and bakery. More acquisition of stores, office complexes, and plazas, most assuredly, will follow. Passive investments that I'm in charge of, hopefully.

* * *

I have always appreciated antiques and fine artifacts. I love surrounding myself with objects that, I feel, give off a special aura. I even have a limited collection of old mortars and pestles, and other tools of the trade once used in drugstores and the pharmaceutical industries.

Over the years, I have acquired so many fine objects that I felt the need to purchase a substantial building to house many of the lots and pieces I've been collecting in Europe, the Far East, and China.

I collect jade, legally obtained old ivory, malachite, coral, and bronzes from the 1700s to about 1900. I acquired some pieces from Sotheby's, others from estate sales where you can often be reassured by their provenances.

I think I know enough about the subject to open a storefront tied into the commercial properties in the Delray Beach area. Atlantic Avenue, I strongly believe, is the next wave, the next Worth Avenue, the next Las Olas for the Florida marketplace. I'm sure there are places like that all over the country, but here is where I happen to be, and where I'm putting a portion of my personal investments at this time.

Also in Delray, I recently purchased a prime piece of property which once housed the former Great Western Bank Building. There, I will establish a fine arts gallery of approximately 17,000 square feet. I intend for it to be a class act, to have the finest showrooms in South Florida, with museum quality objects for sale: Elegant alabaster, jade, ivory, and coral sculptures from the Far East; a jewelry exchange with a menu of rare and exquisite Faberge eggs; and a salon for European paintings. Each genre of art, craft, and fine furniture will have its own section and niche. Theme rooms, if you will.

Because I am a voracious collector, the gallery will definitely be a hands-on operation, off hours from my Rexall Sundown commitments. I'll be using some rooms in the building for my own extensive personal collection. Then I can move about my house, which has been the storehouse for these valuables, without getting impaled on a Chinese horseman's ivory spear or knocking over a priceless vase and reducing it to jigsaw puzzle shards.

I have created more than a new business with my gallery. Its name will be GILLIS SIGNATURE IMPORTS, a tribute to "Pa", my grandfather, who had constructed homes in Boston under GILLIS & SONS and was indeed an imported-rarity in his own right from Antigonish, Nova Scotia.

* * *

From my "toughest man" scuffle with the sailor while I was a high school student, through my first job in a drugstore barely out of my teens, to my daughter's early employment, Walgreens and my life seem to be have been somewhat intertwined. And still is.

After my commitment to purchase the plaza, I learned that it was likely my partners and I would at some point be leasing some property to Walgreens, the company that started me out but did not make the best use of my abilities, I thought. Oh, irony of ironies. And what a euphoric high this brings.

Walgreens is looking to build an approximately 14,000-plus square foot store on our recent property purchase. My life and Walgreens converge yet again. Isn't that something? The terms are in negotiation. All we need now is approval from the city along with some, hopefully, minor concessions to local residents.

As our management negotiates the final phases of that lease with Walgreens, I certainly am tempted to make up for those extra hours I had to work which kept me away from my family. And, yes, I am gloating shamelessly. But in truth, they are a marvelous company, and my start was due to them. Thank you, Walgreens.

It's come full circle. What was that they once told me about not putting Eddie Arcaro on a jackass? Could it be that I have finally arrived?

I now feel comfortable looking at commercial properties and will become involved in purchasing and upgrading more shopping plazas. I have a feeling that this will be more fun for me than taking another business public. I prefer to avoid having to deal again with some of those investment bankers who, in my opinion, are neither investors nor bankers. Sorry, guys.

As I mentioned above, the entire purpose of selling some of my stock was to divest my portfolio and venture into what I really like to do – run businesses from the get-go. I can see where I can make a 12 to 15 percent return on an investment or net on investment, and I have tax depreciation with shopping centers and office buildings. And I have appreciation if I buy the right properties. So to me it's a no-brainer, although it's not all that simple. Or is it?

* * *

I am also studying, along with a couple of people, the possibility of opening up boat washes for those crafts under thirty-five feet. The big boats are handled by captains and require plenty of mates to operate them.

Typical boat owners have to lug their boats in and out of the water and wash them down, which is quite a pain after being out in the salt water all day. That's why I'm thinking of opening up boat washes. I'm looking to work with an individual who owns large Chevron gas stations in the Boca Raton/Delray area. There's a suds that breaks down the saline, and you can wash the boats in no time with less water and cost than a car. So, I'm preparing to open a couple of pilot boat washes just off a pier so a person can initiate the clean-up there and not have to *schlepp* it home.

At the other end of the venture spectrum, I may buy and revive a once-popular charge card, and offer it exclusively to corporate executives and other successful professionals at the top of their careers. I am making a careful study to find the best possible bank that can underwrite the charge card.

I probably will not be happy until I have spent all of my secondary offering personally helping others planting little acorns, doing exciting things with all those funds. I can assure you that I would be bored to death sitting around collecting interest. My pleasures are watching situations grow – getting involved in the action – and most of all, interacting with all types of special people.

The time may soon be ripe once again for a tertiary offering, so I can generate more liquidity to venture into even more new businesses. I love it!

FORTY

Giving Back And Sharing

I believe in sharing the fruits of my success with the community. My involvement with worthy causes are a matter of record: University donations, scholarships, and endowments; National Italian American Foundation; State of Israel Bonds; Alzheimer's Disease Research; City of Hope; March of Dimes; Walk America; AIDS Foundations; Colon Prison Fellowships and the Mental Health Association of Broward County. These are but a few.

Some causes deserve special mention because they are so dear to my heart. I especially enjoy promoting the entrepreneurial spirit amongst college students. That is why I have endowed the School of Business at Florida State University, my once-intended alma mater, with 2 million dollars (that amount to be matched by the State of Florida), and nearly another 2 million-plus dollars to the privately funded Palm Beach Atlantic College to build a prayer and meditation chapel.

And at Florida Atlantic University in Boca Raton, I have helped Dr. Bruce Mallen, Dean of its School of Business, establish a film center, which they have graciously named The Carl DeSantis Business and Economics Center for the Study and Development of the Motion Picture and

Entertainment Industry. Again, as with FSU and PBAC, the State of Florida has matched my 2 million dollar endowment to FAU.

The DeSantis Center will be part of FAU's baccalaureate and MBA program with courses in the marketing, distribution, exhibition, finance, legal, contract negotiations, and economics of the film and TV industries. The center will also put on educational programs, do research, serve as a data center for the entertainment industry, and support the local film festivals in Palm Beach and Ft. Lauderdale to help make South Florida, the community in which I work and live, a welcome place for the movie and TV industry. We are delighted that the legendary film editor-director-producer, Robert Wise, winner of four Academy Awards, has come aboard as FAU's Distinguished Producer/Executive in Residence at the College of Business. Also on the Advisory Board and amongst other industry leaders to join in supporting our center are famed director and current President of the Academy of Motion Pictures Arts and Sciences, Arthur Hiller, and Neil Braun, NBC Television President – each as wonderful a human being as he is talented.

I strongly believe that spirituality should be nurtured along with the intellect at our universities and colleges; therefore, I have also endowed a building at the FAU School of Business where students of all faiths, or none, might take time out to contemplate. I dare not say to pray in this era of political correctness when crèches and menorahs in public places and the singing of Christmas carols in schools are banned. However, if it is true that there are no atheists in foxholes during war, there may also be none during finals when students might very well need a place to ask for aid from the non-denominational Our Lady of the GPA.

Since my early boyhood, I have always enjoyed the fine arts. Thus, I was delighted to have been given an opportunity to contribute to the Miami City Ballet and underwrite its gala in Boca Raton that will launch the first phase of its proposed academic/cultural partnership with FAU. Again, as a result of sharing with my community, I have had the good fortune to meet more outstanding people, amongst them Edward Villella, Artistic Director of the Miami City Ballet, and Theo Fabergé, who has continued his family's tradition of Imperial Easter Eggs, which I had been collecting before he presented me with an award of a special egg for underwriting the gala.

I also wish to give special mention to two medical facilities that I am most proud to be associated with, one local, the other global. I have helped raise funds to establish the Rexall Sundown Pediatric Bone Marrow Center at the University of Miami-Jackson Memorial Hospital Medical Center, which accepts patients from all over the world. We have also donated TV sets, video games, and toys to cheer the children.

The other renowned organization I support is the City of Hope. No other medical research facility has sustained a higher reputation or done more to seek cures for so many diseases over the past decades.

Although I have been given Man-of-the-Year awards for several of the above activities, I do not always win. For two consecutive years, I have been nominated as Entrepreneur of the Year for the State of Florida. I lost for the second time. The winners in both years were very special people. That reminded me of another important lesson in life: There is always someone who can run a bit faster, jump a little higher, and yes, throw a tad farther; but we should all thank our God for whatever blessings He has bestowed upon us.

Yet, although we may never be quite as good as we want to be, we might be better than we think we are.

When a world crisis touches us, we try to do what we can. After the Gulf War, we sent three million dollars worth of our products for Iraqi-Kurd relief. I had wanted to do that quietly, as I was uninterested in any personal glory. Then the person who headed Communications at the time suggested that we send information and samples of what we had done to the local news stations, TV network news, *USA Today,* and the White House.

We received a kind reply from only one person, then Vice President Dan Quayle. A few years later, we had the pleasure of meeting Mr. Quayle privately when he was in the area for a book signing. Regardless of what the readers may think of his politics, pro or con, I can assure you that he is a more intelligent and thoughtful man than the media has portrayed him to be.

I am not one of those who gives only to worthy causes and never to individuals. I do make specific loans to people I care for. Do they pay me back? Not always. But I am not resentful. People are people. That boy in the third grade, to whom I gave my sandwich and dessert, never paid me back with anything. Maybe he couldn't. The main thing is that I helped him in a time of need.

My friends will describe many situations like the night I embraced a homeless Vietnam veteran after hearing his stories, wept with him, and gave him whatever dollars I had in my pocket. Or the time I saw a fellow fixing a flat off the freeway and gave him money to buy a tire because I saw another was worn thin.

Those stories are anecdotal. We've all been there, I'm sure.

You have already read about those businesses I helped

or financially initiated that are becoming enormously successful. I am not infallible and sometimes end up backing
people who tell me that they could be successful if only
they had the capital.

Unfortunately, those individuals, whom I still love, did
not have everything else – or the right stuff. And, each
business may have failed because I did not get involved
hands-on, as I have done with many of my successes. That
should be a salutary lesson for us among others, such as
dear old friends suddenly appearing at your door once
your success has been made known.

The best illustration of the above occurred recently
when someone who had been a school friend since the
second grade came to my office. He assured me that after
praying to his patron saint, he was somehow guided my
way. This was years after he had ignored me when he was
making considerably more money than I. After listening
to his tale of woe, I loaned him a hundred thousand dollars. I have not heard from him since, not even to say
thank you or to offer a reason why he has not paid me
back – which, by the way, I'd accept even if the truth were
shaded. Fortunately, I do not often meet many like him.

Another gentleman, whom I have helped, had worked
with me in the early days of Sundown, but left before we
went public and, therefore, did not reap the same wonderful benefits that came to other loyal employees. I truly
felt guilty in some way because he did not become one of
the millionaires.

I loaned him a significant amount of money for his
ideas and dreams, and his family came up with what they
could. He wanted to establish a chain of discount stores,
the type that carries various sundries and no name brands.
They have not been doing all that well, and it appears I'll

lose about 75 percent of my investment. Okay, all of it! Oh, well, at least a portion of my guilt is being alleviated. I'm only sorry that he did not hit his marks.

I'll say it again. I feel that things do not often go well if I do not become thoroughly involved with the project. But I cannot stop venturing. It's obsessive. I simply love the action.

I go with my feelings, my instincts. It's the same when I visit Las Vegas. Notice, that I mention casinos in this chapter on charities.

Gambling in casinos is not a driving force in my life. I gamble only with my money and an amount that I can afford to lose. The last time I entered a casino was about a year ago.

I play at the tables only when I'm in the right mood. I always play loose. Black Jack is my game. Card counting has been replaced by skills in money management because the multi-deck games can often create long winning and losing streaks. I know the percentages, but sometimes I go on instinct.

I've made more than a "piggy-bankfull" of dollars on one hand splitting sixes (one of my lucky numbers) and getting a third, coupled with double-downs and so on. Yes, all in one hand! P.S., and the dealer had an ace up. Don't try this one; your ability will indeed be questioned.

Unfortunately, in Las Vegas, like much of the rest of the world, the original entrepreneurs have been replaced by bottom line corporate types. As an example, I used to have a comfortable line of credit at Caesar's Palace. I did not play there for about a year and a half, a terrible, unpardonable, and costly injustice as you will see.

On the night of my return to Caesar's, I was playing a few hundred dollars per hand alone with the dealer. I assumed that I still had my original line of credit because without asking any questions they gave me initially the amount of chips I had asked for. I rather quickly lost it and asked for the rest of my limit. They informed me, after the fact, that because I had not been there for a year and a half my limit had been reduced by about 60 percent. The manager would not extend credit to my old limit even when I said that they should have told me my limit had been reduced at the time I sat down at the table. Otherwise, I would never have bet at the level I was playing.

I saw that he was following his casino's SOPs, their instructions. Such employees are small individuals. With very little effort, an intelligent exception can always be made contrary to any book.

I did not make a scene. I simply never went back to Caesar's Palace. And yes, I lost that night – I think they lost too.

FORTY-ONE

Rexall Sundown Prepares For The 21st Century

B ack in 1976, I had an idea. I wanted a lean, "no fat" operation selling high-quality nutritional supplements at lower than market prices. After many years in the retail business, dealing with distribution chains for such respected firms as Walgreens and Super-X, I concluded that the entrenched, traditionally run nutritional companies were not receptive to the real needs of consumers and retailers.

Thus, I created Sundown. Since its inception and the addition of that grand old name, Rexall, Sundown has grown to be the number one seller of vitamins in the United States and is proud of its "All American" status. The strength of this company was, is, and will always be built on the following principals: Quality, value, marketing support, efficiency, merchandising support, believing in people; and most importantly, responsive service to meet the needs of the consumer and retailer, as in the case of our double wrap-around label.

As we approach the second millennium and enter the next century, Rexall Sundown will maintain its dedication to the needs and demands of the educated nutritional buyer. Every Rexall Sundown product will be subjected to the most rigid formulation, inspection, and control system in the industry.

Our intent is to maintain an ongoing relationship with the H. V. Shuster laboratories. Therefore, we promise always to do the following: Comply with the Good Manufacturing Practices mandated by the United States Food and Drug Administration for supplement manufacturers; assay every batch of each product to assure purity and potency; and rigorously inspect our outside suppliers' raw materials, thus guaranteeing their adherence to our own stratospheric standards. I am convinced that at the level we operate, we could be manufacturing pharmaceuticals with little or no changes in our self-imposed rigorous QCs and QAs.

At normal industry prices our quality products would be a good value. But we have gone steps far beyond to maintain our policy of lower prices by controlling the process of manufacturing and packaging every step of the way.

The next century will be even better as we sell our vitamins and nutritional supplements at prices far below the industry average product-by-product to those retailers who will consistently offer fair consumer pricing.

Our worldwide direct buying power will enable us to eliminate layers of importers and other middlemen who add no value or quality to product but increase the prices often times many-fold.

We will continue to contract directly with such companies as Roche, BASF, Takeda, and Henkel to maximize volume discounts for bulk purchases of some of the finest ingredients available worldwide.

We will continue to be innovate and creative. We strive to maintain that seventy-percent of the products we sell are unique to Rexall Sundown. Our special formulations create a higher level of consumer satisfaction and, we feel, with increased health benefits.

We will continue to concentrate our efforts at the other end – first creating the best possible products at the lowest possible cost to the consumer and only afterwards will we plan the comprehensive advertising and promotional strategy that pulls in the customer for that all-important initial sale.

We will continue to take into consideration the needs and requirements of people at all levels of the market-place – wholesalers, retailers, distributors, and consumers.

We will continue to have "consumer friendly" labels. Our patented, double-sided, lacquer coated labels have been specifically developed with the consumer in mind. In addition to conforming with all government require-ments, our labels help the retailer sell the product by describing not only the active ingredients, but by high-lighting the enhancements and special features we've included in the formulation.

* * *

At this point, I want to say that we also tell the consumer what is **not** in the product; i.e., starch, salt, sugar, preserv-atives. Many others have since followed our lead, as, more often than not, we are the initiators of product innovation and improvement. Imitation is indeed the best form of flattery. *Curse their cleverness!*

Our consumer friendly double siding affords assurance that the customers will find the products they are looking for; and the uniform, easy-to-read styling of our labels adds a professional touch to the retailer's vitamin shelf. All this leads to increased confidence of the consumer and increased sales for the retailer.

For the retailer, we have a unique, and yes, patented shelf-system which provides instant organization of our line, plus attractive, sales-inducing copy and information right up front. The shelf system adds a distinctive look to the vitamin section, but, more importantly, it can cause a measurable increase in sales.

In concert with the shelf system, Rexall Sundown's computer-designed planograms maximize the efficiency of a retailer's vitamin section. Products are integrated according to their popularity, topicality, and velocity. Rexall Sundown continually studies the results of the planograms, and is constantly improving the product mix and layout to take advantage of changing demand. Those changes can be made quickly and easily because of the computer-aided layout process. That enables the retailer to take immediate advantage of market swings.

Rexall Sundown provides product-specific shelf-talkers for virtually every product, allowing quick and effective emphasis of any product to take advantage of special offers or consumer interest. Shelf-talkers may provide information, space for pricing, or simply call attention to the product to assure consumer-awareness of its presence.

To aid vision-impaired consumers, Rexall Sundown has incorporated a "magnifier" attached to each rack so that they can read the information on the bottles to assist them in making their vitamin selections.

Comprehensive product information sheets and binders are available for both point-of-sale reference by the consumer and behind-the-counter reference by the pharmacist. Our quarterly publication, *Nutrition News*, written by a pharmacist, informs retail pharmacists about consumer trends and continuing scientific advancements.

As in consumer marketing, the wholesale trade requires not only a good product and marketing support, but also effective service and quick response to its needs. Rexall Sundown prides itself on being, at heart, a service-oriented company. Our products are in stock – period. We do not back order except under extreme conditions, because our entire manufacturing and distribution system is geared to providing product to customers in a continuous stream. Constant forecasting and planning, plus strict manufacturing controls have put Rexall Sundown in the enviable position of being able to fill virtually all orders completely within twenty-four hours of receipt.

To the retailer, this policy offers tighter stock control, fewer dollars committed to inventory resulting in improved inventory turns, and an overall bottom line improvement we believe to be the best in the industry. Rexall Sundown can supply the retailer with merchandising support, pricing, special displays, and consumer responsive signage. All these services are geared to help the retailer maintain the excitement, visibility, and sales that come with the Rexall Sundown line.

Part of our secondary offering was based on having liquidity available to acquire those companies that look to the future with meaningful R&D. In all businesses today, you're seeing major consolidations. There will certainly be casualties along the way. Disciplined companies like Rexall Sundown will begin to acquire more – potentially even larger companies – although in our industry few are larger than we are.

We shall lead, and it is our collective intention of management to take this company to the next level. That's the way we're moving. The smaller companies are often under financed and unable to do proper R&D or keep up with the effective driven leaders. To follow the good manufacturing practices required and our self-imposed, often stauncher regulations do not come without serious dollar outlays. It's very expensive to employ those Quality Assurance and Quality Control people with their accompanying needs.

We are well seeded to move forward so that before the next ten years pass we expect to be, without question, the foremost leader in the health and wellness industry, and will strive to be well over the billion dollars in sales by the millennium. We believe that few companies will be in our peer group. By then, there shouldn't be much more of a shake-out; at that point the voids will have been filled and I feel surely no start-ups of eventual significance will surface.

As this book is being written, Rexall Sundown is the nation's second largest vitamin maker by volume of bottles sold. Number one might be Pharmavite, owned by a well-respected Japanese firm, or P. Leiner a California company owned by venture capitalists.

Outside the USA, and in total, General Nutrition might be larger. They make the majority of their own products. They supply franchises and company owned stores. From the standpoint of the entire marketplace that would make us number two. I hope we stay second for a while – although not too much longer. Ha! As in all spectator sports, people expect you to be number one every year, and, as we all know, Wall Street can be very unforgiving when a front runner falls back into the pack.

Yet, as reported by IRI statistics on March 31, 1997, our Sundown Vitamins have become Number One in the nation in terms of sales volume although we are in limited outlets, but with a plethora of bountiful opportunities going forward.

*   *   *

One message of this book is that we must always have an

environment in this country to encourage the entrepreneurial spirit. I posed a question at the beginning: Are people who start-up successful businesses products of genetics or environment?

I think it is genetic, or Divine Providence if you will, the way gifts in painting, composing, and writing are bestowed either by DNA or the Almighty. I believe, however, those abilities and gifts will appear sooner and flower more brilliantly within a favorable family and social environment. Tragically, they may also be stillborn, stifled at home, or discouraged on the streets and by social institutions.

Over the past two hundred years, people have come to the United States from countries where they were forbidden to create and thrive in their businesses because of race, religion, ethnicity, culture, or gender. More recently, they were not allowed to establish businesses because their countries were ruled by the destructive "isms" of the twentieth century.

State Socialism run by assorted communist parties obliterated free enterprise. Socialist-democratic nations suppressed it. Fascism required businesses to go into partnership with thuggish Party members, if the owners were not exterminated first; authoritarian states do the same, only the partners must come from the ruling elite, not necessarily from any political party.

Yet immigrants and refugees from those same countries where their talents had been stifled have come to the United States and in a short time flourished as successful business folks. That proves my own theory that all wins are based solely on people.

More than twenty years ago when I started this company with my family, the market for vitamins was literally a fraction of what it is today. I would love to tell you that I anticipated the kind of growth we've seen. I certainly did perceive that the market I was entering was one with great potential. But let me assure you that I would have needed a crystal ball to see exactly how much our industry would grow.

A couple of very significant societal factors have influenced our industry, helping it to grow so dramatically. First of all, the whole of the population is aging, and our traditional market is now among the older, learned, sophisticated, cost- and information-conscious Americans. And that market has been swelling steadily in size.

Secondly, as the World War II baby generation is moving into middle age, their focus on well-being grows more pronounced and they continue to demand products that foster a healthy active life style. Today, they have more scientific research available to inform them how vitamins, minerals, and herbals are linked to disease prevention.

Now in their forties, these aging kids, have, in general, an unprecedented level of disposable income. The spiraling cost of health care and the prevalence of cost-conscious managed health care programs have inspired consumers to take their own preventative health care initiatives, thankfully including the regular use of vitamins and nutritional supplements.

This consumer demand for "empowerment" on matters affecting their own good health was a driving force behind recent legislative changes affecting dietary supplements. The Dietary Supplement Health and Education Act of 1994, which we call "DSHEA" provides the regulatory framework for the FDA's regulation of nutritional products. This was all initiated by a strong grass roots support for quality dietary supplements labeled with useful nutritional information.

In the context of our often slow-moving government regulatory agencies, it is difficult to say exactly what changes will result in the long-term. But the spirit of this new regulatory climate is clear: It is a call to action for companies in our industry to pay attention to the products and the information our consumers want and take a proactive stance in fulfilling those needs.

That is what Rexall Sundown is doing. This company was founded on the principle that there is tremendous opportunity for success if you are willing to work hard, provide a quality product at a fair price, and remain ever vigilant in the search for new ideas and opportunities, whenever and wherever they may present themselves. However, our ongoing success has brought with it a new responsibility – to our employees, to our customers and distributors, and now to our shareholders.

We know both ends of the business, which is why we're winning the battle. What has happened is that our competitors have little or no experience as broad product retailers. They're consumers, yet they do not understand how consumers react.

I believe my background in retailing has played an immense role in the success we're having today. So have my instincts, which can come into conflict with my more specialized employees. I do not want to come across as too self-serving, but I must emphasize something to other successful entrepreneurs who may have dropped out of high school or college. Hire them and listen to their advice, but never be intimidated by their MBA or PhD degrees or the term *expert*. When you feel it, go with your gut instinct and winning experience. Do it!

As an example, we now have a substantive Marketing Department. Almost a dozen seasoned veterans. We're looking at how our raw material cost prices have gone up. I've got a list of what was increased this year, and we usually try to do only one price increase or adjustment to maintain our healthy profits and still remain competitive. Nevertheless, our prices don't always have to go north. I generally make sure that the cost of a number of our products goes down when price decreases dictate.

I can assure you that it looks very impressive when you send out a price adjustment letter informing your retail customers that you're dropping the price on 16 items while raising them modestly on 30 or so out of more than 600 in our inventory. It makes us look precisely like what we know we truly are, a caring successful company that evaluates diligently at all levels. And price decreases are as much a part of good business as any of our embellishments.

As for the 16 items we dropped the price on, chances are they wouldn't remain in our inventory unless they suddenly sold with gusto and fell in line with our total sales productivity concept. Another thing, I found early on that if your price list starts with vitamin A, and your drugstore lists products and ingredients alphabetically, a very low price on vitamin A is often the first thing they're going to see, whether it's a big seller or not. And that is the item that should set the standard for your overall pricing policy.

It's like the advice business accountants give to doctors and dentists. Keep the office visit charge at a low constant, which people experience more frequently, but raise the billing price on the other exceptional or one-time services like sutures and root canals.

All right, let's get back to business. Our marketing department worked out new costs and what our prices should be in 1997. They did their homework, and I did mine at home. I had nothing with me except the new costs and a calculator that shows gross profit.

I know what we must make and what consumers will pay and shareholders should be compensated, so I decided to move certain product costs around. We evaluated them with the use of computers, knowing how many we sell of each and their impact on profits. Our financial department together with Marketing did their projections, and I made mine. They spent two weeks doing all their analysis; it took me one solid evening to come up with my price and product changes.

Their conclusions were very close to mine, but theirs were, I felt, misguided on too many items, which is a generic problem within the industry. If Archer-Daniels Midland, Hoffman-LaRoche and/or whoever the suppliers may be for a given product – if they go up 5 percent across the board on vitamin E, it follows that marketing departments will go up 5 percent across the board and add in their suggested acceptable gross profit.

That is **not** how I want it done at Rexall Sundown. I prefer to go up 8 percent on a slower item, and only 2 percent on another. You can't just look at the whole list and go up 5 percent because your cost moved up equally. This is not something you can put into a computer, although projecting sales results can give you a profit model to lean on via computer. **It's an instinctive gut feeling.** And if you don't have it, you're never going to succeed boundlessly in this or any other business. That's my take.

And it's not only about pricing. It's about everything. It's something you cannot learn in school because it cannot be taught. You can read all the textbooks out there, it won't help.

You must have total peripheral vision, see that all-encompassing picture, and prioritize properly.

* * *

Sylvia and I were blessed with three brilliant children who

already have been an integral part of Rexall Sundown's future. I am proud to say they are playing major roles in the running of the company. The most wonderful thing is that each has different strengths to take Rexall Sundown to new heights for generations to come.

Against any potential charges of nepotism, I can assure you that Debbie, Dean, and Damon are where they are because of merit and abilities. Remember, they participated in my business from its very inception when, as children, they filled orders from our bedroom shelves. Ours is not the only family to have been so fortunate. Forbes, Rothschild, and Rockefeller are but a few among many who come to mind.

My profoundly intelligent daughter Debbie, Vice President of the New Products Division, is a registered pharmacist, a career dream I pursued but never truly realized. My oldest son Dean is a seasoned Board Director and more than anyone else is responsible for the existence of our state-of-the-art manufacturing facility, which people from all over the world now visit and praise. And my youngest son Damon, now President of the entire Rexall Sundown Corporation, CEO of Rexall Showcase International, and Board Director, is the rising star in the network marketing industry, and is integral in overall corporate decision making as he weaves his way to top corporate levels.

Before they graduated high school, our children were strongly influenced by the work ethics of their parents at home and later in the early stages of our business. While I was a drugstore manager and just beginning to go into my various entrepreneurial ventures, Sylvia, their mom, worked with Burdines Department Store's Customer Service at minimum wage until we became successful, and in other very responsible positions for various firms during our marriage.

Our children saw what we were doing in business, and appreciated that I was still involved with family. I enjoyed my kids then, and still do. Debbie and Damon used to do paste ups and cut outs – no dolls – and helped laying out ads with dad from the time they were five. On Sundays, Dean was a cashier at the Variety Store.

Dean was for many years our prodigal son, and perhaps the most overtly complex of our three children. He had a good heart and was very independent from the start, a fighter, not in the physical sense, but rambunctious and always into something. That was obvious to me from the age of three or four. Sylvia says he was that way from his moment of birth. My late Aunt Barbara dubbed him "Rocky".

I saw quite early that he had ten times my weaknesses and ten times my strengths. That is why I used to refer to him as ten-by-ten.

Dean is very bright, and might have the highest IQ in our family, whatever that serves, which might well engender arguments from his brother and sister, and rightly so. His greatest strength is that he is fast and brilliant with numbers – all the way to the uppermost levels.

Language was not Dean's forte then, which made him difficult to deal with. It appeared that he was often undiplomatic in his speech or ways, but he had and still has a heart of gold. His communications skills today have improved immensely. After Dean graduated high school, he dropped out of junior college and held a series of short jobs, completely unfocused.

Finally, after we had a talk, Dean went into the Army for three years. He served in the Radio Signal Corps, and was stationed in Germany. While in the Army, Dean took some tests that pre-qualified him for West Point. That was quite rare and an honor to be eligible for an appointment without being recommended by a politician or ranking Army officer.

Dean did not want to make the Army his career. With a bright friend who also was rated high on the scale of potential and is now our operations manager in manufacturing, he finally came back into the family business from being a non-ranked soldier with his younger brother Damon as his boss. Family competition helped spur him to become all he could be.

In the last eight years Dean has realized his potential and then some. He excelled at dollars and cents, purchasing equipment and keeping a tight rein on company expenses. He is integral to the company in watching dollars and is very concerned if he perceives anything has been misspent or misused.

Dean's wife is a CPA, who worked in a senior role for our company. Ever the competitor ready to meet a challenge, he took the equivalent CPA test at home without going to school and excelled in that rigorous exam. He too is always out to prove that he can do it, whatever the challenge may be.

Damon, whom I wrote about extensively in the RSI chapter, is movie handsome without being aware of it, and is head and shoulders more of a people person than Dean. We sent him to a college hundreds of miles away so he would forget the wonderful girl he'd been going with in high school, not marry early, and instead get his degree in Architecture. Six months later, he phoned to tell us that he was getting married to a different girl. Like his parents, he wed early in college. Sometimes mom and dad can't win. Damon won, however. He and his wife are an example for all couples to follow, and with their children, are virtually without equal as a family unit with great values.

After marrying, Damon wanted to stay in school. He worked as a waiter in a restaurant, then became assistant manager in only three months. He is a superb speaker and has always loved business – so much so, that he quit school and came to work for Sundown in the early 1980s. He is rock solid and rarely riled. His silver tongued analogies are almost Biblical in content. Still in his early thirties, he is already a sage and well on his way to corporate stardom.

Debbie is the family's award winner. In Greensboro as a five year old, she won a McDonald's coloring contest. Her prize was a 6 or 10 speed bike, and she got her picture in the local paper.

Debbie won many awards while in school, but was well-rounded and had fun too. A National Merit Scholar, she graduated at the top of her class in high school, and excelled at the University of Florida in pre-pharmacy. Debbie graduated at the top of her Pharmacy class and ended up at Walgreens – a family tradition of sorts, it seems – for about seven years.

Walgreen's sent Debbie to Houston, Texas. After one tornado too many, she returned to Florida and became District Supervisor of Walgreens' pharmacists in South Florida. I heard that Debbie was in the running to become Director of the entire Midwest area before she came to work for Rexall Sundown. That was the year before we went public and began to manufacture our own vitamins. As I said, she is now Vice President of our New Product Division.

Rexall Sundown is not a family business, but we have family in the business. Believe me, that is quite a difference.

FORTY-TWO

My Way ...

Oftentimes, I've been asked for a roadmap and/or a recipe for success. The advice I will try to impart may already have been shared with you by mentors, loving family members, and friends.

First, find something you believe in ardently. Hard work and perseverence will come easily if you truly believe you have found the passion that fuels your fire! Capitalize on your strengths and find solutions for your weaknesses. Today's entrepreneurs are consumed with the strategies that solve problems in business, political, the arts, and yes, even philanthropic fields.

Remember, identify the market-need for your product and service and find out what you can do to fulfill that specific need. I'm talking about good old supply and demand. Most businesses get started by choosing something that's in high-demand and requires minimum capital **with** minor overhead.

Always keep education in the forefront. Educate yourself in every facet of your chosen venture.

Next, make a plan. Sure, you have an idea you're excited about. But be willing to make adjustments along the way. Believe in yourself. I once read, "To begin with an end in mind means to start with a clear understanding of your destination." Only then are you ready for action.

Foremost and mandatory, it's your duty to share – share your knowledge, compassion, and prosperity with your community, its programs, its citizens, its future generations. Remember, a success is empty unless it is shared with others.

And by the way, don't always expect immediacy in your pursuit of success. Set your goals high, but realize that the world **does not** always accomodate your plans. Making a business work requires passion, commitment, timing, **and I may add**, more than a spoonful of good intuition.

If you've got a fairly good gut instinct that works more often than not, go with it. Usually, instinct tends to be right. Certainly in the percentages of life it's going to be on target for you gifted few.

Cliches can be valid, as they are often rooted in truth. He who hesitates is indeed lost all too often in life, be it a personal or business decision. As a good friend once said: "Most people are in the back yard looking for four leaf clovers while opportunity is knocking on their front door." You must get off the fence. Don't ponder for too long. Move forward. Do it! Quit procrastinating.

If you've hired someone who then fails to perform up to your company's standards, the sooner you cut your losses the better off you'll be – and that person too. To prolong it will only aggravate the situation. Handle those situations gingerly and with compassion, but if you fail to act decisively, your indecision can slow productivity and hurt the good of all. I know, I've made those mistakes.

Politely question those who work for you. For example, instead of demanding that a person do a job, you might say: "Could you assist me with this?" Common courtesy is always so very important. I believe it is the key to the success of many individuals. Treat people with the same manners you would want and expect from them. Falseness will eventually obviate itself.

Refrain from speaking negatively when possible. Always look to compliment when you can. You'll have few second chances. But please be genuine when you do.

However, if you find that pleasant courtesies don't work, only then use a stronger hand – take a different approach. It's important that you know all the approaches to take and how individuals react to praise, criticism, or tone of voice. You have seen the same happen in sports. One athlete may be destroyed by an abusive coach; another may be motivated to greater efforts by that same person. You must know people and how to extract from them their very best.

Be as honest and as real as you can. Even nervousness can be the real you. We can all be nervous. This is not a sin. It's being human.

Avoid keeping those people who tend to justify and rationalize their base indefensible actions. From petty theft of office supplies and unauthorized use of "800" lines, to more serious offenses, they will always have a ready excuse: "I didn't get a raise; I got passed over for a promotion; the boss can afford it." *Ad nauseam.* Cut your losses. It's fairer to you and the employee.

Having a superior vocabulary is less important than being an authentic, real person with acumen and empathy.

I have a philosophy about management. Choose the right people so that you can feel secure delegating authority and decision making to them; yet always keep a hands-on interest in what they do. Allow them to make mistakes and feel free to admit they have. If they have wrong opinions, explain and win them over, not only by conversing but by showing. Eliminate fear, otherwise they will have a cover-your-behind mentality that ultimately hurts any business situation.

Nothing succeeds like the **desire** to succeed. Success is measured in many ways. Going only for the brass ring and the big bucks will often impede your ability to do other things. As Baron Rothschild said, anyone can make a million if that's all one wants to do. Know that the true value of your character is far more important than your personal net worth.

Good vocabulary should result in better communication, thus hopefully leading to improved understanding. Inflection and intent must be made clear, which can be difficult in English if I refer to George as a sweet candy salesman. What did I really say?

Communication is a cardinal necessity and can be the absolute cornerstone of success, as I mentioned earlier with my misunderstanding of the word *Street*. It also to get through the most prosaic moments in life. As an example, I had hired an artisan to do some woodwork with Philippine mahogany. While waiting for the wood to arrive, he saw flaws in the lathe work that was on the walls and tried to fix it. As I passed by, I said, "What a lousy job that is." He followed me into the office concerned, and asked me what he was doing wrong. I had to clarify what I had really meant. I had not criticized him but the work done by the people who had originally worked on the walls.

That encounter reminded me to speak always with clear meaning. Before we speak, we should consider what we are really trying to say. Communication skills are essential. We can mis-communicate at the most simple level, as when the wife asks her husband to turn down the air conditioner. What does she mean? Cooler? Not so cool?

I believe in people-power, the potential to work with individuals and fulfilling their needs for the good of an intended purpose. You don't have to be an industrial psychologist, but you must be aware of their feelings and what motivates them. Always work with people on the basis of how you'd like to be treated. Be a model, both as a boss and as a human being.

Be aware that each person has something to offer, some talent or ability that can be developed and utilized – even those who seem to be slow in learning, but whose desire abounds. They may very well possess a genius for some skill or talent that we lack. See if you're able to extract those abilities and work with them – whether they are persons in your firm or those you encounter in life's kaleidoscope of experiences.

Take each person for his or her strengths, regardless of gender, race, or ethnicity, and evaluate them on that basis. You will be surprised at the wisdom you'll receive from all peoples if you toss your prejudices aside.

Enjoy the pleasures of life. They can come in many ways, some quite unexpectedly. In my own particular case, it can even be an object. As I wrote earlier, I have spent countless dollars of my own money on art, the objects I love. Some individual pieces are quite expensive by themselves. Yet it's often a piece for which I may have paid fifty or a hundred dollars that gives me the most pleasure.

Perhaps a lesson can be learned from that. Did I overspend collecting the other pieces? Yet, I never would have found my particular masterpiece if I hadn't. You have to turn over a lot of stones to find one precious gem. But be assured that it does exist.

Be kind to nature. If a plant, in order to flourish, should be in a pot, put it in a pot for its survival first, and only after that for your edification. Wake it. Give it proper sunlight. And if the plant should be in the soil leave it in its natural environment.

Life is teeming all over the planet. I read somewhere that one acre of land could fill volumes of encyclopedias if one were to describe the variety of living things contained within and their symbiotic relationships. Be kind to virtually everything and everyone out there. We live in a wonderful world created by a genius we cannot comprehend, a genius we can only aspire to, never match.

Be it a yellow butterfly that just flew by, or a turtle dove that's down there warbling its sweet song, nature offers so many lessons everywhere. It's our responsibility to discover and learn from each of the Almighty's creations, as King Alfred did from watching a tenacious spider while he hid from his enemies in a cave.

Take the time to accept nature's beauty and enjoy its grandiose pleasures from the most luxuriant rose bushes to the smallest wildflower. Accept each for its own beauty. Know that you are fortunate to enjoy and revel in its miraculous being.

What a pleasant way to awaken and have all your senses stimulated as you look out at nature's exquisite palette. It can set the tone for the entire day, the best possible day.

Apply that lesson to individuals as well. Surround yourself with good auras – be they people or objects.

How you react in life and how you deal with it are reflections of your own internal spirituality. Success doesn't come through dollars alone, but more often is cloaked in spirituality. It's innate in all of us, and we must continue to build upon it.

Do not harbor resentfulness. Eliminate hate from your thought process.

There are only so many hours in the day to accomplish all we have to do and want to do. I freely admit that

I have missed too many moments of the wonderful music I love.

Whatever you aim for, pursue it to the fullest. Be selective of each moment for your own good. At any given time, you may very well want to listen to music you heard thirty years ago, but you can't stop because you're too involved in business. Sure, you'd like to change it, but all you are allowed to have are the memories, that Kodak® moment. I can only assure you my zest and desire to win and succeed is based on **I have to do it now**. Tomorrow is virtually too late.

I recognize that frustration is a part of life. There are not too many Albert Schweitzers or Mother Teresas out in the world, who, despite overwhelming obstacles, devoted their entire lives to helping others. Fortunately, however, there are many anonymous heroes all around us, so let's learn from everyone we can.

If you have learned, then impart whatever knowledge and wisdom you may have. Those you teach may be able to take your information and bring it to another level. If you look at your own past, and I've looked at mine, there have been certain people who have stood out – my mother, grandparents, family, people I've worked with in all walks of life – and I can only thank them for making me a fuller person, richer in all my wins.

Never be overly serious about yourself or life. Always bring wit to the forefront. A good sense of humor brings down barriers. People like it. It's truly a catharsis.

Be a good listener too. Be receptive. You can learn from listening, and while speaking, also listen to yourself, to what you're saying. Be aware that whenever you talk, lecture, and converse, people are listening to you. Speak with clarity and forethought. Avoid hollow, purposeless rhetoric.

I want to emphasize yet again my great belief in people. I have instincts about the individuals I meet and make relatively quick evaluations. I've told you about some of them throughout this book.

Speaking of books – that leads me to writing. I believe that I had found one of my personal niches in writing advertising copy for Sundown products. I especially love to write and receive hand-written letters. Unfortunately, the letter has gone the way of drive-in movies as far as I'm concerned. E-mail communications can never replace the elegant phrase and graceful penmanship of traditional letter writing.

I could always write. We all can pen a lot of wonderful things we can't say verbally. Number one, our mind doesn't work fast enough, and there are things you'll put to pen that you won't say to people.

I regret that letter writing is a dying art. I do have two or three people who write to me on a regular basis, and I hoard them, treasure and re-read each letter. You cannot re-read a telephone conversation. Tape it, perhaps, but it's still conversation.

When I give my motivational speeches to college students, I tell them to be everything they can be, which is typical of a lot of successful people. Don't go for the dollars; the dollars will come. Go for the idea, wholly and with unbridled passion. That's what I try to instill.

Remember that *competitor* is not a bad word. Competition begets innovativeness and brings better products to the masses. That is why I have always envied Gillette.

550 million men use a Gillette blade every morning; no company, not even Schick, is a close second. Gillette truly owns the entire market. They can afford to give away a free razor with its blades. And they do not go out of their way

for older people with poor eyesight and give them clear directions on how to snap the blade into the holder.

With so strong a monopoly, one may well wonder if they don't have built-in obsolescence. Every few years, their new blade seems better – or is it perhaps that the older blades they don't care to market now were not honed so well? Only strong competition can change that status quo. I believe there is a niche or void in the razor blade industry – and in many others – for someone like a Carl DeSantis to fill, which leads me to my final words for all you actual and potential entrepreneurs:

Fill a void, give the customers what they want; do it ethically with integrity, sincerely and with passion, and then the dollars most assuredly will follow.

TOMMOROW'S OPPORTUNITY

If we might have a second chance
To live the days once more,
And rectify mistakes we've made
To even up the score.
If we might have a second chance
To use the knowledge gained,
Perhaps we might become at last
As fine as God ordained.
But though we cannot
retrace our steps,
However stands the score,
Tomorrow brings another chance
For us to try once more.

ANONYMOUS

Appendix A

Some of the countries in which Rexall Sundown's international division distributes or sells:

Antigua	Hong Kong	United Arab
Argentina	Iraq	Emirates
Aruba	Ireland	Venezuela
Australia	Italy	Yemen
Austria	Jamaica	Zaire
Bahamas	Japan	Zambia
Bahrain	Kenya	
Barbados	Lesotho	
Belgium	Lithuania	
Belize	Mexico	
Bolivia	Myanmar	
Botswana	Netherlands	
Brazil	Norway	
Bulgaria	Panama	
Canada	Paraguay	
China	Peru	
Colombia	Philippines	
Congo Republic	Portugal	
Costa Rica	Philippines	
Cyprus	Puerto Rico	
Denmark	Romania	
Dominican Republic	Russia	
Ecuador	Saudia Arabia	
El Salvador	South Africa	
France	South Korea	
Germany	Spain	
Greece	St. Kitts	
Guam	Swaziland	
Guatemala	Taiwan	
Haiti	Trinidad and Tobago	
Honduras	Turkey	

Appendix B

HERBAL ROSTRUM

As we all know, moderate usage of these herbals is best in most cases. If you choose to ingest more than the recommended dosages over an extended period of time, consult your physician or health professional. *Women who are pregnant or nursing should especially heed this advice.*

Aloe Vera

Aloe preparations are derived from the leaf gel and juice of a cactus-like subgroup of the lily family with some 300 species, among them Aloe Vera. **The transparent gel from the inner leaf is applied externally to soothe skin and promote cell repair. When taken internally, Aloe Vera helps promote healthful lower intestinal function.**

Bilberry

Bilberry is derived from the berrylike fruit of a common European shrub (Vaccinium myrtillus), similar to blueberry. Bilberry contains flavonoid compounds called anthocyanosides. **Anthocyanosides are powerful antioxidants which help promote healthy circulatory and eye function.**

Cascara Sagrada

Cascara Sagrada, "sacred bark" in Spanish, is derived from the dried aged bark of a small tree (Rhamnus purshiana) native to the Pacific northwest. **It is typically used as an oral digestive aid and laxative that promotes healthy small intestinal and colon function.**

Cat's Claw

Cat's Claw, also known as uncaria tomentosa, is cultivated in the Peruvian rain forest. **Historically, Cat's Claw has been used by the natives of Peru to aid the digestive and immune system.**

Cayenne

Cayenne, also known as capsicum futescens, is both an herb and a spice obtained from the dried, ground fruit of various hot chili peppers. Cayenne provides the dynamic warming and invigorating benefits of nature's hottest spice without the burning hot taste. **Popular use of Cayenne in the United States as a digestive and circulatory stimulant dates back to the late 1700s.**

Chamomile

Chamomile is an ancient and widely used herb made from the flowers of either of two annual plants (German chamomile, or Matricaria recutita, and Roman chamomile, or Anthemis nobilis). **Taken as a tea, it has long been used for its natural calming and soothing effects to combat the pressures of a busy, active or stressful lifestyle.**

Cranberry

The American cranberry, also known as the trailing swamp cranberry, is referred to scientifically as Vaccinium macrocarpon Ait (family Ericaceae). **It is typically used as an aid in maintaining a healthy urinary tract.**

Dandelion

Dandelion is a bitter but nutritious herb prepared from the roots, leaves, and other parts of the well-know yellow flowered weed (Taraxacum officinale). **Traditionally, it has been used as a digestive tonic that promotes healthy lower intestinal function when taken internally.**

Dong Quai

Dong Quai, a favorite Chinese herb for women, is derived form the root of Chinese angelica (Angelica sinensis). Used for thousands of years, Dong Quai is one of the most important female tonic remedies in Chinese medicine. **It is used to provide energy, for gynelco-logical problems, and to regulate hormones. Dong Quai is often taken by women entering menopause or before menstruation.**

Echinacea

Echinacea angustifolia (E. purpurea), usually referred to simply as Echinacea, is derived primarily from the roots of the purple cone-flower. It is an increasingly popular herb in Europe and North America. **Echinacea provides superior herbal support for healthy immune function and promotes general well-being during the cold and flu season.**

Eyebright

Eyebright preparations are derived from a northern plant (Euphrasia officinalis) with somewhat eye-shaped flowers. **It has tra-ditionally been used to make eyewash, and also helps promote gen-eral well-being during the cold and flu season.**

Fennel Seeds

Fennel preparations are produced from seeds of a tall, stalky plant (Foeniculum vulgare) native to the Mediterranean. **Fennel is pri-marily used as a digestive aid, and is popular among women.**

Feverfew

Feverfew preparations are derived from the leaves and flowers of a bushy perennial (Tanacetum parthenium), and is a member of the daisy family. It was known to the ancient Egyptians and Greeks as a valuable herbal remedy. **Today, Feverfew has become popular due to its effectiveness as a remedy for migraine headaches. Feverfew has also been used for its anti-inflammatory properties in the treat-ment of arthritis, and as an anti-spasmodic to relieve menstrual cramps.**

Garlic

One of nature's most valuable foods that has been used since Biblical times and is found in the literature of the ancient Hebrews, Greeks, Babylonians, Romans, and Egyptians. **Garlic assists in diges-tion and helps maintain healthy serum cholesterol and fat levels. It also helps promote healthy circulatory function.**

Ginger

Ginger is derived from the underground stems of a tropical plant (Zingiber officinale) native to the Orient. It has been used since ancient times by the Greeks and Chinese. **Ginger has been recognized for its ability to enhance well-being naturally by promoting healthy and calming digestive function. It is also used for nausea, prevention of sea sickness, and aids in cases of vertigo.**

Ginseng

Ginseng is one of the Orient's most prized herbs for well being – used as a tonic for extra energy. There are many types of ginseng: Eleuthrococcus senticosus (Siberian ginseng), Panax ginseng (Chinese or Korean ginseng), and Panax japonicum (Japanese ginseng). **One of nature's most popular herbs, it is chosen by individuals with active lifestyles worldwide to help promote energy and endurance. Ginseng is also well known for its ability to support normal body functions under environmental and physical stress.**

Ginkgo Biloba

Ginkgo preparations are derived from the fan-shaped leaves of one of the world's most ancient tree species (Ginkgo Biloba). It has been used by the Chinese for thousands of years for a variety of conditions. **Ginkgo helps maintain brain function, memory, and alertness by stimulating blood circulation in the brain. Ginkgo also works as an antioxidant, promoting cell repair function.**

Golden Seal Root

Golden seal preparations are derived from the yellow root of a small perennial plant (Hydrastis canadensis) native to eastern North America. It is one of the more widely used herbs. Golden Seal contains a number of important alkaloids, including hydrastine, berberine, and tetrahydroberberine. **Golden Seal is reported to help maintain healthy respiratory function.**

Gotu Kola

Gotu Kola is a principally Asian plant (Hydrocotlyle asiatica, Centella asiatica). It should not be confused with kola, an unrelated caffeine-containing herb. For thousands of years, Gotu Kola has been a popular herb in India and Pakistan. **The Gotu plant contains** glycosides, which help promote healthy skin as well as connective tissue function and repair.

Hawthorn

Hawthorn preparations are derived from the flowers, leaves or berries of a thorny shrub (Crataegus oxyacantha) native to Europe. Hawthorn contains procyanidins and flavonoids, which provide important antioxidant functions in the body. Hawthorn helps stabilize collagen, the protein found in abundance in body joints. **Hawthorn also helps promote healthy heart and circulatory function.**

Kava Kava

Kava Kava is an herb native to the South Pacific islands. Island cultures have used Kava Kava for centuries for its natural calming and soothing effects. **When you are ready to unwind at the end of the day from the pressures of a busy, active, or stressful lifestyle, you should consider the benefits of Kava Kava, a natural sedative.**

Licorice Root

Licorice is an herb prepared from the underground stem and roots of an Oriental and European perennial (Glycyrrhiza glabra L.) of the pea family. **Licorice is reported to help promote peptic function, but excessive consumption should be avoided unless otherwise directed by a medical practitioner.**

Milk Thistle

Milk Thistle is a traditional remedy prepared from the seeds of a thorny, weedlike plant (Silybum Marianum). It is often taken in the form of silymarin, a standardized extract of a complex compound found in the seeds. **Studies confirm that silymarin helps maintain healthy liver function.**

Nettle Root

Nettle root supplements are derived from the upper levels and stems of a stinging, weedlike plant found around the world. **Nettle root has become quite popular in recent years for proper urinary function.**

Passion Flower

Passion Flower preparations are made from the leaves of a climbing vine (Passiflora incarnata). **Passion Flower has enjoyed a reputation as a natural calming and soothing herb that helps reduce the effects from the pressures of a busy, active, or stressful lifestyle.**

Pygeum

Pygeum is a large evergreen tree, growing in the higher plateaus of Southern Africa. Traditionally, this herb has been taken as tea, but it can now be found in supplement form. **Pygeum contains naturally occurring phytosterols useful for maintaining a healthy prostate gland.**

Saw Palmetto

Saw Palmetto is derived from the dark berries of a small southeastern palm tree (Serenoa repens). **The berries contain a variety of fatty acids and sterols which have anti-inflammatory and anti-androgyne properties – both of which are helpful for prostate and urinary function.**

St. John's Wort

St. John's Wort preparations are derived from the leaves and flowers of a common North American and European perennial (Hypericum perforatum). **It has been used for centuries for a variety of ailments including nervous disorders, kidney problems, and burns. Recent studies have identified that the leaves and flowers contain a variety of active components which have been shown to be effective in the treatment of anxiety and depression. St. John's wort has become a popular natural alternative to conventional prescription drugs, having far fewer side effects.**

Valerian Root

Valerian Root consists of the dried rhizome and roots of Valeriana officinalis L, a plant which has been used for more than 1,000 years for its calmative effects. **Valerian Root has been recognized as an aid for restlessness and for sleep.**

Appendix C

Recipe For Success

Most important is to properly blend the mixture. Different results will occur if the amounts used are not in direct proportion to your passion and quest to succeed. Note also that proper quantitative coming together with the ingredients below will at the very least bring joy to you and others; and most likely as a fall-out, you could achieve financial independence.

Fill a void to your fullest.
Totally believe in your pursuit.
Pursue your goals with definable benchmarks.
Be fair and honest in all your deeds.
Build meaningful relationships with those who share your expectations and spirituality.
Treat everyone, at first, as a trusted friend.
Give more than you take.
Give praise often.
Sustain humility.
Look for a genius in each person you encounter; it's there!
Always give homage to God.
Treat all others fairer than you would want to be treated.
Spirituality must always be omnipresent.
Face your fears and exorcise those that impair your growth and impede your life's goals.

Be panoramic in your thought procceses;be wide-angle in your vigilance.

Evaluate fairly, then empower the deserving.

Pay all your debts.

Teach, but teach more often by example.

Exude good vibrations.

Harbor no hatred.

Dissuade negative biases.

Repress anger.

Forgive.

Each day, love a lot more, dislike a lot less.

Time is our most precious and fleeting gift; use it wisely.

Finally, adding some addiitonal good sense of your own might just make the results of this recipe award winning.

By Carl DeSantis

Order Information

Other Books by Transmedia Publishing:

THE CUBAN COP

KING OF THE CONDO

THE PSORIASIS & ECZEMA SOLUTION

SPIN MAN

If you are unable to find **Vitamin En*Rich*ed** in your local bookstore, please send $22.00 plus $3.50 shipping and handling to:

TransMedia Publishing, Inc.
6001 Broken Sound Parkway, NW, Suite 414
Boca Raton, Florida 33487
Phone: 561-998-4888
Fax 561-998-5661
E-Mail: TransMedia@worldnet.att.net
www.transmediapr.com